Bay Leaves

Published By
THE JUNIOR SERVICE LEAGUE
OF
PANAMA CITY, FLORIDA

P. O. BOX 404
PANAMA CITY, FLORIDA 32401
1975

Eleventh Printing, November, 1993
Southern Living® **Hall of Fame** edition
20,000 Books

The purpose of the Junior Service League shall be to foster interest among its members in the social economic, cultural, and civic conditions in their community and to make effective their volunteer service.

The profits from the sale of the Junior Service League's cookbooks, *BAY LEAVES* and *BEYOND THE BAY* enable the League to fund projects like the following:

CHILD SERVICE CENTER: The Junior Service League and the United Way clothe approximately 300 school children with new clothing and shoes.

HAPPY HANGER: A clothing source of nearly new clothing for students referred by school personnel.

KIDS ON THE BLOCK: Comprised of eight puppets used by the Junior Service League to help children understand the problems of being disabled or handicapped.

UNITED CEREBRAL PALSY CENTER: The Junior Service League has been a long time supporter of the CP Center, giving of our time and finances.

BAY LEAVES COMMITTEE

Mrs. David J. Turner
Chairman

Mrs. Benjamin W. Redding
Co-chairman

Recipe Chairman
Art Editor
History Editor

Mrs. E. Clay Lewis, III
Mrs. Raymond W. Wagner
Mrs. Malcolm M. Traxler

Food Editors

Miss Holly Bingham
Mrs. James E. Carter
Mrs. B. Philip Cotton
Mrs. Theodore G. Elchos
Mrs. Betty Ereckson
Mrs. George Goodreau
Mrs. Ronald G. Groom
Mrs. W. Gerald Harrison
Mrs. William E. Holland, III
Mrs. William E. Lark
Mrs. R. William Lawrence

Mrs. Rayford Lloyd, Jr.
Mrs. Dayton Logue
Mrs. Warren Middlemas, Jr.
Mrs. James R. Patterson
Mrs. James E. Preston
Mrs. Jack N. Segler
Mrs. Philip H. Smith
Mrs. Stephen M. Smith
Mrs. Tim Smith
Mrs. Raymond Syfrett
Mrs. Steve Wilson

Sustaining Advisor
Sustaining Co-ordinators

Mrs. Albert M. Lewis, Jr.
Mrs. Foster Kruse
Mrs. Nellie Laird

The Junior Service League of Panama City, Inc., expresses grateful appreciation to its members and friends who contributed their recipes, their time, and their efforts, all of which have made this book possible.

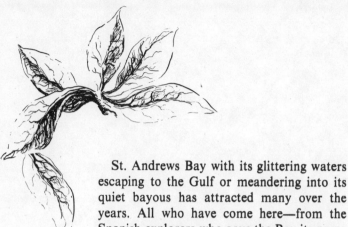

St. Andrews Bay with its glittering waters escaping to the Gulf or meandering into its quiet bayous has attracted many over the years. All who have come here—from the Spanish explorers who gave the Bay its name to the present day visitor—have been drawn by the unique beauty of its peaceful shores lined with moss hung oaks, magnolia, and bay trees.

Along these shores fishermen could draw in their nets in the age old manner of St. Andrew himself or cast out into its depths to reap the abundance of shrimp, mullet, scamp, snapper, oysters, and scallops.

Into this setting on St. Andrews Bay at the turn of the 20th Century, Panama City was born, thrived, and acquired a reputation for its gracious hospitality and leisurely living.

Within the leaves of this book, we have tried to capture the flavor of those early days with some traditional and contemporary recipes that we hope will enhance that reputation. To your enjoyment and the endeavors which this book will support, we dedicate BAY LEAVES.

TABLE OF CONTENTS

Appetizers

PINEAPPLE REFRESHER

. . .a dramatic beginning for a seafood dinner. . .

Juice of 10 lemons
4 cups sugar
1 pint cream
Grated peel of 1 orange

Pinch of salt
1 large can crushed pineapple, drained
2 quarts milk or enough to fill
freezer can

Mix ingredients together and freeze either in an electric freezer or in a container in the freezer. If using the latter method, stir frequently. Serve either in sherbet glasses or in a scooped out fresh pineapple. Fresh mint makes a pretty garnish. Serves 12.
Mrs. Warren Middlemas, Jr. (Martha)

SHRIMP MADELEINE

2 dozen shrimp
2 tablespoons green onions,
chopped
2 tablespoons green pepper,
chopped
2 tablespoons celery, chopped
½ pound fresh mushrooms

4 tablespoons lemon juice
2 teaspoons Worcestershire sauce
1 stick butter
2 tablespoons parsley, snipped
Salt
White pepper

Peel and clean uncooked shrimp, leaving on tails. Saute green onions, green pepper, and celery in butter for 4 or 5 minutes. Add shrimp. Sprinkle with salt and white pepper. Cook, stirring often until the shrimp turn pink. Add mushrooms and cook until just heated. Add parsley, lemon juice, and Worcestershire sauce. Mix well. Serves 4 as an appetizer.
Mrs. H. Mack Lewis (Eleanor)

SHRIMP ORIENTALE

1 pound shrimp, cooked
4 tablespoons butter
4 teaspoons flour
1 cup light cream
2 tablespoons tomato paste
6 tablespoons dry vermouth
1½ tablespoons chives, chopped

1½ tablespoons parsley, snipped
1 small can water chestnuts, chopped
1½ teaspoons Worcestershire sauce
Salt
Pepper
4 pastry shells

Melt butter. Stir in flour until smooth. Add cream. To this sauce add remaining ingredients and mix well. Serve hot in small baked pastry shells. Serves 4.
Mrs. Robert H. Marcy (Edith)

DOLMADAKIA

...a good Lenten dish...

4 cups onion, chopped (about
  6 onions)
1 cup olive or cooking oil
1 cup rice, uncooked
2 teaspoons dill, crushed
1 cup parsley, snipped

2 teaspoons mint, crushed
1 teaspoon salt
Dash of pepper
3 cups boiling water
¼ cup lemon juice
1 16-ounce jar grape leaves

Cook onions in oil until soft. Add rice and one cup of the water to the same pan. Cook 8 minutes. Add dill, mint, parsley, salt, and pepper. Cook 4 minutes. Allow to cool 5 minutes. Spoon one teaspoon of this filling near stem end of washed grape leaf with wrong side of leaf up and shiny part down. Fold sides in and then roll up loosely. Layer closely in a heavy Dutch oven. Add 2 cups boiling water and lemon juice. Place a Pyrex dish directly on top of them. Cover and simmer one hour or until rice is done. (Watch closely, as you may have to add more water.) Cool in pan. Sprinkle with more lemon juice. Remove and cool. Serve garnished with lemon wedges as a first course or as an hors d'oeuvre. Serve with yogurt, if desired. This makes about 50.
Mrs. Bill Janos (Cathy)

CHAFING DISH CRAB

6 tablespoons butter
3 tablespoons all-purpose flour
2½ cups half and half
1 pound fresh crabmeat
¼ cup dry sherry or white wine
Juice of ½ lemon

⅓ cup green onions, chopped
2 cups fresh mushrooms, sliced
4 ounces cream cheese
Salt
Pepper

Sauté onions and mushrooms in butter. Stir in flour and cook until mixture is blended. Pour in half and half and cook, stirring constantly, until mixture thickens. Add cream cheese; stir until melted. Add crabmeat. Season to taste with wine, lemon juice, salt, and pepper.
Mrs. Rayford Lloyd, Jr. (Genie)
Mrs. Benjamin W Redding (Dee)

CRAB PUFFS

24 2-inch bread rounds
Mayonnaise
24 thin slices of cherry tomatoes
Salt

Pepper
1 6½-ounce can crabmeat, drained
    and flaked
Lemon juice

Broil bread rounds on one side until lightly browned. Cool. Spread untoasted side with mayonnaise. Place a slice of tomato on bread. Sprinkle with salt and pepper. Top with 2 teaspoons of crabmeat, ½ teaspoon mayonnaise, and a few drops of lemon juice. Broil until mayonnaise puffs and starts to brown.
Mrs. Clay Smith (Gayle)

HOT CRAB SPREAD

1 8-ounce package cream cheese
1 tablespoon milk
½ teaspoon horseradish
2 tablespoons onion, minced

1 can crabmeat
Salt
⅓ cup slivered almonds

Soften cheese with milk. Add other ingredients and top with almonds. Bake at 375 degrees for 15 minutes. Serve warm with Triscuits or any other bland cracker.
Mrs. James R. Corn   *Annandale, Virginia*
Mrs. Elbert Dukate (Gwen)

FRESH SHRIMP MOLD

1½ cups cooked shrimp, finely
    chopped
1 can tomato soup
1½ tablespoons unflavored gelatin
¼ cup cold water

3 3-ounce packages cream cheese,
    softened
1 cup mayonnaise
¾ cup celery, finely chopped
½ cup onion, finely chopped

Dissolve gelatin in cold water. Heat soup to boiling point and add softened gelatin. When cool, add cream cheese and mayonnaise. Mix well. Stir in remaining ingredients. Pour into a 4-cup mold. (A fish mold is nice.) Chill for at least 2 hours. Serve with crackers.
Mrs. Herbert Mizell, III (Carol)

SHRIMP MOLD

2 4½-ounce cans shrimp
1 2-ounce jar pimiento
2 hard-cooked eggs
1 cup celery pieces
1 3-ounce package lemon gelatin
½ cup boiling water

½ cup light cream
½ cup mayonnaise
3 slices onion, finely chopped
1 teaspoon salt
1 5-ounce jar pimiento cheese spread

Chop shrimp, pimiento, eggs, celery, and onions. Dissolve gelatin in boiling water. Add mayonnaise, cream, salt, and cheese spread. Mix well. Grease a one-quart mold with mayonnaise. Pour mixture into mold and congeal.
John Henry Sherman, Jr.

SHRIMP SPREAD

1 8-ounce package cream cheese
4 tablespoons mayonnaise
2 tablespoons catsup
2 teaspoons prepared mustard
Dash of garlic powder

2 cups cooked shrimp, finely chopped
½ cup celery, finely chopped
2 teaspoons onion, grated
Dash of celery salt
Salt

Mix above ingredients together. Serve on buttered bread or use as a dip.
Mrs. Harry A. Smith (Mable)
Mrs. Franklin Harrison (Linda)

CREAMY SHRIMP DIP

2 8-ounce packages cream cheese
3 ounces cream cheese with chives
1 can frozen cream of shrimp soup
1½ cups cooked shrimp, chopped
1 teaspoon dry mustard

1 teaspoon Worcestershire sauce
¼ teaspoon garlic powder
¾ teaspoon paprika
Salt
Pepper

Thaw soup; combine with remaining ingredients. Chill at least two hours before serving.
Note: This also makes a delicious spread on tea sandwiches.
Mrs. C. L. Jinks, Jr. (Mary Catherine)

PICKLED SHRIMP

2½ pounds fresh shrimp, unpeeled
½ cup celery tops
¼ cup mixed pickling spice

3½ teaspoons salt
2 cups sliced onions
7 or 8 BAY LEAVES

Cover shrimp with boiling water. Add celery, spices, and salt. Cover and simmer for 5 minutes. Drain. Peel and devein shrimp under cold water. Alternate layers of cleaned shrimp and onions in a shallow dish. Add BAY LEAVES. Marinate at least 24 hours in the following pickling marinade.

Pickling Marinade:

1¼ cups salad oil
¾ cup white vinegar
3 tablespoons capers and juice

2½ teaspoons celery seed
1½ teaspoons salt
Dash of Tabasco

Combine ingredients and mix well. Pour over shrimp. Cover and chill. These will keep at least two weeks in the refrigerator. Serve with crackers.
Mrs. Rowe Sudduth (Gay)

TINY PARTY PUFFS

1 cup water
½ cup butter
1 cup flour, sifted

Dash of salt
4 eggs

Stir butter in boiling water until melted. Add flour and salt all at one time. Stir well until mixture is smooth and forms a soft ball. Cool slightly. Add eggs, one at a time, beating well after each addition. Continue beating until mixture is shiny. Drop by teaspoonfuls onto a lightly greased baking sheet. Bake at 375 degrees for 50 minutes. Allow to cool in a warm place away from drafts. When cool, fill with shrimp salad and decorate with parsley or softened cream cheese. Makes 36 puffs.

Shrimp Filling:

1½ cups cooked shrimp, finely chopped
½ cup celery, finely chopped

1 teaspoon caraway seeds
2 teaspoons lemon juice
¾ cup mayonnaise

Combine above ingredients and mix well. Refrigerate at least one hour.
Mrs. James Preston (Sandra)

OYSTERS IN CHAFING DISH

1 gallon oysters
1 pound butter
1 jar creamed horseradish

1 can cream of mushroom soup
Dash of Worcestershire sauce
Salt

Put all ingredients in saucepan except oysters. Heat until the butter melts. Pour in the well-drained oysters but do not cook. Let stand over low flame in chafing dish and serve with crackers. Wonderful for cocktail parties.
Mrs. Milton Gray (Helen)
Mrs. Hugh Nelson (Lila)

GRAB BAG DIP

2 cups mayonnaise
½ cup horseradish
½ teaspoon monosodium glutamate
2 teaspoons dry mustard
2 teaspoons lemon juice

½ teaspoon salt
1 can mushrooms, drained
1 can black olives, drained
1 jar cocktail sausages, drained
1 recipe meat balls

Mix first 6 ingredients together and heat in a double boiler to make sauce. Add other ingredients, heat thoroughly, and serve in a chafing dish. Spear with bamboo straws.
Meat Balls:
¼ cup dry bread crumbs
1 pound ground chuck
1 egg
¼ cup water

1 teaspoon minced, dry onions
1 teaspoon salt
Pepper

Combine all ingredients. Shape into balls, and brown in a small amount of grease in a hot skillet, shaking constantly.
Mrs. Robert Walsh (Kitty)

SOUR CREAM-HORSERADISH DIP

8 ounces sour cream
1 container horseradish dip

3 or 4 green onions, finely chopped
1 package dry Italian dressing mix

Mix all ingredients together. Delicious with crudités.
Mrs. Tim Smith (Mary Ann)

SHRIMP DIP

2 pounds shrimp
¾ cup celery, chopped
½ cup onions, chopped
1 cup mayonnaise

Lemon juice to taste
16 ounces cottage cheese
Salt

Cook and clean shrimp. Chop fine. Cream all ingredients except cottage cheese until fluffy. Add cheese. Serve with crackers or potato chips. Flavor improves if made the day before.
Mrs. J. C. Harris (Ruby)   *Cove Hotel*

FULTON'S FOLLY

5 ounces dried beef, shredded
8 ounces cream cheese
3 medium Kosher dill pickles, diced

7 tablespoons pickle juice
Anchovy paste to taste

Cream the cheese with pickle juice. Use mixer to blend and slowly add shredded beef and diced pickles to mixture. Blend in anchovy paste until smooth. Serve with crackers. Good also as sandwich spread on rye bread served with cold beer.
A. Lloyd Fulton

BROCCOLI DIP

2 packages frozen, chopped broccoli
1 small onion, chopped
2-3 ribs of celery, chopped
1 6-ounce roll garlic cheese
1 can cream of mushroom
  soup
1 4-ounce can mushrooms, drained
¾ cup slivered almonds

1 small can water chestnuts, quartered
Pimiento for color
½ teaspoon salt
¼ teaspoon pepper
2 tablespoons butter
1 teaspoon monosodium glutamate
1 teaspoon Worcestershire sauce
¼ teaspoon Tabasco

Cook broccoli according to package directions. Let cool in strainer and drain well. Combine all ingredients. Warm thoroughly and serve in a chafing dish.
Mrs. Robert Allman   *Atlanta, Georgia*

DILL DIP

1 cup sour cream
1 cup mayonnaise
1 package Fritos Green Onion
    Dip Mix

½ teaspoon Worcestershire sauce
1 tablespoon dillweed
6 drops Tabasco
½ teaspoon seasoned salt

Mix all ingredients together and chill. Fresh dill may be used, if available.
Good used with cauliflower, celery, and carrots.
Mrs. Gene Crist (Jan)

CUCUMBER DIP

1 cucumber
1 8-ounce package cream cheese

Green onions, chopped
Seasoned salt

Peel and grate cucumber. Mix with softened cream cheese. Add onions and
salt to taste.
Mrs. William E. Lark (Ruthie)

GUACAMOLE

2 avocados, mashed
1 tablespoon lemon juice
2 tablespoons lime juice
1 tablespoon onion, grated
1 teaspoon salt

¼ teaspoon chili powder
Dash of cayenne pepper
⅓ cup mayonnaise
¼ cup ripe olives, chopped
4 slices of crisp bacon, crumbled

Blend all ingredients thoroughly. Serve with warmed corn chips or spoon over
shredded lettuce as a salad.
Mrs. H. Mack Lewis (Eleanor)

YOU'D-NEVER-GUESS-IT'S-SPINACH DIP

1 package frozen spinach,
    uncooked
¼ cup parsley
½ cup onion, chopped

1 teaspoon salt
½ teaspoon pepper
2 cups mayonnaise
Tabasco, to taste

Thaw and squeeze all liquid from spinach. Mix all ingredients in blender.
Serve with carrot sticks, celery, and cauliflower.
Mrs. Charles Robinson   *Summerville, South Carolina*

STUFFED TOMATOES
. . .delicious as an hors d'oeuvre or garnish around roast. . .

36 firm cherry tomatoes
Salt
½ teaspoon curry powder
½ teaspoon chili powder

1 medium onion, grated
1 ripe avocado
2 tablespoons lemon juice

Cut a thin slice from the top of each tomato and reserve the slices. Scoop out the pulp. Sprinkle shells with salt; invert on a rack and let drain 15 minutes. In a bowl, mash the pulp of the avocado with a silver fork until smooth. Stir in lemon juice, salt, curry powder, chili powder, and onion. Beat well. Fill each tomato with mixture and replace tops.
Variation:

¾ cup cottage cheese
½ cup bleu cheese, crumbled
½ teaspoon onion, grated

Chives
Salt
Pepper

Fill tomatoes with mixture and sprinkle with chopped chives.
Mrs. Sterrett Procter   *Lafayette, Louisiana*

STUFFED MUSHROOMS

3 pounds medium-sized mushrooms   2 jars Smithfield Ham Spread

Remove stems from mushrooms. Clean caps with a damp cloth. Fill with ham spread. Place under broiler for about 3 minutes. A favorite at cocktail parties! Serves 60.
Mrs. Clark Whitehorn (Ginny)

MARINATED MUSHROOMS I

1 pound fresh mushrooms
¼ cup olive oil
½ cup salad oil
⅓ cup red wine vinegar
2 tablespoons lemon juice

1 teaspoon tarragon
1 clove garlic, chopped
1 teaspoon salt
½ teaspoon sugar
3 teaspoons chives, chopped

Combine all ingredients except mushrooms. Pour over the mushrooms and marinate several hours, turning occasionally. Drain and serve. The leftover marinade may be used again or as a salad dressing.
Mrs. Joe Cornett (Marianne)

MARINATED MUSHROOMS II

⅓ cup red wine vinegar
⅓ cup salad oil
1 onion, sliced
1 teaspoon salt
2 teaspoons dried parsley flakes

1 teaspoon prepared mustard
1 tablespoon brown sugar
2 6-ounce cans whole mushrooms, drained

Combine all ingredients except mushrooms. Bring to a boil. Add mushrooms and simmer 5 minutes. Pour into a bowl. Cover and chill overnight, stirring occasionally. Drain and serve with picks.
Mrs. Benjamin W. Redding (Dee)

HOLIDAY CHEESE BALL

4 3-ounce packages cream cheese
¼ pound Roquefort cheese
2 tablespoons Worcestershire sauce
1 small onion, grated
⅛ teaspoon garlic, pressed

1 cup pecans, finely chopped
1 cup parsley, minced
3 or 4 drops Tabasco
Salt

Mix all cheeses with half of the pecans and half of the parsley. Work in Worcestershire, onions, garlic, and Tabasco. Add salt to taste. Shape into a ball. Mix remaining parsley and pecans and pat on outside of ball. Chill 24 hours before serving.
Miss Eloise Wall   *El Dorado, Arkansas*

GARLIC CHEESE BALL

1 pound hoop cheese, grated
1 3-ounce package cream cheese, softened
1 clove garlic, crushed
1 onion, finely chopped
Mayonnaise

Red pepper
Salt
Pepper
Worcestershire sauce
Paprika

Combine cheeses and enough mayonnaise to make a creamy consistency. Add remaining ingredients, mixing well. Shape into a ball and sprinkle with paprika. Let season for two days in refrigerator. Before serving let stand at room temperature at least 1 hour.
Mrs. John Rainey (Peggy)

HOT CHEESE PUFFS

4 ounces cream cheese
1 teaspoon onion, grated
¼ cup mayonnaise
1 tablespoon chives, chopped
⅛ teaspoon cayenne pepper
2 tablespoons Parmesan cheese
½ small loaf white bread

In a bowl, combine all ingredients except bread. Mix well. Cut bread into 1½-inch rounds and spread with cheese mixture. Bake in 350 degree oven for 15 minutes, or longer for crispier puffs.
Note: To make ahead, cut bread, spread with cheese mixture, and freeze. Bake when ready to use.
Mrs. Scott Nabors (Gayle)

TIROPETES

(Cheese Triangles)

1 pound filo (thin pastry)
1 pound Feta cheese
1 8-ounce package cream cheese
1 8-ounce carton cottage cheese
1 cup Romano cheese
4 tablespoons plain flour
3 eggs, well beaten

Beat eggs with electric mixer until fluffy. Add cream cheese, cottage cheese, Romano cheese, and flour and continue beating until well blended. Crumble Feta cheese with fork and combine with egg mixture. Cut filo into 6x12-inch strips. For each triangle, brush half the filo strip with melted warm butter. Fold over other half of filo to make a strip about 3 inches in width. These may be made smaller or larger depending on size desired. Brush with butter. Place 1 teaspoon cheese mixture at one end of each strip, folding strip diagonally until triangles are formed. Brush tops with melted butter and place on an ungreased baking sheet. Bake at 375 degrees for 20 or 25 minutes or until golden. Makes 40 triangles. Serve warm.
Note: To freeze, place unbaked buttered triangles in a plastic container, separating layers with waxed paper, and place in freezer. When ready to serve, place frozen triangles on an ungreased pan and bake. May be frozen for at least 2 months.
Mrs. John Cleondis (Caliope)

CHEESE GOURMET

1 ball Edam cheese
½ cup good white wine
1 teaspoon cumin, dill, or
caraway seeds

Cut off top of cheese. Remove inside of cheese and beat in electric mixer until creamy. Add preferred seeds and wine. Refill cheese shell and replace top. Wrap in waxed paper. Let cheese ripen for 2 or 3 days and serve with crackers.
Mrs. Clark Whitehorn (Ginny)

FRESH FRUIT DIP

. . . .delicious as a dip or as a dressing for fresh fruit. . . .

⅓ cup sugar
4 teaspoons cornstarch
¼ teaspoon salt
1 cup unsweetened pineapple juice

¼ cup orange juice
2 eggs, beaten
2 3-ounce packages cream cheese

Combine dry ingredients in a saucepan. Blend in fruit juices. Cook, stirring constantly until thick and bubbly (about 5-8 minutes). Slowly stir some of this hot mixture into the eggs. Return to saucepan and cook over low heat, stirring constantly for 3-5 minutes or until mixture thickens slightly. Cool 5 minutes. Soften cream cheese and beat into cooled mixture. Chill. Makes 2 cups.

Doug and Lois Dick   Four Winds Restaurant

PINEAPPLE CHEESE BALL

2 8-ounce packages cream cheese
1 large can crushed pineapple, drained

1 medium onion, grated
Pecans, chopped

Soften cream cheese. Drain pineapple thoroughly. Mix all ingredients together. Form into a ball, roll in chopped pecans, and chill. Serve with crackers. This may also be used as sandwich spread.

Mrs. Charles D. Price, III   Dothan, Alabama

TOASTED CHEESE FINGERS

½ pound American or Cheddar cheese, grated
½ cup mayonnaise
1 tablespoon Worcestershire sauce
1 teaspoon mustard

1 tablespoon Durkee Sauce
Salt
Pepper
Thin bread slices

Mix cheese with mayonnaise. Add seasonings. Remove crusts from thinly sliced bread. Cut bread into three strips. Spread one strip with cheese mixture. Top with another strip and brush with melted butter. When ready to serve, toast in oven for 5 minutes at 400 degrees. Serves 6-8.

Mrs. D.E. McCloy   Monticello, Arkansas

CHEESE AND OLIVE NUGGETS

¼ pound sharp Cheddar cheese
¼ cup soft butter
½ rounded cup flour
⅛ teaspoon salt

½ teaspoon paprika
Dash of cayenne pepper
35 small stuffed green olives

Grate cheese. With your hands, mix all ingredients together except olives. Shape dough around each olive. Refrigerate or freeze. Bake at 400 degrees for 12-15 minutes.
Jan Newberry Cooley

CHEESE WAFERS

2 sticks margarine, softened
2 cups sharp Cheddar cheese, grated
2 cups sifted flour
¼ teaspoon salt

¼ teaspoon red pepper
1 tablespoon sugar, (optional)
Pecans

Cream butter and cheese. Sift dry ingredients together. Add to butter and cheese. Shape into small balls. Press ½ pecan into each ball. Bake on ungreased cooky sheet at 300 degrees for about 30 minutes. Do not overcook.
Mrs. Sidney A. Daffin, Jr. (Carlyne)

ARTICHOKE NIBBLES

2 jars marinated artichoke hearts
1 small onion, finely chopped
1 clove garlic, minced
4 eggs
¼ cup fine, dry bread crumbs
2 teaspoons minced parsley

¼ teaspoon salt
⅛ teaspoon pepper
⅛ teaspoon oregano
⅛ teaspoon hot pepper sauce
½ pound sharp Cheddar cheese, shredded

Drain marinade from 1 jar of artichokes into a skillet. Drain the other jar and discard marinade. Chop all artichokes and set aside. Add onion and garlic to skillet. Sauté until clear. Beat eggs; add crumbs and seasonings. Stir in cheese, parsley, artichokes, and onion mixture. Turn into a greased 7x11-inch pan. Bake at 325 degrees for 30 minutes. Allow to cool in pan. Cut into 1-inch squares. Serve hot or cold.
Mrs. Abbott Browne (Mary Belle)

GREEN CHILI PIE

1 can green chilies, chopped
4 eggs, well beaten

1 10-ounce package Cheddar cheese, grated

Lightly grease a 9-inch pie pan with butter. Spread chilies evenly over bottom of pan. Layer cheese evenly. Drizzle beaten eggs over cheese. Bake at 275 degrees for 1 hour. Cut into bite-sized pieces. To make a hotter pie, use 2 cans of green chilies.
Philip Allen Cotton

VEGETABLE FONDUE

1 pound sharp Cheddar cheese
1 pound mozzarella cheese
½ cup butter

½ cup milk
Cauliflower, broccoli, and brussel sprouts, cut into bite-sized pieces

Using an electric fondue pot for even heat, *slowly* melt cheeses with butter and milk. Stir constantly. Keep sauce hot and serve immediately with parboiled vegetables. Chunks of French bread may also be used.
Mrs. Sidney Daffin, III (Jane)

CHAFING DISH MEAT BALLS

1 pound ground beef
1 small onion, finely chopped
½ teaspoon horseradish
Salt
Pepper
1½ slices bread, broken
½ cup milk (approximately)
1 cup catsup

2 tablespoons Worcestershire sauce
½ cup fruit syrup (from any canned fruit)
½ cup water
4 8-ounce cans button mushrooms
3 6-ounce cans pitted black olives or large green olives, not stuffed

Combine ground beef, onion, horseradish, salt, pepper, bread, and milk and shape into small meat balls. Fry, turning frequently to preserve shape. Drain on paper towels. Make a sauce using catsup, Worcestershire, fruit syrup, and water. Arrange meat balls in a chafing dish with mushrooms and olives. Pour sauce over all and heat.
Mrs. Jack Blackwell (Theola)

PINEAPPLE MEAT BALLS

½ cup milk
1 slice bread
2 pounds ground beef
1 egg

2 teaspoons salt
2 teaspoons pepper
Dash of garlic salt
2 tablespoons salad oil

Pour milk over crumbled bread. Add meat, egg, salt, pepper, and garlic salt. Mix well. With wet fingers, form into walnut-sized balls. (Mixture will be soft.) Brown in hot oil, shaking pan so balls will keep their round shape.
Pineapple Sauce:
1 can beef bouillon
1 No. 2 can pineapple chunks
½ cup green pepper, chopped
½ cup wine vinegar
½ cup sugar

2 tablespoons soy sauce
½ teaspoon salt
1 teaspoon monosodium glutamate
2 tablespoons cornstarch

Mix bouillon, undrained pineapple chunks, green pepper, vinegar, sugar, soy sauce, salt, and monosodium glutamate. Simmer 15 minutes. Moisten cornstarch in a small amount of water and stir into boiling liquid. Simmer and stir until sauce is clear and thickened. Add browned meat balls and simmer 10-15 minutes until flavors are blended and meat balls are heated through. Serve in chafing dish.
Mrs. George Logue, Sr. (Gladys)

OLIVE-CURRY ROUNDS

4½ ounces ripe olives, chopped
¼ cup green onions, minced
¾ cup Cheddar cheese, grated
4 tablespoons mayonnaise

Salt
1 teaspoon curry powder
Garlic rounds

Combine all ingredients thoroughly. Spread thickly on garlic rounds. Bake in 400 degree oven for 5-6 minutes or until cheese is bubbly.
Mrs. Fred Lindholm (Jayne)

BOURBON HOT DOGS

2 pounds Oscar Meyer Wieners
1½ cups catsup

½ cup brown sugar
½ cup bourbon

Cut wieners into bite-sized pieces. Simmer uncovered in skillet for ½ hour in sauce made of catsup and brown sugar. Add bourbon and cook in covered skillet ½ hour longer. Refrigerate overnight. Serve hot in chafing dish.
Note: Tiny meatballs are also good in this sauce.
Mrs. Charles Lahan (Ann)

SMOKED SALMON PARTY BALL

1 1-pound can salmon
1 8-ounce package cream cheese, softened
1 tablespoon lemon juice
2 teaspoons onion, grated

1 teaspoon prepared horseradish
¼ teaspoon salt
¼ teaspoon liquid smoke
½ cup pecans, chopped
3 tablespoons fresh parsley, snipped

Drain salmon, removing all skin and bones. Thoroughly mix salmon, cream cheese, lemon juice, onion, horseradish, salt, and liquid smoke. Form into a ball and chill overnight. Combine pecans and parsley. Roll ball in this mixture. Chill. Serve with crackers.
Mrs. Oliver Oxford   Americus, Georgia

CHICKEN BALLS

1 cup pecans, finely ground
1 cup chicken, finely ground
2 tablespoons pimiento, finely chopped

1 tablespoon onion, finely chopped
¼ teaspoon salt
⅛ teaspoon hot pepper sauce
½ cup cream of mushroom soup

Combine ¼ cup pecans with remaining ingredients. Use less soup, if needed, for proper consistency. Mix well. Make small balls and roll in remaining ¾ cup nuts. Cover and chill overnight. Makes 24.
Mrs. J. C. Harris (Ruby)   Cove Hotel

SAUSAGE BALLS

1 pound hot sausage
3 cups Bisquick

10 ounces extra sharp Cheddar cheese

Grate cheese and allow to soften. Mix all ingredients well with hands. Shape into small balls. Bake 15-20 minutes at 350 degrees.
Mrs. Harold E. Wager (Margaret)
Mrs. D. L. Boone   Montgomery, Alabama

Editors' Variation: For a sausage ball with a less smooth appearance but more "sausage taste," use only 2 cups Bisquick.

MEXICAN QUICHE

1½ cups Monterey Jack cheese, grated
1 cup mild Cheddar cheese, grated
1 4-ounce can green chilies, chopped
1 cup half and half
3 eggs, slightly beaten
¼ teaspoon salt
⅛ teaspoon cumin
1 9-inch pie crust, partially baked

Sprinkle all the Monterey Jack and half of the Cheddar over bottom of partially baked pie crust. Spread chilies over cheese. Beat half and half with eggs and other ingredients. Pour into crust and sprinkle remaining cheese on top. Bake at 325 degrees for 40 minutes or until center is set. Let stand for 15 minutes before cutting.
Mrs. Bill Casey (Robin)

SIMPLY ELEGANT CAVIAR

This recipe is from a novel I read once and it's the only thing I remember about the book (including the title)!

Caviar
Whipped cream cheese
Chopped chives
Thin lemon slices
Melba toast

Use the best caviar available. Serve in a crystal bowl which is embedded in ice. Each guest assembles his own while sipping chilled, dry champagne.
Mrs. Sidney Daffin, III (Jane)

EGG RING WITH CAVIAR

10 hard-cooked eggs
½ cup mayonnaise
Paprika
Worcestershire sauce, to taste
1 small onion, finely grated
2 cans black caviar
Red caviar to garnish (optional)
Salt

Finely chop eggs. Blend with mayonnaise. Add Worcestershire sauce, onion, and salt (not too much, as caviar is salty). In center of serving plate, mound the black caviar. If desired, garnish with red caviar. Spoon egg salad around caviar. Sprinkle with paprika. Serve with Melba toast rounds. Serves 20.
Mrs. Clay Smith (Gayle)

Beverages

COVE HOTEL CRANBERRY PUNCH

4 cups sugar
2 cups water
6 quarts cranberry juice

3 48-ounce cans pineapple juice
1 quart ReaLemon
1 quart vodka

Make a simple syrup by adding 4 cups of sugar to 2 cups of boiling water, stirring frequently. Combine other ingredients except vodka. Freeze. One hour before serving, remove punch from freezer. When it reaches an icy consistency, add vodka and serve. Makes 3 gallons.
Mrs. J. C. Harris (Ruby)   *Cove Hotel*

FRUIT BOWLE

1 bottle white wine
1 bottle champagne
1 bottle ginger ale

5 tablespoons Cognac
Fresh fruit of the season
Sugar to taste

Cut fruit into bite-sized pieces, enough to cover bottom of punch bowl. Sprinkle sugar over fruit. Pour Cognac over this and allow to soak overnight. When ready to serve, add wine, champagne, and ginger ale. Serve cold in punch bowl.
Mrs. Kurt Gerstle   *Biebermühle/Pfalz, West Germany*

SANGRIA

1 bottle Burgundy
4 oranges, squeezed
½ cup water

¼-½ cup sugar
Maraschino cherries
1 orange, sliced

Mix Burgundy, orange juice, water, and sugar together. Garnish with orange slices and Maraschino cherries. Add ice and serve cold.
Mrs. Norman Gross

HOLIDAY CHAMPAGNE PUNCH
Potent!

1 fifth Southern Comfort
½ cup light rum
1 cup pineapple juice
1 cup grapefruit juice

½ cup lemon juice
2 quarts champagne or soda
  water

Chill ingredients overnight. You may mix ahead, but add the champagne at the last minute. Pour over ice in punch bowl. Float thin slices of citrus on top.
Mrs. Warren Middlemas, Jr. (Martha)

CHAMPAGNE PUNCH

1 bottle sauterne
½ bottle peach brandy
1 quart lemon sherbet

1 bottle soda water
1 bottle champagne
1 bottle ginger ale

Mix all ingredients together. Chill and pour over large chunk of ice in punch bowl. Float fresh fruit on top.
Mrs. B. Philip Cotton (Salie)

ANNIVERSARY PUNCH

1 fifth champagne
1 fifth sherry
½ pint cherry brandy

1 bottle soda water
1 small package frozen
  strawberries

Mix all ingredients together. Chill and pour over a chunk of dry ice in bottom of punch bowl. Makes 2 quarts.
Mrs. Everette Williams (Carolyn)

RUM PUNCH

2 quarts freshly squeezed orange
  juice
40 ounces frozen lemon juice
1 pint Curaçao

1 cup grenadine
1 fifth dark rum
2 fifths light rum

Mix all ingredients together. Serve over ice. Garnish with slices of orange and lemon and sprigs of mint. Serves 25.
Mrs. Rayford Lloyd, Jr. (Genie)

GOLDEN PUNCH

2 small cans frozen pink lemonade
1 small can frozen limeade
1 46-ounce can pineapple juice

1 large bottle ginger ale, chilled
13½ ounces Tang
1 quart ice water

Mix all ingredients together. Chill. Garnish with mint or may be served over a frozen fruit ring. Serves 25-30.
Mrs. Harry A. Smith (Mable)
Miss Joan Fleming

COVE HOTEL PUNCH

1 12-ounce can of frozen orange juice, undiluted
3 small cans lemonade, (follow directions)

1 can apricot nectar
1 46-ounce can pineapple juice
½ gallon orange sherbet
2 quarts ginger ale

Mix first four ingredients together and chill. Put ice cubes in bottom of bowl along with sherbet and mash sherbet. Add chilled juice mixture and pour ginger ale over all. Stir well. Serves 40.
Mrs. J. C. Harris (Ruby)   *Cove Hotel*

COFFEE FRAPPÉ

1 gallon vanilla ice cream
1 pint cream, whipped

1 quart double-strength coffee

Chill coffee and pour over ice cream which has been broken into chunks. Stir in whipped cream and serve. It should be about the consistency of a milk shake. This can be made ahead and frozen. Serves 35.
Mrs. J. C. Harris (Ruby)   Cove Hotel

ORANGEADE

...nice for a summer brunch or luncheon...

4 cups water
2 cups orange juice
¼ cup lemon juice

¾-1 cup sugar
Maraschino cherry juice for color

Mix all ingredients together. Garnish with mint leaves, orange or lemon slices, and Maraschino cherries. Makes 1½ quarts.
Mrs. James E. Carter (Jeri)

PINK PUNCH

1 package frozen strawberries	1 large can pineapple juice
1 package frozen raspberries	1 bottle claret or rose´
1 package frozen peaches	2 cups gin
1 cup sugar	1 large bottle ginger ale
1 cup rum	Lemon or orange slices

Combine first five ingredients and let stand overnight. Squeeze through cheesecloth. Add remaining ingredients. Serve over ice. Makes 6 quarts.
Mrs. Chester Harvey (Susie)

FRUIT JUICE PUNCH

Basic Recipe:

1 large can frozen lemonade	1 46-ounce can pineapple juice
3 large cans water	Sugar to taste
1 46-ounce can grapefruit-pineapple juice	2 large bottles ginger ale

Pink:
Use pink lemonade instead of lemonade. Use pink grapefruit-pineapple juice instead of grapefruit-pineapple juice.

Yellow:
Add 1 46-ounce can of orange juice to basic recipe.

Green:
Add 1 large or 2 small cans frozen limeade and 3 large or 6 small cans of water to basic recipe.

Lavender:
Add 1 quart bottle of grape juice to basic recipe.

Christmas Punch:
Use the recipe for the pink punch and add 1 large bottle of cranberry juice cocktail. Spirits may be added for desired flavor.

If more color is desired, add a few drops of food coloring. This mixture may be made ahead of time and frozen. The ginger ale should be added just prior to serving. Serves 35-40.
Mrs. B. M. Fields (Margaret)

BANANA PUNCH

6 cups water
4 cups sugar
6 bananas
Juice of 4 lemons

1 46-ounce can pineapple juice
1 6-ounce can frozen orange juice
4 large bottles ginger ale

Boil water and sugar 4 minutes. Cool. Mix together bananas and lemon juice in blender. Add cooled sugar water and freeze. (May be frozen for a month.) Thaw in refrigerator overnight and add orange juice, pineapple juice, and ginger ale. Makes 2 gallons.
Mrs. Thomas H. Gregory   *St. Petersburg, Florida*

KAHLUA

4 cups sugar
1½ ounces instant espresso coffee
2 cups water

1 vanilla bean
1 fifth vodka

Mix sugar and coffee well. Add water and boil until coffee is dissolved. Add 3 inches vanilla bean to hot liquid. Cool. Add one fifth vodka. Let stand 30 days in a glass gallon container.
Mrs. William Russ Mathis (Sally)   *Orlando, Florida*

EGGNOG

This makes a good thick "eat with a spoon" kind of eggnog.

10 eggs yolks
10 tablespoons sugar
10-12 teaspoons whiskey

1 pint whipped cream
Nutmeg

Separate eggs. Beat yolks in mixing bowl until lemon colored. Add sugar to egg yolks and beat on medium speed until sugar is melted. Add whiskey, one teaspoon at a time, until all is added. Beat egg whites until stiff and dry. Fold into egg yolk mixture. Fold in whipped cream. (You may place whipped cream on top instead, if you wish.) Sprinkle with nutmeg and serve immediately. Serves 10.
Mrs. Clell Warriner, Jr. (Jean Ann)
Variation: Add 1 cup vanilla ice cream before serving.
Mrs. Paul Eubanks (Maedelle)

MILK PUNCH

1 cup brandy (bourbon or rum
  is also good)
2 cups cold milk
6 tablespoons powdered sugar

½ teaspoon vanilla
6-8 ice cubes, coarsely crushed
Nutmeg

Pour spirits into blender with all ingredients except nutmeg. Blend well. Pour into glasses or cups and sprinkle with nutmeg. Makes about 5½ cups punch.
The Editors

AMARETTO ALEXANDER

12 ounces Amaretto liqueur
1 pint half and half

6 ounces white crème de cacao
1½ quarts vanilla ice cream

Combine Amaretto, crème de cacao, and half and half in blender. Put a scoop of ice cream in each sherbet glass and the remainder in blender. Blend well. Pour in glass and serve. Serves 10.
Mrs. Chesley S. Fensom (Darlene)

VELVET HAMMER

½ gallon vanilla ice cream
9 ounces vodka

5 ounces white crème de cacao
1 ounce triple sec

Combine all ingredients in blender. Makes 8 or more drinks.
Mrs. Lynn C. Higby (Dedee)

BULL SHOT

1 can beef bouillon
2 teaspoons Worcestershire sauce
1 teaspoon lemon juice

Dash of Tabasco
Dash of celery salt
5½ ounces vodka

Combine first five ingredients and chill thoroughly. Before serving, add vodka.
Mrs. J. C. Harris (Ruby)   *Cove Hotel*

BLOODY MARY PITCHER

1 46-ounce can tomato juice
2 cups vodka
4 tablespoons Worcestershire sauce
1 teaspoon salt

½ teaspoon pepper
2 to 2½ teaspoons Tabasco
1½ teaspoons celery salt
Juice of 3 large limes

Combine all ingredients and chill several hours. Stir well and serve over ice. Garnish with lime slices. Serves 10.
Mrs. Philip H. Smith (Ann)

WHISKEY SOUR

1 6-ounce can frozen lemonade
   concentrate
6 ounces whiskey

4 cups crushed ice
Maraschino cherries
Orange slices

Mix first three ingredients in blender until slushy. Less ice can be added if a stronger drink is desired. Pour into sour glasses and garnish with a cherry and orange slices. Vodka or rum may be substituted for whiskey.
Mrs. Theodore G. Elchos (Jimmie)

TOM AND JERRY FOR TWO
This recipe is very old and makes a wonderful Christmas drink.

1 egg, separated
½ jigger Jamaican rum
1 teaspoon powdered sugar
¼ teaspoon powdered allspice

Brandy
Milk or water, heated
Nutmeg

Mix together egg yolk, rum, sugar, and allspice. Beat egg white until stiff. Add ¼ ounce brandy and combine with rum mixture. Divide equally into 2 Tom and Jerry mugs. Add ½ ounce brandy to each mug. Stir hot water or milk into mugs and top with nutmeg.
Mrs. William D. Carter (Carmen)

FRENCH CHOCOLATE

2½ ounces Baker's chocolate   ¾ cup sugar
1 cup water   ½ cup heavy cream, whipped
¼ teaspoon salt   Hot milk

Mix chocolate with water and cook over low heat until thick, stirring constantly. Add salt and sugar and continue to cook 4 more minutes. Cool. Fold in ½ cup whipped cream. Store in refrigerator. To use, place 1 tablespoon of chocolate mixture in a cup and fill with hot milk. Stir well. Top with additional whipped cream and serve.
The Editors

VIENNESE COFFEE

4 cups French chocolate   Sugar to taste
1½ cups strong coffee   1 cup heavy cream, whipped
1 cup Cognac

Mix chocolate and coffee together. Add Cognac and sugar. Serve very hot with whipped cream on top. Serves 8.
The Editors

HOT BUTTERED RUM

1 cup apple cider   1 ounce rum
1 teaspoon butter-brown sugar   1 cinnamon stick
  mixture

Heat apple cider. Add 1 teaspoon butter-brown sugar mixture. Pour into mug. Add rum and serve with cinnamon stick. Makes one serving.
Butter-Brown Sugar Mixture:
1 stick butter   1 pound brown sugar

Melt butter in saucepan. Add sugar. This may be kept in refrigerator and used as needed.
Mrs. Bill Chatoney (Billie Kay)

HOT SPICED BREW

1 orange, sliced ¼-inch thick
Whole cloves
2 quarts apple cider
2 7-ounce bottles 7-Up
2 cups orange juice
¼ teaspoon nutmeg

¼ teaspoon cloves
1 teaspoon cinnamon
½ teaspoon allspice
¼ cup brown sugar
24 whole sticks of cinnamon (use as swizzle sticks)

Stud orange slices with whole cloves. Save these for garnish. Combine cider, 7-Up, orange juice, spices, and brown sugar in a 4-quart pan. Heat, stirring frequently, until piping hot. Slowly pour this mixture into a punch bowl. Float orange slices on top or cut slices into smaller pieces and put into cups if no bowl is being used. I fix mine in a large coffee maker and then add an orange slice to each cup. Serve hot. Makes 24 servings.
Mrs. Don Fay (Gail)

HOT MULLED CIDER

¼ cup brown sugar (or more to taste)
¼ teaspoon salt
2 quarts Indian Summer cider

1 teaspoon whole allspice
1 teaspoon whole cloves
3-inch stick of cinnamon
Dash of nutmeg

Combine sugar, salt, and cider. Tie spices in a small piece of cheese cloth; add to mixture. Slowly bring to a boil. Simmer covered 20 minutes. Remove spices. Serve hot. Makes 2 quarts.
Mrs. Malcolm M. Traxler (Martha Lee)

INSTANT RUSSIAN TEA

1 cup Tang
1 cup instant tea
1 cup sugar

1 teaspoon cinnamon
1 teaspoon ground cloves
1 package lemonade mix

Mix all ingredients together. Store in a jar. To make beverage, add 2 or 3 teaspoons to one cup hot water. The diet-conscious may omit sugar and use unsweetened lemonade mix. Add sugar substitute to each cup as it is made.
Mrs. Harry Murphy (Ozelle)

Soups

SEAFOOD GUMBO

7 tablespoons flour
6 tablespoons oil
2 medium onions, chopped
4 ribs of celery, chopped
1 medium green pepper, chopped
1 clove garlic, chopped
2 14½-ounce cans Hunt's whole tomatoes
1 15-ounce can Hunt's tomato sauce
1 large package frozen, chopped okra

2 quarts water
6 crabs, cleaned
1 pound crabmeat
3 pounds shrimp, peeled and deveined
1 pint oysters
3 teaspoons salt
BAY LEAVES
Red pepper, to taste
Tabasco
Parsley flakes

In a heavy bottomed 4-quart pot, make a dark roux of flour and oil, stirring constantly so as not to burn. When brown, add celery, onions, green pepper, and garlic. Stir this with roux until vegetables become slightly browned. Add juice from tomatoes and tomato sauce. Cut up tomatoes into small pieces and add water. Bring mixture to a boil stirring frequently. Add crab bodies (excellent for flavor) and seasonings and boil gently for 1 hour. Taste for additional seasonings and add okra and cook for another hour. Add peeled, raw shrimp, crabmeat, and oysters. Cook for 30 minutes longer, tasting again for seasonings. The crab bodies may be removed before adding the seafoods. Add more water if gumbo becomes too thick. Serve over rice with French bread and a green salad.
Mrs. David Turner (Patty)
Mrs. Dayton Logue (Ann)

BAY LEAVES OYSTER STEW

For the very best oyster stew, have your oysters shucked at an oyster bar or shuck your own.

1 pint oysters
2 tablespoons Pillsbury Sauce and Gravy Flour
2 teaspoons salt

Dash of white pepper
Dash of Beau Monde (optional)
1 quart milk, scalded
Butter

In a large saucepan, melt 4 tablespoons butter. Blend in flour, salt, pepper, and Beau Monde. Stir in oysters and their liquor; simmer until edges curl. Slowly add milk to oyster mixture. Remove from heat, cover, and allow to stand for 15 minutes. Reheat briefly and pour into heated bowls containing a lump of butter. Dash with paprika or black pepper.
The Editors

FISH COURTBOUILLON

4 pounds red fish
¼ cup flour
½ pound butter
2 tablespoons green onions, chopped
2 large onions, finely chopped
½ cup celery, chopped
1 large green pepper, chopped
½ teaspoon allspice

1½ quarts water
1 tablespoon parsley, minced
1 large can stewed tomatoes
Salt
Red pepper
2 BAY LEAVES
1 teaspoon rosemary
¼ cup dry sherry
Lemon slices

Melt butter and blend in flour. Sauté onions slowly until light brown, stirring constantly. Add all remaining ingredients except fish. Cook about 20 minutes. If thicker consistency is desired, thicken with cornstarch or arrowroot. Fillet and skin fish and cut into 2½-inch squares. Add fish to mixture and cook slowly, stirring gently so as not to break fish. Cook about 20 minutes longer. Just before serving garnish fish with lemon slices and add sherry. Serve with rice or French bread.
Mrs. Sterrett Procter   *Lafayette, Louisiana*

DUCK GUMBO

4 large or 6 small ducks
1 gallon chicken stock
2 cups onions, chopped
1 cup green pepper, chopped
1 cup celery, chopped
2 pounds okra, chopped
½ onion
½ green pepper

1 cup Pillsbury Sauce and Gravy
  Flour
½-¾ cup vegetable oil
1 12-ounce can tomato paste
1 pound ground, hot sausage
Salt
Pepper
Tabasco, to taste

Soak ducks in salted water for several hours or overnight. Boil ducks in chicken stock in a large pot with 2 cups onions and 1 cup green pepper until very tender. Remove from stock and separate meat and skin from bones. Reserve stock. Chop meat. Discard onion and green pepper. Make a roux by browning flour and oil in an iron pot. Cook over medium heat, stirring constantly with a wooden spatula until mixture is a rich brown color. Turn off heat and add 2 cups stock from duck. Continue stirring until smoothly mixed. Add remaining stock, onions, pepper, celery, and okra to soup and simmer for 1 hour, stirring occasionally. Brown sausage and drain. Add duck, sausage, and tomato paste. Season to taste. Cook 30 minutes longer, stirring frequently. Serve over rice. Serves 18-20.
Merritt Pope

SHRIMP CHOWDER

2 pounds shrimp, cooked
3 medium onions, thinly sliced
5 medium potatoes, diced
1 cup boiling water
3 teaspoons salt
¼ teaspoon black pepper

3 tablespoons bacon fat
1 quart milk
¼ pound sharp Cheddar
  cheese, grated
2 tablespoons parsley, minced

In a deep pot heat bacon fat and saute' onion slices until barely tender. Add diced potatoes, salt, pepper, and boiling water. Simmer covered for 15 minutes or until potatoes are tender. Heat milk and grated cheese in a heavy pot until the cheese is melted and the milk is scalded. Be very careful that the milk does not boil, or the milk will curdle. Add the cheese and milk to the potatoes. Add shrimp and parsley and heat only until the shrimp are warmed through. Serves 4.
Mrs. William J. Boyle (Marise)

FISH CHOWDER

1½-2 pounds snapper,
  cut into chunks
2 tablespoons oil
2 slices salt pork
  (don't omit!)
1 medium onion, chopped
1 clove garlic, minced

Salt
Pepper
1 teaspoon chili powder
1 quart water
2 cups potatoes, peeled and cut
  into chunks
1 large can tomato sauce

In a deep heavy pot, lightly cook salt pork in oil. Add onion, garlic, salt, pepper, and chili powder and cook until onions are just tender. Add water and potatoes and simmer until the potatoes are about half done. Add the tomato sauce and fish and simmer until the liquid is a little reduced and potatoes and fish are done.
Mrs. Rayford Jones (Frances)

SPLIT PEA SOUP

1 meaty ham bone or several
   ham hocks
2 cups dried split peas
1½ quarts cold water

1 onion, diced
1 small carrot, (optional)
Salt
Pepper

Soak peas in water overnight. Drain and add cold water and remaining ingredients. Simmer 3-4 hours. Add more water if soup is too thick. Serves 8.
Mrs. Harvey Brewton (Lillie)

GAZPACHO

½ cup olive oil
4 teaspoons lemon juice
6 cups V-8 juice
2 cups beef broth
½ cup onion, grated
2 tomatoes, peeled and cubed
2 cups green peppers, diced

2 cucumbers, diced
2 cups celery, diced
Tabasco, to taste
Salt
Pepper
Croutons

Combine oil and lemon juice. Add other ingredients except croutons. Chill at least 4 hours before serving. Garnish with croutons.
Mrs. J. C. Harris (Ruby)   *Cove Hotel*

POLISH SAUSAGE AND POTATO SOUP

2 tablespoons butter or margarine
1 pound kielbasa (Polish sausage),
   sliced
1 cup onion, chopped
2 cups celery and leaves, chopped
4 cups cabbage, shredded
2 cups carrots, sliced

1 BAY LEAF
½ teaspoon dried leaf thyme
2 teaspoons salt
1½ cups beef bouillon
5 cups water
3 cups potatoes, pared and cubed

In a large kettle, melt butter and add kielbasa, onion, and celery. Cook until very tender. Add remaining ingredients except potatoes. Cover and cook for 1½ hours. Add potatoes; cover, and cook 20 minutes longer. Good and filling.
Mrs. Charles Alexander (Teeny)

SPRINGTIME VEGETABLE SOUP

2 quarts chicken stock
2 tablespoons flour
3 tablespoons oleo
3 ribs of celery, sliced
10 green onions, sliced
   (tops included)
3 carrots, sliced diagonally
2 small yellow squash, sliced
3 cups fresh green beans, cut
   into 1-inch pieces

½ teaspoon sugar
1 tablespoon parsley, snipped
1 teaspoon salt
Pepper
⅛ teaspoon sage
½ teaspoon marjoram
2 egg yolks
1 cup heavy cream

In a soup kettle melt oleo and sauté celery, green onions, and carrots for 5 minutes. Sprinkle flour over mixture and stir. Add stock while stirring and bring to a boil. Except for egg yolks and cream, add remaining ingredients. Bring to a boil again, reduce heat, and simmer 30 minutes. In a small bowl, blend egg yolks and heavy cream. Slowly add to soup, stirring constantly, until well blended. Adjust seasoning. *Do not boil!* Serves 8. Serve with fresh sliced bread and a variety of cold cuts or cheese.
Holly Bingham

BRUNSWICK STEW

½ pound onions, chopped
1 stick margarine
1 teaspoon salt
1 teaspoon pepper
1 tablespoon hot sauce
3 ounces vinegar

1 3-ounce can tomato paste
1 cup barbecue sauce
1 cup creamed corn
1 pound potatoes, cooked and
   mashed until lumpy
1 chicken, cooked and diced

Sauté onions in margarine. Add other ingredients except potatoes, meat, and water; cook 30 minutes. You may need to add a small amount of water to prevent sticking, especially when using fresh corn. Add potatoes and chicken; cook 15 minutes. Add water (2-3 cups as necessary) and cook 1-2 hours. Also very good with fresh pork. A very spicy and thick stew.
Mrs. Carl Funchess (Ruth)

MARY BELLE'S BRUNSWICK STEW

1 ounce salt pork, chopped	3 large onions, chopped
1 3½-pound stewing hen	Salt
2 large potatoes, peeled	Pepper
1 14-ounce can tomatoes	2 packages frozen, baby lima beans
½ teaspoon red pepper	2 cans whole kernel, white corn

Sauté salt pork and reserve fat. Using a heavy kettle, boil hen in the smallest amount of water possible until done. Remove from kettle and add to the broth whole potatoes, tomatoes, red pepper, onions, salt, pepper, and sautéed salt pork with the fat. Simmer for 3 hours; remove potatoes, add lima beans, and simmer 2 hours more. Mash potatoes and return to kettle. Remove meat from bone and cut into bite-sized pieces. Add meat and corn to broth; heat and serve.
Mrs. Abbott L. Browne (Mary Belle)

FRENCH ONION SOUP AU GRATIN
...as served at St. Andrews Bay Yacht Club...

4 large onions	Salt
¼ cup butter	Pepper
1 tablespoon flour	French bread or English
1½ quarts beef broth or	muffins
consommé	Parmesan, Gruyère, Swiss, or
BAY LEAVES	Romano cheese

Peel and thinly slice onions into rings. In a large saucepan, sauté the onion rings in butter very gently over low heat, stirring constantly with a wooden spoon until they are an even golden brown. Sprinkle flour over the onions and stir until blended. Gradually add the beef broth, stirring constantly until soup begins to boil. Lower the heat and simmer soup for about 20 minutes. Add BAY LEAVES, and other seasonings to taste. Serve in individual French Onion Soup crocks. Top with either toasted French bread or ½ of a toasted English muffin. Cover the bread with grated cheese or a combination of cheeses. Bake in a 400 degree oven until cheese browns.
Bob McCorkendale

VICHYSSOISE

...creamy, cold potato and leek soup...

1 quart chicken stock
1 pint heavy cream
1 bunch fresh leeks *or* green onions
3 medium-sized potatoes

Salt
Pepper
Chives, finely chopped

Peel potatoes and chop fine. Wash leeks and mince. Simmer potatoes and leeks in chicken stock for about 1 hour. Season to taste. Strain to remove any lumps. Place in refrigerator until chilled (about 1 hour). Remove from refrigerator, add cream, and thoroughly blend. Serve in chilled individual bowls, sprinkling each with chopped chives.
Note: If too thick, thin with milk.
Mrs. Sterrett Procter   *Lafayette, Louisiana*

HODGE'S CHILI

2 pounds lean, ground beef
3½ tablespoons chili powder
2 teaspoons salt
1 teaspoon sugar
1 large onion, chopped
½ green pepper, chopped
2 8-ounce cans tomato sauce
1 can Ro-Tel tomatoes

1 cup water
1 clove garlic, minced
1 teaspoon oregano
1 teaspoon comino seed
2 cans kidney beans, undrained
2 tablespoons cooking oil
2 tablespoons flour

Brown beef. Add other ingredients except beans, cooking oil, and flour; cover and simmer 1 hour. In a small bowl, mix cooking oil and flour together until smooth; add undrained kidney beans. Add bean mixture to kettle. Cover and simmer, stirring occasionally for about 30 minutes. Serves 8-10.
Mrs. Dixon McCloy (Hodge)

Salads & Salad Dressings

FLORIDA CRAB MOLD

2 envelopes unflavored gelatin
½ cup cold water
⅔ cup chili sauce
¾ cup water
½ cup mayonnaise
½ cup sour cream
½ cup tomato juice
2 teaspoons instant minced onion
2 tablespoons lemon juice
¼ teaspoon salt

¼ teaspoon dillweed
1 cup celery, diced
½ cup ripe olives, sliced
2 cups lump crabmeat

Salad greens
Olives to garnish
Hard-cooked eggs

Soften gelatin in the cold water. Heat the chili sauce with ¾ cup water; stir in the softened gelatin until thoroughly dissolved. Remove from heat and add mayonnaise, sour cream, tomato juice, onion, lemon juice, salt, and dill. Chill until the mixture is partially set. Stir in celery, ripe olives, and crabmeat. Turn mixture into a 6-cup ring mold and chill until firm. To serve, unmold on salad greens; garnish with whole olives and hard-cooked eggs. The mold can be made 2 days before using. Serves 8.
Mrs. Charles W. Ireland (Caroline)

CRAB LOUIS

½ cup mayonnaise
½ cup sour cream
2 tablespoons chili sauce
2 tablespoons salad oil
1 tablespoon vinegar
1 tablespoon horseradish
1 tablespoon fresh lemon juice
1 tablespoon parsley, snipped

2 teaspoons onions, grated
½ teaspoon salt
4 drops Tabasco sauce
1 pound lump crabmeat
1 medium head iceberg lettuce
Watercress sprigs
Lemon wedges

Combine all of the ingredients through Tabasco. Cover and refrigerate. If frozen, thaw crabmeat and pat dry with paper towel. Break lumps into bite-sized pieces. Keep refrigerated until ready to use. Arrange shredded lettuce on individual salad plates. Mound crabmeat and top with sauce. Garnish with watercress and lemon wedges.
Mrs. C. T. Clayton, Jr.   *Birmingham, Alabama*

SHRIMP SALAD

2 cups shrimp, chopped
1 cup celery, diced
1 teaspoon lemon juice

Salt
Pepper
Mayonnaise

Mix lightly all ingredients except mayonnaise and refrigerate. Just before serving, drain and toss with enough mayonnaise to hold ingredients together. Serve on crisp lettuce. Garnish with tomato and lemon wedges, hard-cooked eggs, or ripe olives. Serves 4.
Variation: Crabmeat or tuna may be used in place of shrimp.
Mrs. James E. Carter (Jeri)

TOSSED SHRIMP SALAD

2-3 pounds shrimp, boiled
1 medium head of lettuce,
   broken

1 jar of marinated artichoke
   hearts, quartered
1 small avocado, sliced

Toss above ingredients with:
1 pint sour cream
Juice of ½ lemon
Mrs. Eugene Kreiser (Ella)

1 package Good Seasons Bleu Cheese
Dressing Mix

SHRIMP AND POTATO SALAD

1 cup boiled shrimp, chopped
3 cups cooked potatoes, cubed
1 cup celery, diced
½ cup sweet mixed pickle relish
2 hard-cooked eggs, chopped
   or sliced

1 teaspoon salt
½ cup sour cream
2 tablespoons mayonnaise
½ envelope Italian salad
   dressing mix

Mix together the potatoes, celery, relish, eggs, and salt. To sour cream, add mayonnaise and dry Italian dressing mix. Combine the potato mixture with sour cream; refrigerate. To serve, add the shrimp and serve in a salad bowl lined with lettuce. Serves 8.
Mrs. Malcolm M. Traxler (Martha Lee)

BOBBIE'S SHRIMP SALAD

2 pounds cooked shrimp
6 hard-cooked eggs
½ small jar cubed salad pickles

Salt
Pepper
Kraft Mayonnaise

Peel and devein shrimp. Cut shrimp and eggs into large pieces. Add pickles, salt, and pepper to taste and enough mayonnaise to hold salad together. Serve on lettuce leaves with quartered tomatoes.
Mrs. M. G. Nelson (Bobbie)

SHRIMP AND RICE SALAD

1 cup cooked rice
⅓ cup green onions, minced
1 teaspoon curry powder
2 tablespoons salad oil
1½ tablespoons vinegar
4 cups cooked shrimp

1 cup celery, finely chopped
½ cup ripe olives, chopped
½ cup green pepper, chopped
¾-1 cup mayonnaise
Lemon-pepper, optional

To rice, add onions, curry powder, oil, and vinegar. Mix well and refrigerate overnight. Toss cooked shrimp with celery, olives, and green pepper. Mix the marinated mixture with mayonnaise and add to shrimp mixture. Serve on lettuce leaf. Serves 4-6.
Mrs. Gordon Hill (Mary)
Holly Bingham

AVOCADO-SHRIMP ASPIC

1 tablespoon unflavored gelatin
2 tablespoons cold water
1 cup boiling water
1 cup sieved avocado
1½ tablespoons lemon juice

Dash of Tabasco
¾ teaspoon salt
½ teaspoon Worcestershire sauce
1 pimiento, minced
1½ cups shrimp, cooked

Soften gelatin in cold water. Add boiling water and stir to dissolve gelatin. Add avocado, seasonings, and pimiento. Chill until mixture just begins to thicken. Add shrimp. Pour into a cold, wet mold. Chill until firm. Serves 8.
Mrs. A. V. Hooks (Mildred)

SHRIMP ASPIC

1 tablespoon unflavored gelatin
½ cup cold water
1 can tomato soup, heated
2 3-ounce packages cream
   cheese, softened

½ cup mayonnaise
1 cup celery, finely chopped
Minced onion, to taste
Salt
3 cups cooked shrimp, finely chopped

Dissolve gelatin in water. Add to hot tomato soup. Mix in softened cream cheese. Allow mixture to cool and add remaining ingredients. Place in an 8-inch square glass dish in refrigerator until set. Serves 6-8.
Mrs. John Colmery (Maxine)

SHRIMP-STUFFED ICEBERG

1 medium head iceberg lettuce
1 teaspoon instant minced onion
1 teaspoon lemon juice
1 8-ounce package cream cheese,
   softened

Dash of Tabasco
1 4½-ounce can shrimp
2 tablespoons dill pickle, chopped
1 tablespoon parsley, minced
2 tablespoons mayonnaise

Core, rinse, and drain lettuce thoroughly. Soften onion in lemon juice. Mix with cream cheese, mayonnaise, and Tabasco. Drain and chop shrimp. Blend shrimp, pickle, and parsley into cheese. Pull out center leaves from lettuce to make a cavity about 3 inches in diameter. Pack cheese mixture into lettuce and place in bowl, cored side up. Chill at least 4 hours. Keeps well for several days. To serve, cut into wedges. Serves 6-8.
Variation: Substitute chopped ham for the shrimp; add 2 tablespoons chopped stuffed olives and 2 or 3 tablespoons grated Cheddar cheese.
Holly Bingham

HOT SEAFOOD SALAD

1 green pepper
1 small onion
1 cup celery
1 cup mayonnaise
Buttered bread crumbs

½ teaspoon Worcestershire sauce
Dash of soy sauce
2 cups mixed seafood (shrimp, crab,
   or lobster)

Chop pepper, onion, and celery and mix with remaining ingredients except bread crumbs. Pour into a casserole dish and cover with toasted, buttered bread crumbs. Bake for 30 minutes at 350 degrees. Serves 6.
Mrs. Julian Bennett (Agatha)

TOMATO ASPIC

1½ envelopes unflavored
   gelatin
2 cups tomato juice
¼ cup vinegar
½ teaspoon salt

⅓ cup cold water
Celery, diced
Cucumber, diced
Olives, diced
Onions, diced

Dissolve gelatin in water. Heat tomato juice. Add gelatin and stir until completely dissolved; add vinegar and salt. Add to mixture diced celery, cucumber, olives, and onions, to taste. Chill until firm. Would also be good without vegetables.
Mrs. Reynolds E. Pitts (Jean)

ASHVILLE SALAD

1 can tomato soup
1 small carton cottage cheese
2 envelopes unflavored gelatin
¼ cup cold water
1½ cups celery, finely chopped
1 green pepper, finely chopped
1 small bottle stuffed olives,
   sliced

1 small onion, finely chopped
1 cup mayonnaise
1 tablespoon lemon juice
½ teaspoon salt
Dash of red pepper
Dash of garlic salt

Combine tomato soup with cottage cheese in a double boiler and stir until melted. Dissolve gelatin in water and add to soup mixture. Cook for about 20 minutes, stirring occasionally. Chill until partially set. Combine remaining ingredients and add to the gelatin mixture.
Mrs. Dorothy Logue Durham

MOLDED SALMON SALAD

1 3-ounce package lemon gelatin
1 teaspoon sugar
1½ cups boiling water
3 tablespoons vinegar
¼ teaspoon salt

¼ teaspoon dry mustard
½ cup mayonnaise
1 cup celery, chopped
1 cup cucumber, diced
1 large can salmon, flaked

Dissolve gelatin in boiling water and add vinegar. Chill. Combine salt, sugar, mustard, and mayonnaise. When gelatin is partially thickened, fold in mayonnaise mixture. Add remaining ingredients. Turn into molds, which have been rinsed in cold water. Chill until firm. Serve on lettuce, and garnish with pimiento, paprika, or radish roses.
Mrs. Ralph Segrest, Jr. (Jane)

CONGEALED SALMON

1 16-ounce can red salmon
2 cans tuna
5 or 6 sweet pickles, chopped
2 tablespoons sweet pickle juice
1 onion, grated
1 cup celery, chopped

4 hard-cooked eggs, chopped
1 cup mayonnaise
3 envelopes unflavored gelatin
¼ cup cold water
¼ cup hot water

Dissolve gelatin in cold water and add hot water. Mix all ingredients together and pour into slightly oiled fish mold. Refrigerate overnight. Serves 15.
Mrs. George Logue, Sr. (Gladys)

PARTY SOUFFLÉ TUNA

¾ cup ripe olives
1 3-ounce package lemon gelatin
1 cup hot water
½ cup cold water
½ cup mayonnaise
1 teaspoon prepared horseradish

2 tablespoons vinegar
¼ teaspoon salt
1 7-ounce can tuna
1 cup celery, chopped
3 hard-cooked eggs

Cut olives into small pieces. Dissolve gelatin in hot water; blend in cold water. Add mayonnaise, vinegar, salt, and horseradish. Beat with rotary egg beater. Pour into refrigerator tray and place in freezer compartment for 15-20 minutes or until partially set. Pour into bowl and beat until light and fluffy. Fold in olives, tuna, celery, and eggs. Put into a 1-quart mold and chill until firm. Serves 6-8.
Mrs. J. C. Harris (Ruby)   *Cove Hotel*

MARY ANNE'S SALAD

1 small head of cabbage,
    coarsely shredded
1 green pepper, sliced
    into strips
1 red onion, sliced into rings

1 rib of celery, chopped
¼ cup olive oil
Salt
Freshly ground pepper

In a large skillet, sauté cabbage, green pepper, and onion in olive oil until slightly wilted. Season with salt and pepper.
Mrs. Jimmy Christo (Mary Anne)

SAUERKRAUT SALAD

1 2½-pound can sauerkraut
1½ cups sugar
⅔ cup cider vinegar
1 cup celery, chopped

1 cup green pepper, chopped
½ cup onion, chopped
1 small jar pimiento, chopped

Rinse sauerkraut well in cold water and drain. Boil sugar and vinegar until clear. Combine other ingredients and pour syrup over them. Refrigerate and serve cold. Will keep for two weeks in refrigerator.
Mrs. E. Clay Lewis, III (Marsha)
Mrs. Edward L. Pipkin (Shirley)

MARINATED SLAW

1 head cabbage, finely shredded
1 large onion, sliced into rings
1 green pepper, cut into strips
½-¾ cup sugar
1 cup vinegar

¾ cup oil
2 teaspoons dry mustard
2 teaspoons celery seed
2 teaspoons salt

Combine cabbage, green pepper, and onion rings. Pour sugar over this. Combine last five ingredients in a saucepan. Bring to a boil. Mix and marinate for 24 hours, stirring occasionally.
Mrs. Newton Allen (Jane)
Mrs. Jill Jackson

ASPARAGUS-CUCUMBER MOLD

1 can asparagus soup
1 cup cucumber, chopped
¼ cup celery, chopped
1 small onion
½ cup boiling water

¼ cup parsley, minced
1 3-ounce package lime gelatin
½ cup mayonnaise
Salt
Pepper

Dissolve gelatin in water. Cool. Whip soup and mayonnaise together. Add salt and pepper. Stir in gelatin; add cucumber, onion, celery, and parsley. Pour into a mold and chill until firm. Serve on lettuce.
Mrs. Sam Fleming (Irene)

BROCCOLI SALAD

2 packages frozen broccoli florets
4 hard-cooked eggs
¾ cup mayonnaise
1 envelope unflavored gelatin
1¾ teaspoons salt

1 cup condensed consommé
2 teaspoons lemon juice
4 teaspoons Worcestershire sauce
Dash of Tabasco

Soften gelatin in a little cold water and then dissolve in boiling consommé. Add lemon juice, Worcestershire, and Tabasco. Chill until mixture begins to thicken. Mash eggs and cooked broccoli together. Add to gelatin mixture. Pour into a round mold or eight individual molds. Good served with Sour Cream-Horseradish Dressing (see index).
Mrs. John Robert Middlemas (Kendall)

CUCUMBERS IN SOUR CREAM

2 large cucumbers
1 onion
½ teaspoon salt
½ teaspoon sugar

1 tablespoon tarragon vinegar
Pepper
Sour cream to hold together
1 teaspoon paprika

Slice onions and cucumbers paper thin. Cover with crushed ice and water for at least 15 minutes. Drain. Combine remaining ingredients. Toss with onions and cucumbers. Serve immediately.
Mrs. Florence Hood   Moultrie, Georgia

WILTED LETTUCE

1 head of lettuce
6 strips of bacon
½ cup red wine vinegar

Salt
Pepper
3 hard-cooked eggs, chopped

Wash and thoroughly dry lettuce. Tear into small pieces; cover and chill. Cut bacon into small pieces, fry until crisp. Drain, reserving bacon drippings. Arrange bacon on top of lettuce with chopped eggs. Add vinegar, salt, and pepper to hot drippings in skillet. Pour over lettuce and toss quickly. This requires last minute preparation, so begin just as the meat finishes cooking.
The Editors

CAESAR SALAD

2 heads romaine lettuce
1 head iceberg lettuce
2 bunches scallions, chopped
3 tomatoes, cut into wedges

1 pound bacon, fried and crumbled
1 box garlic croutons
Parmesan cheese, grated

Make salad and toss in bacon, adding croutons last. Add dressing and sprinkle salad with cheese.

Dressing:

1 cup Wesson Oil
1 egg
1 teaspoon sugar

1 teaspoon garlic powder
1 teaspoon salt
Juice of 1 lemon

Make dressing, blending all ingredients well. Refrigerate at least one hour.
Mrs. George Christo (Judy)

ITALIAN SALAD

¼ cup bleu cheese
1 hard-cooked egg, chopped
¼ cup pepperoni or other Italian sausage, finely chopped
¼ cup ripe olives, chopped

Watercress
Iceberg lettuce
Endive lettuce
Romaine lettuce

Just before serving combine roughly broken pieces of greens in a large salad bowl. Top with remaining ingredients. Serve with Italian Salad Dressing (see index). Serves 6-8.
Holly Bingham

LUNCHEON CHICKEN SALAD

1 3-ounce package lemon gelatin
1 package unflavored gelatin
1 cup ginger ale
1 tablespoon lemon juice
1½ cups mayonnaise

2 cups cooked chicken, diced
⅓ cup celery, chopped
⅔ cup seedless grapes
½ cup pecans, chopped
⅓ cup green pepper, chopped

Dissolve lemon gelatin in 1 cup hot water. Add unflavored gelatin, ginger ale, and lemon juice, mixing thoroughly. Blend in mayonnaise. Chill until partially congealed in a 12x9-inch dish. Fold in chicken with remaining ingredients and refrigerate until firm. Serves 6.
Mrs. John Fishel (Louise)

SUMMER POTATO SALAD

2 teaspoons sweet basil
2 teaspoons summer savory
2 teaspoons marjoram
2 cups mayonnaise
4 medium onions, chopped
Cider vinegar

2 teaspoons celery salt
8 cups potatoes, cooked and diced
4 hard-cooked eggs, chopped
1 teaspoon salt
1 teaspoon pepper

Make seasoned mayonnaise by mixing together the basil, savory, marjoram, and mayonnaise. Chill for 2 hours. Cover onions with vinegar and let stand for 15 minutes. Toss the potatoes with chopped eggs, salt, pepper, celery salt, and drained onions. Add seasoned mayonnaise and mix to coat all ingredients.
Mrs. John Henry Sherman (Ruth)

CHICKEN SALAD

1 large hen
1 large onion
1 rib of celery
1 cup celery, finely chopped
½ pint mayonnaise
Almonds

Salt
Pepper
Capers (optional)
Sweet pickled onions (optional)
Pecans (optional)

Boil hen with cut onion and celery rib. Allow hen to cool in stock. Remove meat from bones. Cut chicken and combine with other ingredients. Makes about 25 sandwiches. Cut chicken coarsely to make 8 salad plates.
Mayonnaise:
2 egg yolks
1 pint Wesson Oil
Wine vinegar, to taste
Juice of 1½ lemons

Paprika
Salt
Pepper

Beat egg yolks in small mixing bowl. Pour in oil *very* slowly as you mix. After half of the oil is added, add salt, vinegar, lemon juice, paprika, and pepper. Then proceed to add remaining oil. Taste to see if more seasonings are required.
Mrs. Warren Middlemas, Jr. (Martha)

CHINESE VEGETABLE SALAD

1 can Chinese vegetables
1 can French-style green beans
1 can Le Sueur peas
1 can bean sprouts
1 can sliced mushrooms
1 can water chestnuts, sliced

2 onions, sliced into rings
¾ cup sugar
¾ cup white vinegar
Salt
Pepper

Drain vegetables and place in layers in a large bowl. Boil sugar and vinegar until sugar is dissolved. Pour mixture over vegetables and refrigerate overnight. Drain before serving.
Mrs. Frank H. Bromberg, Jr.   *Birmingham, Alabama*

POTATO SALAD

7 medium potatoes, peeled and cubed
1 cup celery, chopped
½ cup green pepper, chopped
1 small jar pimiento, chopped

1 heaping tablespoon celery seed
⅓ cup Wesson Oil
2 tablespoons sweet pickle juice
½-¾ cup mayonnaise
Salt

Cook potatoes. Cool. Add oil and toss. Add celery, green pepper, pimiento, celery seed, pickle juice, mayonnaise, and salt. Mix thoroughly. Chill before serving. Serves 6-8.
Mrs. R. William Lawrence (Linda)

MARY'S POTATO SALAD

3-4 medium potatoes
1 medium cucumber, sliced
1 medium onion, thinly sliced
½ pint mayonnaise
½ pint sour cream

2 teaspoons celery seed
2 tablespoons Worcestershire sauce
2 tablespoons vinegar
Salt
Pepper

Boil potatoes in jackets. Peel and slice. Layer potatoes, cucumbers, and onions. Mix other ingredients well and pour over vegetables. Cover and chill. Serves 8.
Mrs. Leon Mathis (Mary)

SALADE NIÇOISE

2 pounds potatoes, boiled and
  sliced
2 cups cut green beans, cooked
1 cup artichoke hearts
1 cup pitted, black olives
1 large onion, thinly sliced
3 7-ounce cans tuna, drained
1 pint cherry tomatoes
Salad greens

1 large green pepper, sliced into
  rings, (optional)
4 hard-cooked eggs
½ cup pimiento, chopped
2 cans rolled anchovies with
  capers
¼ cup parsley, snipped
3 cups Garlic Dressing (see index)

Combine potatoes, beans, artichoke hearts, and onions with Garlic Dressing. Marinate mixture in refrigerator for about 2 hours, stirring occasionally and gently. Line salad bowl with greens. Drain the marinated vegetables, reserving the dressing for later use and spoon over the greens. Place tuna in center of bowl. Arrange remaining ingredients around tuna. Sprinkle lightly with parsley. Serve with Garlic Dressing.
Mrs. Charles W. Ireland (Caroline)

HEARTS OF PALM AND ARTICHOKE HEARTS

1 can hearts of palm, drained
1 can artichokes, drained

6 pimiento strips

Place diced hearts of palm and sliced artichoke hearts on lettuce leaf; garnish with pimiento strips. Pour dressing over salad. Serves 6.
Dressing:

1 cup salad oil
⅓ cup vinegar
1 teaspoon lemon juice
½ teaspoon salt
½ teaspoon celery salt

¼ teaspoon dry mustard
¼ teaspoon cayenne pepper
1 teaspoon sugar
1 clove garlic, mashed
Dash of paprika

Combine ingredients in a jar; cover and shake. Makes 1½ cups.
Mrs. Harry A. Smith (Mable)

HOT CHICKEN SALAD

4 cups cold chicken, diced
2 tablespoons lemon juice
¾ cup mayonnaise
2 cups celery, chopped
4 hard-cooked eggs, sliced
½ teaspoon Accent

¾ cup cream of chicken or
   mushroom soup
1 teaspoon onion, chopped
1 small jar pimiento
1 cup cheese, grated
1½ cups crushed potato chips

Combine all ingredients except cheese and potato chips. Place in refrigerator overnight. Before serving, top with cheese and potato chips and bake at 350 degrees for 30-40 minutes.

Mrs. Larry Armstrong   *Humble, Texas*

PRESSED CHICKEN

1 large hen
1 clove garlic
2 medium onions, chopped
2 ribs of celery, chopped
1 teaspoon salt
½ teaspoon paprika
¼ teaspoon pepper
3 tablespoons unflavored gelatin

1½ tablespoons of lemon juice
1 cup celery, chopped
6 hard-cooked eggs
¾ cup mayonnaise
1 small jar of pimiento
Stuffed olives
4 cups chicken broth

Boil hen with garlic, onions, salt, pepper, paprika, and celery. Cook until tender. Strain and reserve broth. Dissolve gelatin in 1 cup of cooled broth over hot water. Add lemon juice to remaining 3 cups of cooled broth. Add a small amount of broth at a time to mayonnaise and blend. Add to the gelatin mixture. Bone chicken and cut into large pieces. Chop eggs and pimiento. Reserve some pimiento and 1 cup chopped celery. Put a layer of this mixture in a 2-quart dish. Cover with a little gelatin mixture and congeal slightly. Continue until all gelatin and chicken are used. Top with the remaining gelatin mixture and when congealed, garnish with stuffed olive slices and pimiento. Cut into squares and serve on lettuce. Sprinkle with paprika. Serves 8.

Mrs. Albert Lewis, Jr. (Jean)

CHICKEN OR TURKEY MOUSSE
....as was served at the Dixie Sherman Hotel....

4 envelopes unflavored gelatin
5 cups milk
1 cup butter
6 tablespoons flour
3 cups mayonnaise
3 teaspoons salt
1 teaspoon onion, grated

Dash of pepper
6 cups chicken or turkey, diced
2 cups celery, finely chopped
1 cup stuffed olives, sliced
1 cup almonds, finely chopped
1½ cups cream, whipped

Soften gelatin in ½ cup of milk for 5 minutes. Melt butter and blend in flour. Add remaining milk slowly, stirring constantly. Cook until smooth and thick. Remove from heat. Add gelatin and stir until dissolved. Blend mayonnaise into mixture. Cool. Carefully fold in remaining ingredients. Pour into a loaf pan and chill until firm. Serves 20.
Mrs. Walter Green (Marjorie)

APRICOT SALAD

2 No. 303 cans apricots (reserve juice)
1 No. 2 can crushed pineapple (reserve juice)
2 3-ounce packages orange gelatin

2 cups hot water
1 cup apricot juice
1½ cups miniature marshmallows

Mix gelatin with hot water; add 1 cup of apricot juice. Cool in mold until partially congealed. Add apricots, marshmallows, and pineapple. Chill.
Topping:
½ cup sugar
2 tablespoons flour
2 tablespoons butter

1 cup mixed juices
1 cup whipping cream, whipped

Mix thoroughly the above ingredients, except cream. Cook until thick. Let cool and fold in whipped cream. Unmold salad and cover with topping.
Mrs. Paul Gwinn   Pine Bluff, Arkansas
Mrs. Prentice Melder (Mary Lou)

BLACK CHERRY MOLD

1 No. 2 can pitted black cherries
(reserve juice)
1 3-ounce package cherry gelatin
1 cup port wine

1 package unflavored gelatin
½ cup nuts, chopped
1 8-ounce package cream cheese

Heat reserved cherry juice and wine. Pour over gelatins, stirring until dissolved. Add cherries and nuts to gelatin mixture and pour into mold. Serve with softened cream cheese on top.
Variation: A small can of crushed, well-drained pineapple is also very good in this.
Mrs. Casper E. Harris (Sue)

SPRING DELIGHT SALAD

1 3-ounce package lemon gelatin
1 3-ounce package lime gelatin
3 cups boiling water
1 No. 2 can crushed pineapple,
undrained

1 cup pecans, chopped
24 large marshmallows
1 teaspoon vinegar
2 3-ounce packages cream
cheese

Cut marshmallows into small pieces. Pour water over gelatin and marshmallows; stir until dissolved. Chill. Blend cheese with vinegar until smooth. Add undrained pineapple and blend; add pecans. Chill. When gelatin is ready to thicken, combine the two mixtures and mold as desired.
Mrs. T. Woodie Smith (Lois)

CHRISTMAS SALAD

2 3-ounce packages black cherry
gelatin
1 cup freshly ground cranberries
1 cup freshly ground oranges,
reserving juice

1 cup crushed pineapple,
undrained
1 cup pecans, chopped
1 teaspoon ground orange rind
1 cup red wine

Make gelatin according to package directions, using wine and juice from pineapple and orange as part of the liquid. Refrigerate gelatin mixture until it begins to thicken; stir in remaining ingredients. Chill in decorative mold; turn out on shredded lettuce and decorate with thinly sliced oranges for a colorful dish.
Mrs. Ray Wagner (Nancy)

APRICOT FLUFF

1 6-ounce package orange
   gelatin
1 No. 303 can apricot halves
1 No. 2 can crushed pineapple
1 cup apricot-pineapple
   juice
½ cup Cheddar cheese,
   grated

1 cup boiling water
½ cup miniature marshmallows
⅓ cup sugar
1 package Dream Whip
3 tablespoons flour
1 egg, beaten

Combine gelatin and water. Drain fruits and reserve one cup of the juice. Add remaining juice to gelatin. Cut apricots and add to pineapple. Combine with gelatin. Pour into a dish. Sprinkle marshmallows on top. Mix flour, sugar, juice, and egg together. Cook, stirring constantly until thickened. Cool. Prepare Dream Whip by package directions, omitting the vanilla. Fold topping into cooked mixture and pour over gelatin. Sprinkle cheese on top and chill for several hours.
Mrs. Milton Acton (Lois)
Mrs. A. L. Aldrich   *Hueytown, Alabama*

CINNAMON-APPLE SALAD

2 cups water
2 3-ounce packages cherry gelatin
¼ cup red cinnamon candies
1 15-ounce jar sweetened
   applesauce

¼ teaspoon lemon juice
1 8-ounce package cream cheese
½ cup mayonnaise
½ cup pecans, chopped

Dissolve gelatin in boiling water. Reduce heat to medium low and add candies, stirring until melted. Remove pan from heat; stir in applesauce and lemon juice. Pour 2 cups gelatin mixture into a ring mold or glass dish. Cover and chill until set. Beat cream cheese, gradually adding mayonnaise. Stir in nuts. Spread filling evenly over the firm gelatin mixture in mold. Cover and chill 1 hour longer. Heat reserved gelatin mixture over low heat, stirring until dissolved. Set pan in bowl of ice cubes and stir until mixture reaches the consistency of unbeaten egg whites. Spoon over cream cheese mixture. Cover and chill until set. Serves 8-10.
Mrs. George Gore (Madelyn)

CREAMY CARROT-NUT SALAD

2 3-ounce packages orange
  gelatin
2 cups boiling water
¾ cup sour cream
¼ cup mayonnaise

1 13-ounce can crushed pineapple,
  undrained
½ cup golden raisins, plumped
2 cups carrots, finely shredded
½ cup nuts, chopped

Pour boiling water over gelatin, stirring until dissolved. Spoon mayonnaise into a bowl with sour cream. Gradually add gelatin mixture, stirring until blended. Chill until mixture begins to thicken slightly, then stir in remaining ingredients. Turn into a 2-quart mold or individual molds. Serve on lettuce. Serves 10-12.
Note: Raisins may be plumped by placing them in a strainer and pouring warm water over them.
Mrs. Albert Lewis, Jr. (Jean)

SOUR CREAM CRANBERRY SALAD

First Layer:
1 3-ounce package of orange
  gelatin
1 cup boiling water

3 tablespoons sugar
2 teaspoons lemon juice
¾ jar orange-cranberry relish

Dissolve gelatin in boiling water. Stir in remaining ingredients. Pour into a round mold that has been rinsed in cold water. Chill until partially set.
Second Layer:
½ cup cranberry juice
1 3-ounce package orange gelatin
1 small carton cottage cheese
1 cup celery, diced

¼ teaspoon salt
½ cup pecans, chopped
1 teaspoon lemon juice
1 cup sour cream

Boil cranberry juice and pour over gelatin. Stir until dissolved. Add remaining ingredients except sour cream. Carefully fold in sour cream. Pour over first layer. Chill. Unmold and serve on lettuce.
Mrs. Ernest Bennett   *Hartsell, Alabama*

CRANBERRY SALAD

1 can whole cranberry sauce
1 can crushed pineapple, undrained

1 6-ounce package raspberry gelatin
1½ cups boiling water

Dissolve gelatin in boiling water. Add pineapple and cranberry sauce. Congeal.

Topping:
2 envelopes Dream Whip
1 8-ounce package cream cheese,
   softened

¾ cup pecans, chopped

Mix Dream Whip according to package directions. Fold in cream cheese; add nuts. Spoon topping on congealed salad. This is best made the day before. Use a 16x12x2-inch pan. Serves 16-22.
Mrs. D. B. James (Gertie)

DATE SALAD

2 3-ounce packages cream cheese
1 cup mayonnaise
2 tablespoons gelatin
¼ cup cold water

1 20-ounce can pineapple chunks
   (reserve juice)
½ package chopped dates
1 cup nuts, chopped

Mix cheese with mayonnaise. Soak gelatin in cold water. Heat pineapple juice and add to gelatin, stirring until dissolved. Cool and add first mixture. Add dates, nuts, and pineapple. Chill in mold.
Mrs. Gayle Sudduth (Betty)

SWEET AND TANGY FRUIT SALAD

3-4 bananas, sliced
1 can Awake concentrate, thawed
1 package frozen strawberries

1 can pitted dark, sweet cherries,
   with juice
1 large can fruit cocktail, drained

Marinate bananas in Awake serveral hours or overnight. Add remaining ingredients. This will keep in refrigerator for several days.
Mrs. Eugene Kreiser (Ella)

GREEN CONGEALED SALAD

...perfect with Shrimp Stacks...

1 1-pound 4-ounce can crushed pineapple
½ cup lemon juice
2 3-ounce packages lime gelatin
1 cup pecans, chopped

2 tablespoons lemon rind, grated
2 cups cottage cheese
1 cup celery, chopped
2 teaspoons horseradish
½ teaspoon salt

Drain juice from pineapple into a 4-cup measuring cup. Add lemon juice and enough boiling water to make 3 cups of liquid. Add gelatin and dissolve. Chill mixture until slightly thickened. Spoon about 1½ cups gelatin into a bowl and fold in pineapple, nuts, and grated lemon rind. Pour into a lightly greased loaf pan. Chill until just firm. Keep remaining gelatin at room temperature. When layer in loaf pan is firm, beat remaining gelatin until fluffy. Fold in cottage cheese, horseradish, celery, and salt. Spoon over layer in pan. Chill until firm and serve with Banana Dressing.

Banana Dressing:

½ cup mayonnaise
1 banana, mashed
2 cups nuts, chopped

3 tablespoons heavy cream
1 tablespoon lemon juice

Blend all the above ingredients well and serve with salad. Dressing and salad may be made a day before serving.

Mrs. Ben James   Ruston, Louisiana
Mrs. Jack Dyer (Jill)

MYSTERY SALAD

1 3-ounce package raspberry gelatin
½ cup hot water
Dash of Tabasco

1 pound can Del Monte stewed tomatoes

Dissolve gelatin in hot water. Add tomatoes, cutting large tomatoes into smaller pieces. Add Tabasco and pour into 6 small oiled molds. When congealed, serve on crisp lettuce with the following dressing.

Dressing:

⅔ cup sour cream
¼ teaspoon sugar

1 teaspoon horseradish
¼ teaspoon salt

Combine ingredients and mix well.
Mrs. Florence Hood   Moultrie, Georgia

PINEAPPLE-LIME SALAD

1 3-ounce package lime gelatin
¾ cup boiling water
1 cup evaporated milk
1 cup creamed cottage cheese
½ cup nuts, chopped

½ cup mayonnaise
1 tablespoon lemon juice
1 8½-ounce can crushed
   pineapple

Dissolve gelatin in boiling water. Cool slightly; stir in milk. Chill until thick but not firm. Fold in remaining ingredients and pour into an 8-inch square pan or 8 individual molds. Chill until firm. Cut into squares, or unmold, and serve on lettuce leaves. Serves 8.
Mrs. George Dudley (Ruth)

ORANGE-PINEAPPLE CREAM CHEESE SALAD

1 3-ounce package orange-pineapple
   gelatin
2 3-ounce packages cream cheese
1 small can mandarin oranges
1 medium-sized can crushed
   pineapple

⅔ cup pecans, chopped
½ cup mayonnaise
1 cup boiling water

Thoroughly cream cheese and add gelatin. Mix well. Add boiling water. Cool slightly. Add mayonnaise, nuts, and fruit. Stir and refrigerate.
Mrs. Beatrice M. Cowgill

SPICED PEACH SALAD I

Men like this, especially when served with wild game!

1 6-ounce package lemon gelatin
1 jar spiced pickled peaches,
   chopped (reserve juice)
1 jar Royal Ann cherries, pitted
   and chopped (reserve juice)

1 cup nuts, chopped
4 oranges, peeled and chopped
   (reserve juice)

Combine juices to make a little over 3 cups liquid. Prepare gelatin according to package directions using the juice as part of the liquid. Add the chopped ingredients and pour into 2 ring molds. Congeal. Serves 14-16.
Mrs. Ralph Garrison   *Eufaula, Alabama*

SPICED PEACH SALAD II

1 large can peach halves
(reserve juice)
¼ cup vinegar
¼ teaspoon salt
4 two-inch cinnamon sticks

¾ teaspoon whole cloves
2 3-ounce packages orange gelatin
1 5-ounce jar pineapple cream
cheese
¼ cup pecans, chopped

Add enough water to peach juice to make 1½ cups liquid. Add vinegar, salt, cinnamon, and cloves to liquid; simmer 10 minutes and strain. Add enough boiling water to make 3 cups of liquid and in this dissolve gelatin. Pour ½-1 inch of the gelatin into a flat mold, large enough to space peaches, or use individual molds. Chill remaining gelatin until thick. Make 7-8 cheese balls, roll in nuts and place in center of each peach. Cover with remaining gelatin mixture and chill until firm.
Note: Be sure to coat nut balls with gelatin.
Mrs. Creed Greer (Selby)

PICKLED PEACH SALAD

½ envelope unflavored gelatin
1 3-ounce package lemon or apple
gelatin
1 cup celery, diced

1 small can crushed pineapple
1 jar pickled peaches, sliced
½ cup nuts, chopped
1 cup boiling water

Drain and reserve juice from peaches and pineapple. Dissolve both gelatins in boiling water. Add ⅓ cup peach juice and ⅔ cup pineapple juice. When cooled, fold in celery, nuts, peaches, and pineapple. Pour into mold and refrigerate. Serves 8.
Mrs. William B. Singer   *Lumpkin, Georgia*

ORANGE-GRAPEFRUIT SALAD RING

2 3-ounce packages orange gelatin
1½ cups boiling water
1 6-ounce can frozen orange juice,
thawed

1 cup cold water
1 11-ounce can mandarin oranges
1 1-pound can grapefruit sections,
drained

Dissolve gelatin in boiling water; add juice and cold water. Drain oranges, reserving syrup. Add syrup to gelatin mixture. Chill until partially set; fold in fruit sections. Pour into a 6½-cup ring mold. Chill until set. Unmold and serve with mayonnaise. Serves 8-10. Delicious with barbecued chicken.
Mrs. Charles E. Collins (Marion)

TEA GARDEN SALAD

1 3-ounce package orange gelatin
1 cup hot freshly made black tea
1 cup juice drained from oranges
  and pineapple

1 11-ounce can mandarin orange
  sections
1 9-ounce can crushed pineapple
1 5-ounce can water chestnuts

Dissolve gelatin in hot tea. Add mixed fruit juices. (Add some orange juice to make 1 cup if needed.) Stir gelatin mixture and chill until partially set. Drain and cut water chestnuts into thin slices. Add chestnuts, pineapple, and orange sections to gelatin. Spoon into 8 well-oiled molds. Refrigerate until set and serve with the following dressing.

Dressing:

1 cup whipped cream
½ cup mayonnaise

Grated rind of 1 orange
Pinch of mace

Fold mayonnaise into cream; add orange rind and mace. Refrigerate. If recipe is doubled, use combination of orange and lemon gelatin.

Mrs. Tom Bingham (Martha)

STRAWBERRY SOUR CREAM SALAD

2 6-ounce packages strawberry
  gelatin
3 cups hot water
1 16-ounce package frozen
  strawberries
1 8-ounce can crushed pineapple,
  undrained

2 cups cold water
3 large bananas, mashed
½ cup walnuts, chopped
1 pint sour cream

Dissolve gelatin in hot water. Add frozen strawberries, stirring until dissolved. Add crushed pineapple and cold water. Pour half of the mixture into a 13x9x2-inch pan or two 1½-quart molds. Chill until cool and add half of the bananas and walnuts. Refrigerate until firm. Spread sour cream evenly over congealed mixture. Mix remaining bananas and nuts to the remaining gelatin mixture and pour over the sour cream. Chill until firm. Cut into squares and serve on lettuce. Yields 16-20 servings.

Mrs. Florence Stewart

ORANGE COTTAGE SALAD

1 pound cottage cheese, drained
1 3-ounce package orange gelatin
1 small can mandarin oranges

1 20-ounce can crushed pineapple
1 large carton Cool Whip

Sprinkle gelatin over cottage cheese and stir. Drain canned fruit and chop oranges. Add fruit to cottage cheese mixture. Fold in Cool Whip. Chill and serve on lettuce.
Mrs. T. Woodie Smith (Lois)

ELOISE'S FRUIT SALAD

2 cans pitted, white cherries, drained
2 oranges, peeled, sectioned, and cut into pieces

2 cups pineapple bits, drained
24 marshmallows, cut into thirds

Combine above with Orange Cream Salad Dressing and chill 24 hours.
Orange Cream Salad Dressing:

⅓ cup fresh orange juice
½ tablespoon lemon juice
¼ cup sugar
2 egg yolks

Salt
White pepper
¾ cup whipped cream

Cook orange juice, lemon juice, and sugar for 3 or 4 minutes, stirring constantly. Remove from heat and cool slightly. Add egg yolks, one at a time, beating well each time. Cook over hot water, stirring constantly, until mixture is creamy. Season with salt and white pepper; chill. Fold in whipped cream. Serves 8-12.
Mrs. Clell C. Warriner, Jr. (Jean Ann)

FROZEN FRUIT SALAD I

1 large can Pet Milk
1 large can fruit cocktail, drained
3 tablespoons lemon juice
1 small jar cherries

16 marshmallows, cut into small pieces
½ cup mayonnaise
½ cup nuts

Place milk in freezer and when partially frozen, whip until stiff, folding in lemon juice, marshmallows, mayonnaise, and drained fruit. Pour into a tray and freeze for 3 hours or more.
Letitia Corbett Moody

FROZEN FRUIT SALAD II

1 8-ounce package cream cheese
½ cup mayonnaise
1 No. 303 can fruit cocktail
1 small jar cherries, halved
1 cup small marshmallows

1 can mandarin oranges
½ cup pecans, chopped
½ teaspoon allspice
1 cup whipping cream

Soften cream cheese and blend with mayonnaise. Drain all fruits. Add allspice, marshmallows, nuts, and all fruit. Whip cream and fold into fruit mixture. Freeze.
Mrs. Ray Kelly (Tina)

FROZEN GRAPE SALAD

2 3-ounce packages cream cheese
2 tablespoons mayonnaise
2 tablespoons pineapple juice
24 marshmallows, cut up

1 No. 2 can crushed pineapple
1 cup cream, whipped
2 cups seedless grapes, chopped

Combine cream cheese and mayonnaise. Beat in pineapple juice. Add marshmallows and drained pineapple. Fold in whipped cream and grapes. Pour into a 1-quart refrigerator tray. Freeze until firm. Serve on lettuce with mayonnaise to which a small amount of cream has been added.
Mrs. Tom Bingham (Martha)

FRESH BING CHERRY SALAD

1 8-ounce package cream cheese
1 cup sour cream
¼ cup sugar
¼ teaspoon salt
1½ cups Bing cherries, drained

1 No. 303 can apricot halves, drained
1 9-ounce can crushed pineapple, drained
2 cups tiny marshmallows

Soften cream cheese and beat until fluffy. Stir in sour cream, sugar, and salt. Remove pits from cherries and cut in half. Add cherries, apricot halves, pineapple, and marshmallows to creamed mixture. Pour into a loaf pan and freeze 6 hours or overnight. Slice and serve on lettuce. Makes 8 servings.
Mrs. John E. Carroll   Kissimmee, Florida

THOUSAND ISLAND DRESSING

1 pint mayonnaise
2 hard-cooked eggs, grated
1 green pepper, finely chopped

1 tablespoon parsley flakes
1 tablespoon onion, finely grated
Paprika
1 bottle chili sauce

Mix all ingredients together and store in refrigerator. Makes 1 quart.
Mrs. Tim Smith (Mary Ann)

AVOCADO DRESSING

1 avocado, mashed (keep the seed)
½ cup sour cream
1 tablespoon lemon juice
⅓ cup oil

1 clove garlic, mashed
½ teaspoon chili powder
½ teaspoon sugar
¼ teaspoon salt

Blend or whip all ingredients until well mixed and smooth. Place seed in the dressing to retain the color.
Mrs. Creed Greer (Selby)

ROQUEFORT DRESSING

1 cup sour cream
2 tablespoons mayonnaise
1 tablespoon vinegar
½ teaspoon garlic salt

⅛ teaspoon salt
½ teaspoon sugar
1 small wedge Roquefort cheese

Combine first 6 ingredients. Crumble cheese into mixture and chill.
Mrs. James E. Carter (Jeri)

BLENDER RUSSIAN DRESSING

¼ small onion
¼ cup vinegar
½ cup sugar
1½ teaspoons salt

1½ teaspoons dry mustard
½ teaspoon celery salt
1½ teaspoons celery seed
1 cup salad oil

Combine onion and vinegar in blender and chop. Add remaining dry ingredients and blend. Set on lowest speed and *slowly* add oil. This recipe was given to me by Mrs. J. Wayne Reitz, wife of a former president of the University of Florida. She served it over quartered lettuce; however, it is also delicious over a tossed or fresh fruit salad.
Mrs. Raymond Syfrett (Ann)

SOUR CREAM-HORSERADISH DRESSING

½ cup sour cream
1 cup mayonnaise
1 heaping tablespoon horseradish
Dash of dry mustard

2 cloves garlic, pressed
1 tablespoon chives
Dash of Tabasco

Combine all ingredients except chives in blender. Add chives and refrigerate.
Serve on broccoli or asparagus salad.
Mrs. Ronald E. Tew (Marti)

GARLIC DRESSING

Serve with Salade Niçoise.

2 cups olive oil
½ cup tarragon vinegar
¼ cup fresh lemon juice
2 cloves garlic, minced

1 tablespoon dry mustard
1 teaspoon sugar
1 tablespoon salt
Coarsely ground black pepper

Combine mustard, sugar, salt, and a generous amount of pepper. Add garlic,
vinegar, and lemon juice; stir until thoroughly blended. Add oil and mix well.
Stir or shake vigorously just before using.
Mrs. Charles W. Ireland (Caroline)

ITALIAN SALAD DRESSING

1 cup olive oil
¼ cup wine vinegar
2 cloves garlic
½ teaspoon salt
½ teaspoon black pepper, coarsely
 ground

½ teaspoon monosodium glutamate
Pinch of sweet basil
¼ cup green onions, minced
2 tablespoons parsley, minced

Blend above ingredients; store in a cruet and refrigerate overnight. Remove
garlic cloves just before serving. Use with Italian Salad.
Variation: Olive oil combined with vegetable oil may be used for a milder
taste.
Holly Bingham

STONEHENGE COUNTRY DRESSING

1½ cups mayonnaise
⅔ cup heavy cream
1 tablespoon dry mustard
¼ teaspoon thyme
¼ teaspoon savory
¼ teaspoon pepper

2 tablespoons Sago cheese, grated
2 tablespoons onion, finely chopped
1 tablespoon salt, or less
2 tablespoons white vinegar
1 cup Gruyère cheese
½ clove garlic, minced

Place all ingredients in a mixing bowl and blend with a mixer or wire whisk.
This is delicious served with a fresh mixed garden salad!
Mrs. Buford Ennis (Dot)

VINAIGRETTE FOR FRESH ASPARAGUS

1 teaspoon salt
¼ teaspoon paprika
1 tablespoon tarragon vinegar
2 tablespoons cider vinegar
6 tablespoons olive oil

1 tablespoon green pepper,
minced
1 tablespoon parsley
1 teaspoon chives

Combine all ingredients in a bottle and shake well. Serve hot or cold over
freshly cooked asparagus. This is great for basting fish.
Mrs. J. C. Harris (Ruby)   *Cove Hotel*

HOMEMADE MAYONNAISE

1 egg
2 tablespoons fresh lemon juice
¼ teaspoon salt
Pinch of cayenne pepper

½ teaspoon dry mustard
1 teaspoon Gulden's spicy
brown mustard
1 cup safflower oil

Combine egg, lemon juice, salt, cayenne, mustards, and ¼ cup of the oil.
Blend for 15 seconds on chop or #3 speed. Immediately add remaining oil.
Pour rapidly so that oil is poured in another 15 seconds. Blend on liquify for 3
seconds.
Mrs. Florence Hood   *Moultrie, Georgia*

FRENCH DRESSING

1 teaspoon salt
1 medium onion, grated
3-5 cloves garlic, minced
1 cup catsup
Salad oil

3 teaspoons Worcestershire sauce
3 tablespoons A. 1. sauce
Dash of paprika
1 cup sugar
1 cup vinegar

Combine all ingredients except oil in a 1-quart jar. Fill jar with salad oil and shake well. Store in refrigerator. This sauce is good on hot beets, beans, and other vegetables.
Mrs. Murray Crowder (Harriet)

CAESAR SALAD DRESSING

1 pint mayonnaise
2 eggs
½ teaspoon curry powder
¼ teaspoon garlic powder

½ cup Parmesan cheese
2 tablespoons anchovy paste
½ envelope onion soup mix

Mix above ingredients in blender. Serve with croutons over romaine lettuce.
Mrs. Harvey Mathis (Marjorie)

POPPY SEED SALAD DRESSING

½ cup sugar
1 teaspoon dry mustard
1 teaspoon salt
1 cup salad oil

3 tablespoons vinegar
2 teaspoons poppy seeds
1 tablespoon lemon juice
1 teaspoon paprika

Combine all ingredients but oil. Add oil a little at a time mixing with a wire whisk. Yields 1½ cups.
Mrs. Ira A. Hutchinson (Allene)

TOMATO SOUP FRENCH DRESSING

1 can tomato soup
¾ cup vinegar
½ cup sugar
1½ cups Wesson Oil

1 teaspoon salt
½ teaspoon onion juice
1 clove garlic, minced

Combine all ingredients in a jar and shake well. Makes 1 quart.
Mrs. Tom K. Hannah   *Eustis, Florida*

Sauces

LEMON SAUCE

1½ cups water	Juice of 2 lemons
1 cup sugar	2 eggs
2 tablespoons flour	Lump of butter

Over low heat combine flour, sugar and ¾ cup water. Add eggs. Beat well and stir until thickened; add remaining water, lemon juice, and butter.

Mrs. J. C. Harris (Ruby)   *Cove Hotel*

HARD SAUCE

½ cup butter	2 teaspoons vanilla
1 cup confectioners' sugar	¼ teaspoon rum flavoring

In a medium bowl, cream butter and sugar together and beat until fluffy. Add vanilla and rum flavoring. Serve over Purple Plum Mincemeat Pie. Yields 1 cup.

Mrs. Ray Wagner (Nancy)

PLUM SAUCE

7 pounds plums (barely ripe)	1 teaspoon allspice
1 pint vinegar	1 teaspoon cinnamon (optional)
4 pounds sugar	

Wash and cover plums with water and boil for five minutes. Plums may be pitted now, if desired. Drain well and put plums in boiler with remaining ingredients. Cook until thickened, about 25-30 minutes. Put sauce in sterilized jars and seal.

Note: Spices put in a small bag will make a clearer sauce. The liquid, if drained after 5 minutes of cooking, may be used to make jelly.

Mrs. F. A. Bridges   *Dawson, Georgia*

CARAMEL SAUCE

½ cup sugar	1 cup brown sugar, packed
¼ cup butter	1 cup whipping cream

Dissolve sugars in butter and cream over low heat in double boiler. Sauce thickens as it cools.

Note: Delicious served over angel food cake with a dollop of whipped cream or over ice cream.

Mrs. Jack Segler (Patty)

ALMOND SAUCE
. . .delicious on angel food cake. . .

5 tablespoons butter, melted
3 tablespoons cornstarch
1 pint milk
1 cup sugar

5 egg yolks
¼ teaspoon salt
1 teaspoon almond extract
1 pint whipping cream

Combine butter and cornstarch in a saucepan. Add sugar, salt, and slowly add milk. Heat almost to boiling. Beat yolks and slowly pour custard into them while stirring. Return mixture to boiler and simmer until slightly thickened. Do not boil. When cool, add almond flavoring and fold in stiffly beaten cream. Serves 16.
Mrs. J. C. Harris (Ruby)   *Cove Hotel*

CHOCOLATE SAUCE

2 cups sugar
1 14-ounce can evaporated milk
4 1-ounce squares of chocolate

¼ cup butter
½ teaspoon salt
1 teaspoon vanilla

Combine sugar, milk, chocolate, and salt. Cook over medium heat, stirring constantly until mixture thickens. Remove from heat. Add butter and vanilla. Serve hot over vanilla ice cream.
Mrs. Aubrey Heim (Ann)

SPICY CHERRY SAUCE FOR HAM

¾ cup sugar
Dash of salt
2 tablespoons cornstarch
¾ cup orange juice
1 inch stick cinnamon

½ teaspoon whole cloves
1 No. 2 can pitted, tart, red
cherries
¼ teaspoon red food coloring
Juice of 1 lemon

Combine sugar, salt, and cornstarch; stir in orange and lemon juice. Add undrained cherries, spices, and food coloring. Cook, stirring constantly, over medium heat until mixture thickens and comes to a boil. Boil 2 minutes; remove stick cinnamon and cloves. Serve warm with ham. Makes 3 cups.
Mrs. James A. Poyner, Sr. (Nell)

MINT SAUCE FOR LAMB

4 tablespoons fresh mint,
finely chopped
1 tablespoon sugar

¼ teaspoon salt
3 tablespoons vinegar, heated

Place mint in a bowl and add sugar. Cover and let stand for 1 hour. Add salt to hot vinegar. Pour over mint. Let stand several days before using.
Mrs. T. Woodie Smith (Lois)

WINE SAUCE FOR GAME AND FOWL

⅓ cup currant jelly
⅓ cup catsup

⅓ cup sherry

In a saucepan, melt jelly. Add catsup and sherry. Serve warm.
Mrs. Casper E. Harris (Sue)

GEECHEE SAUCE

¼ pound butter, melted
5 teaspoons mustard
3 cloves garlic, minced
2 teaspoons salt

½ teaspoon pepper
4 teaspoons Worcestershire sauce
¼ cup vinegar
Dash of hot sauce

Combine all ingredients in a saucepan. Bring to a boil. Great for basting chicken while grilling over charcoal.
Mrs. Benjamin W. Redding (Dee)

AUTHENTIC TERIYAKI SAUCE

8 ounces soy sauce
6 ounces or more water
1½ ounces bourbon
2 tablespoons sugar

1 tablespoon Accent
1 tablespoon confectioners' sugar
Garlic clove, crushed

Combine all ingredients. Marinate beef or chicken 12 to 24 hours before barbecuing.
Mrs. Charles Ireland (Caroline)

REMOULADE SAUCE

1 egg, hard-cooked
2 shallots, finely chopped
4 cloves garlic, minced
¼ cup spinach, cooked
2 cups mayonnaise

1 tablespoon Worcestershire sauce
1 tablespoon Creole mustard
1 tablespoon lemon juice
1⅓ ounces anchovy paste
Dash of Tabasco

Finely chop egg, shallots, garlic, and spinach and combine with remaining ingredients. This is used with shrimp salad moistened with mayonnaise and placed on a bed of lettuce.
Mrs. Jack Dyer (Jill)

SHRIMP COCKTAIL SAUCE

1 cup mayonnaise
⅓ cup catsup
¼ teaspoon dehydrated
horseradish

3 tablespoons Worcestershire sauce
Salt
Pepper

Whip ingredients together with a fork. Serve with boiled shrimp. Also good with crab claws.
Mrs. Charles Anderson (Janet)

BAHAMA FISH SAUCE

2 medium onions, sliced
1 pimiento, chopped
1 green pepper, diced
6-8 bird peppers, chopped
¾ cup olive oil

1½ cups tomato paste
1 teaspoon salt
1½ teaspoons thyme
1½ teaspoons red pepper

Sauté onion, pepper, and pimiento in oil until onion is transparent. Add remaining ingredients and simmer. Ladle over baked fish.
Note: Bird peppers are the tiny round peppers put in vinegar to make hot pepper sauce, usually found in oyster bars.
Mrs. Charles Ireland (Caroline)

BONNE FEMME SAUCE

...excellent with shrimp, scamp, or black grouper...

1 small onion, chopped
½ pound mushrooms, chopped
½ cup dry white wine
2 tablespoons fresh lemon juice
½ cup water
3 tablespoons flour

1 cup half and half
2 tablespoons Parmesan cheese, grated (optional)
2 tablespoons parsley, snipped
½ teaspoon salt

Melt butter in a large skillet and cook onions until tender. Add mushrooms and cook for 3 minutes. Slowly stir in wine, lemon juice, and ½ cup of water. Reduce to low heat. Combine in a small bowl flour, salt, and half and half. After mixture is well blended, pour through a strainer into sauce in skillet. Cook, stirring constantly, until mixture has thickened. Pour sauce over platter of freshly poached fish. Sprinkle with cheese and parsley and broil for approximately 3 minutes.
Mrs. Lambert Anderson (Evelyn)

SHRIMP SAUCE

1 cup mayonnaise
¾ cup catsup
1 medium onion, grated
⅓ cup pickle relish
1 tablespoon Worcestershire sauce

Dash of Tabasco
1 teaspoon horseradish
Salt
Pepper

Combine all ingredients and chill.
Mrs. William E. Lark (Ruthie)

CRAB LOUIS SAUCE

1 cup mayonnaise
1 tablespoon chives, chopped
1 tablespoon onion, grated
1 tablespoon lemon juice
½ cup chili sauce
1 teaspoon green pepper, minced

1 teaspoon Worcestershire sauce
¼ teaspoon Tabasco
1 tablespoon capers
Salt
Pepper

Combine all ingredients. Chill. Serve with crabmeat as a salad.
Mrs. Merritt Pope (Edna)

TARTAR SAUCE

⅓ cup onion, grated
⅔ cup Kosher pickles, grated
4 tablespoons mayonnaise

Salt
Pepper

Combine all ingredients and chill.
Mrs. Charles Anderson (Janet)

SKORDALIA

...Greek garlic sauce...

4-5 garlic cloves
¼ teaspoon salt
18 slices of day-old bread
¾ cup Wesson Oil

4 teaspoons cider vinegar
1 teaspoon lemon juice
1-2 tablespoons cold water

In a bowl, crush garlic well and add salt. Garlic will almost disappear after being crushed. Set aside. Remove crust from bread and soak one piece at a time in a small container of water, just long enough to wet. Squeeze out excess water and place soaked bread in mixer and begin beating slowly. Add only 2-3 slices of bread at a time, beating well after each addition. Use 2 or 3 slices of soaked bread to remove the crushed garlic from the container. Keep adding bread a little at a time until it begins to be smooth looking. Then *slowly* add oil, not more than one tablespoon at a time and beat continually. Add lemon juice and vinegar. Add cold water and continue beating. Sauce should be the consistency of mayonnaise, or, if thinner sauce is desired, add more water, especially if sauce is to be used as a dip. This sauce is delicious served on top of fried fish, fried eggplant, fried yellow squash, beets, cucumbers, or even used as a salad dressing. The amount of garlic and vinegar may be increased according to your own taste, if desired. This will keep in the refrigerator for two weeks or longer.
Mrs. Olympia G. Elchos   *Vicksburg, Mississippi*

LOUISE'S MUSTARD

4 ounces Coleman's Dry Mustard
1 cup lightly packed brown sugar
2 tablespoons flour

1 cup cider vinegar
1 can beef consommé,
3 eggs

Combine ingredients in blender. Cook in a double boiler until thick, stirring occasionally. Refrigerate when cooled.
Mrs. Leslie R. Nicholas (Louise)

BARBECUE SAUCE I

¾ cup onion, chopped
½ cup salad oil
¾ cup catsup
¾ cup water
⅓ cup lemon juice

3 tablespoons sugar
3 tablespoons Worcestershire sauce
2 tablespoons prepared mustard
2 teaspoons salt
½ teaspoon pepper

Cook onion in salad oil until tender. Add remaining ingredients and simmer for 15 minutes.
Mrs. A. H. Lisenby (Elizabeth)

BARBECUE SAUCE II

1 cup catsup
¼ cup Worcestershire sauce
4 tablespoons wine vinegar
4 tablespoons Italian salad
  dressing

1 cup Coca Cola
Tabasco to taste
¼ teaspoon oregano
¼ teaspoon dry mustard

Combine all ingredients. Cook until sauce thickens and serve over hot chicken, sausage, pork, or beef.
Joe Goodwin   *Ruston, Louisiana*

BARBECUE SAUCE III

2¼ cups catsup
2½ tablespoons Worcestershire
  sauce
¾ teaspoon cayenne pepper
¾ teaspoon chili powder
½ cup tarragon vinegar

1 cup sugar
1 tablespoon minced onion
6-8 cloves garlic
2 strips salt pork
1 cup salt pork liquor

To obtain liquor boil salt pork in 1½ cups water. Add remaining ingredients to liquor and bring to a boil. Makes 1 quart.
Mrs. Paul H. Eubanks (Maedelle)

HORSERADISH SAUCE

¾ cup consommé
½ cup dry white wine
½ cup fresh horseradish, grated
1 cup sour cream
Seasoned salt

Pepper
3 tablespoons fine bread crumbs
1 teaspoon dry mustard
1 egg yolk

Combine consommé, wine, and horseradish with sour cream. Simmer about 15 minutes and add crumbs and seasonings. For a thicker sauce, add beaten egg yolk mixed with a little of the sour cream and stir until smooth.
Mrs. Florence Hood   *Moultrie, Georgia.*

PAPRIKA SAUCE
...good used with meats...

2 shallots, chopped
1 clove garlic, minced
1 tablespoon butter
2 tablespoons flour

2 tablespoons paprika
1 cup chicken bouillon
1 cup sour cream
Lemon juice to taste

Sauté shallots and garlic in butter. Mix flour and paprika with bouillon. Cook until thickened. Remove from heat and fold in sour cream. Add lemon juice. Store in refrigerator.
Mrs. Florence Hood   *Moultrie, Georgia.*

HOMEMADE MUSTARD

1 cup Coleman's Dry Mustard
1 cup vinegar

2 eggs
1 cup sugar

Combine mustard and vinegar. Let stand overnight. Beat eggs and sugar together and combine the two mixtures. Cook in double boiler for 15 minutes, stirring occasionally. Keeps indefinitely in refrigerator. Makes 3 cups. Good with cheese and crackers.
Mrs. Morton Carl   *Opelika, Alabama*

STEAK SAUCE

½ cup oil
¼ cup Kitchen Bouquet
Salt
Pepper

Accent
Lemon and orange peel
Garlic
Charcoal Seasoning

Combine all ingredients. Brush on steaks and broil.
Mrs. Peter H. Brower (Judy)

ALMOND BUTTER FOR ASPARAGUS

½ cup butter
½ cup slivered almonds
2 tablespoons cucumber, grated

2 teaspoons lemon juice
½ teaspoon salt

Combine butter and almonds in broiler pan and broil until almonds are crisp and golden. Add cucumber, lemon juice, and salt to almonds and serve immediately.
Mrs. John Robert Middlemas (Kendall)

HOLLANDAISE SAUCE

1 stick butter
4 egg yolks
¼ cup lemon juice

¼ cup whipping cream
Dash of salt

Melt butter in double boiler. Stir in egg yolks and salt. Add lemon juice while beating with an electric mixer. After mixture begins to thicken, remove from heat. Beat in whipping cream. This can be made ahead of time, refrigerated, and reheated. When reheating, beat with electric mixer to avoid lumps.
Mrs. Lynn C. Higby (Dedee)

ALMOST HOLLANDAISE SAUCE

3 tablespoons butter
2 tablespoons flour
¾ cup hot water
½ teaspoon salt

¼ teaspoon Accent
Juice of 1 small lemon
2 egg yolks

Melt butter in double boiler. Add flour, stirring gently. Slowly add water, salt, and Accent. Simmer until ready to use. Add egg yolks and lemon juice. Cook for 3 minutes.
Mrs. Arthur A. Reams (Elinor)

Cheese & Eggs

QUICHE LORRAINE

Crust:

1¼ cups flour, sifted
½ cup butter, softened
1 tablespoon ice water

1 egg yolk
1 teaspoon salt

Lightly beat egg yolk, butter, and salt together. Pour flour into a large bowl and make a well in the center. Pour egg mixture into the well and with fingers work into a smooth paste, gradually working in all of the flour. Sprinkle with ice water and gather into a ball. Wrap in waxed paper and chill in refrigerator for 30 minutes. Roll dough and line a 9-inch pie plate with the dough. Flute edges and prick sides and bottom. Bake at 450 degrees for 5 minutes. Cool and place in freezer for at least 1 hour.

Filling:

1 tablespoon butter
2 small onions, finely chopped
1 cup cooked ham, finely diced
1 cup Gruyère cheese, grated
4 eggs (room temperature)

2 cups heavy cream
½ teaspoon salt
½ teaspoon cayenne pepper
½ teaspoon white pepper

Melt butter and sauté onions until they are transparent. Place ham in frozen pie shell. Sprinkle cheese and onion on top of ham. Beat eggs, cream, and seasonings and pour over onion-cheese mixture. Bake on lower shelf in oven at 450 degrees for 15 minutes. Reduce heat to 350 degrees and bake until custard is set. Insert knife, and if it comes out clean, pie is done. If pie is frozen before baking, bake at 450 degrees for 15 minutes. Reduce heat to 350 degrees and bake for 50 minutes on upper shelf of oven until custard is done. May be served hot, cold, or at room temperature. The French usually serve it at room temperature.

Mrs. Arthur A. Reams (Elinor)

CHEESE GRITS CASSEROLE

1 cup grits
1 teaspoon salt
4 cups water
1 garlic cheese roll

½ stick oleo
2 eggs, beaten
½ cup milk

Cook grits in boiling, salted water as directed on box. Blend in cheese and oleo, stirring until melted. Add milk and eggs. Bake in a 1½-quart casserole at 350 degrees for 45 minutes.

Mrs. C. L. Jinks, Jr. (Mary Catherine)
Mrs. Ronny Harrell　　　　　*Donalsonville, Georgia*

CHILI RELLENOS

2 4-ounce cans whole green chilies
½ pound Monterey Jack cheese
2 eggs, separated
Shortening
1 jar Green Chili Salsa
Flour
Salt
Pepper

Season flour with salt and pepper. Carefully stuff chilies with cheese, which has been cut into thin strips. Beat egg whites until stiff; fold in beaten egg yolks. Dip stuffed chilies into egg mixture, then roll in flour. Fry in hot oil until golden brown on both sides. Serve hot with heated Salsa as topping.
Mrs. James E. Carter (Jeri)

GARLIC CHEESE GRITS

2 cups quick grits
2 sticks butter
1 Kraft garlic cheese roll
1 Kraft Jalepeños cheese roll
1 teaspoon Worcestershire sauce
½ cup milk
2 eggs, beaten
Paprika

Cook grits according to package directions. Add butter, cheese rolls, and Worcestershire. Mix beaten eggs with milk and stir into grits. Place in a buttered casserole. Sprinkle with paprika. Bake at 350 degrees for 25 minutes. Serves 12.
Mrs. E. Clay Lewis, III (Marsha)

CHEESE AND RYE CASSEROLE

12 slices party rye bread
Butter, softened
Prepared mustard
2 4-ounce packages shredded
    Cheddar cheese
½ cup Parmesan cheese
3 eggs
3 cups milk
1 teaspoon Worcestershire sauce
½ teaspoon salt

Spread bread on one side with butter and other side with mustard. In a casserole dish place one layer of bread, then cheese, then another layer of bread. Beat eggs slightly; add milk, salt, and Worcestershire sauce. Pour over bread and let stand covered in refrigerator at least 8 hours. Bake uncovered at 350 degrees for 1 hour.
Mrs. Sam Ridley (Marge)

WELSH RABBIT (RAREBIT)

1½ tablespoons flour
½ cup evaporated milk
½ teaspoon salt
½ teaspoon dry mustard
1 teaspoon Tabasco
Garnishes:
Pimiento
Mushrooms
Green peppers
Tomatoes

1 teaspoon Worcestershire sauce
4 cups sharp Cheddar cheese, grated
¾-1 cup beer, wine, or ale
English muffins

Hard-cooked eggs
Bacon
Anchovies

In a double boiler combine flour, milk, salt, mustard, Tabasco, and Worcestershire; cook until mixture has thickened. Add cheese and stir until melted. Add beer as needed. Serve hot over toasted muffins and top with any of the desired garnishes.

Note: This may also be used as an hors d'oeuvre. Serve from a chafing dish with corn chips, omitting garnishes.

Mrs. A. D. Teal, Jr.   *Deland, Florida*

INSTEAD OF EGGS BENEDICT

. . .great for a Sunday brunch. . .

2 cans cream of chicken soup
Salt
Pepper
1 cup milk
4 teaspoons instant minced onions
4 dashes of Tabasco sauce

1 teaspoon prepared mustard
8 ounces Swiss cheese, shredded
12 eggs
12½-inch slices French bread,
   halved and buttered
Parsley, snipped

Combine soup, milk, onions, Tabasco, mustard, salt, and pepper in a saucepan. Cook, stirring until smooth and thoroughly heated. Remove from heat. Stir in cheese until melted. Pour 1 cup of sauce into each of *two* 10x6x1¾-inch baking dishes. Break 6 eggs into sauce in each casserole. Carefully spoon remaining sauce around eggs. Stand French bread slices around edge of casseroles with crust up. Bake at 350 degrees for 20 minutes or until eggs are set. Garnish with parsley. Serves 12.

Mrs. Sterrett Procter   *Lafayette, Louisiana*

BREAKFAST CASSEROLE

¼ cup onion, chopped
2 tablespoons butter
2 tablespoons flour
1½ cups milk

1 cup sharp cheese, shredded
6 hard-cooked eggs, sliced
1½ cups potato chips, crushed
10-12 slices of bacon, crumbled

Fry bacon until crisp; drain and set aside. Sauté onion in butter; blend in flour and milk. Stir until thick; add cheese. Place eggs in a 10x6x1½-inch baking dish. Cover with half of the cheese sauce, potato chips, and crumbled bacon. Repeat layers and bake at 350 degrees for 15 to 20 minutes.
Mrs. Robert Gary Lee (Jean)

FLUFFY BAKED OMELET

6 eggs, separated
1 tablespoon flour
1 tablespoon cornstarch
1 cup milk

2 tablespoons butter
½ teaspoon salt
Coarsely ground pepper

Beat egg yolks. Add flour, cornstarch, salt, and pepper. Beat until smooth. Gradually add milk, stirring constantly. Beat egg whites until stiff but not dry. Fold into egg yolk mixture. Melt butter in a heavy 9-inch skillet. Pour in egg mixture and bake at 350 degrees for 20 minutes. Fold onto hot platter. Serve immediately. Serves 6.
Florence Bell Stewart

EGG AND SAUSAGE CASSEROLE
This was good served at a "Pre-Masters' Brunch."

6 hard-cooked eggs, sliced
Salt
Pepper
1 pound hot sausage (bulk type)

1½ cups sour cream
½ cup dry bread crumbs
1½ cups Cheddar cheese, grated

Place eggs in a buttered casserole. Season to taste. Brown sausage in a skillet. Drain and sprinkle over eggs. Pour sour cream over sausage. Mix crumbs and cheese. Sprinkle over casserole. Place in oven to heat thoroughly and brown under broiler. Serves 6.
Variation: For 18-20 people increase to:

1½ dozen eggs
2 1-pound packages sausage
3 large cartons sour cream

1 pound cheese, grated
1½ cups bread crumbs

Mrs. W. L. Clark   *Augusta, Georgia*

Seafood

JANICE'S CRAB CASSEROLE

2 cups cooked rice	¼ cup slivered almonds
1 cup mayonnaise	¼ cup green pepper, chopped
½ cup milk	½ cup onion, chopped
½ pound crabmeat	1 stick butter, melted
2 cups boiled shrimp	Cracker crumbs
1 cup tomato juice	

Combine all ingredients except butter and crumbs. Place in a 9x12-inch dish. Combine cracker crumbs with melted butter and cover casserole. Bake uncovered for 1 hour at 350 degrees. Serves 4-6.
Mrs. W. Gerald Harrison (June)

CRABMEAT BETTYE

...a good luncheon dish...

1 pound lump crabmeat	2½ cups heavy cream sauce
1 pound fresh mushrooms	Anchovy paste
4 English muffins	1 cup bread crumbs
4 tablespoons butter	1 ounce white wine (optional)

Split English muffins, toast lightly, and butter generously. Chop mushrooms and saute in 4 tablespoons butter for 5 minutes; add crabmeat, wine, and mushrooms to cream sauce. Spread a thin layer of anchovy paste on muffins and mound crabmeat mixture on top. Sprinkle with crumbs, dot with butter, and bake about 15 minutes at 350 degrees. Can be prepared ahead of time and baked when ready to serve.
Bettye P. McInnis   Minden, Louisiana

IMPERIAL CRAB

2 pounds lump crabmeat	½ teaspoon white pepper
1 teaspoon dry mustard	1 teaspoon Worcestershire sauce
1 teaspoon salt	¾ cup mayonnaise

Combine ingredients and toss lightly. Generously fill 8-9 crab shells. Brush top slightly with additional mayonnaise. Bake in 375 degree oven for 20-25 minutes or until brown. Serve at once!
Mrs. Charles W. Ireland (Caroline)

CRAB ACAPULCO

¼ cup butter, melted
¼ cup flour, sifted
1⅔ cups milk
¾ teaspoon salt
1 teaspoon Worcestershire sauce
Dash of cayenne pepper
2 tablespoons fresh lime or lemon
    juice

3 tablespoons sherry
2 cups crabmeat
4 avocados
Sesame seeds
Nutmeg

Mix flour and butter together. Gradually blend in milk and cook, stirring constantly until thick and smooth. Add salt, Worcestershire, cayenne pepper, lime juice, and sherry. Stir. Add crabmeat and mix well. Cut avocados in half, remove seed, and peel. Place in a shallow baking dish. Sprinkle with salt and fill each half with crabmeat mixture. Sprinkle with sesame seeds and nutmeg. Bake at 300 degrees for 15 minutes.
Mrs. Abbott L. Browne (Mary Belle)

DEVILED CRABMEAT

2 tablespoons margarine
½ cup celery, chopped
¼ cup green pepper, chopped
¼ cup onion, chopped
1½-2 tablespoons flour
1 cup warm cream
Celery salt or celery seed
½ teaspoon Worcestershire sauce
1 teaspoon sherry or white
    wine

1½ tablespoons parsley, snipped
12 ounces crabmeat
1 teaspoon onion juice
Salt
Pepper
Tabasco to taste
2 hard-cooked eggs, thinly sliced
Paprika
Cracker crumbs

Melt margarine and saute celery, green pepper, and onion. Add flour all at once, stirring constantly over low heat. Add cream slowly, stirring until it thickens. Add seasonings, crabmeat, and sliced eggs. Place in individual baking shells or casserole. Sprinkle with paprika and cracker crumbs and dot with margarine. Place in 400 degree oven or under broiler for a few minutes. Makes 8 shells to serve 4 people.
Mary Kathryn Upchurch   Bedias, Texas

BAKED DEVILED CRAB

2 cups crabmeat	12 or more crackers
2 hard-cooked eggs	Salt
1 small onion, grated	Pepper
½ cup fresh parsley, snipped	Juice of 1 lemon
1 tablespoon prepared mustard	Canned milk to moisten
1 stick butter, melted	Paprika

Combine ingredients and moisten with milk. Sprinkle with paprika. Bake at 350 degrees for 35 minutes in individual baking shells.

Mrs. George Alford   *Fort Walton Beach, Florida*

DEVILED CRAB

1 pound crabmeat	½ cup celery, chopped
2 eggs	1 medium onion, chopped
¾ cup cracker crumbs	Tabasco
1 cup mayonnaise	Worcestershire sauce
1 tablespoon lemon juice	Salt
¼ cup green pepper, chopped	Pepper

Combine all ingredients lightly and fill crab shells or ramekins. Bake in a 350 degree oven until lightly browned. Serves 4-6.

Mrs. Merritt Pope (Edna)

SAPPHIRE VALLEY CRAB REMICK

1 pound lump crabmeat	½ teaspoon onion juice
Juice of 1 lemon	Dash of Tabasco
6 pieces of bacon, fried crisp	1 cup chili sauce
1 teaspoon celery salt	2 teaspoons tarragon vinegar
2 teaspoons dry mustard	½ cup mayonnaise
⅛ teaspoon cayenne pepper	Parsley, chopped

Drain crabmeat and remove any remaining shell. Divide between 6 or 8 small casseroles or shells and sprinkle lemon juice over all. Place crumbled bacon on crab. Place in 350 degree oven until warm. Blend remaining ingredients except for parsley and spread over crab. Place under the broiler for a few minutes; sprinkle parsley on top. Serve immediately. Serves 6 or 8.

The Editors

CRABMEAT A LA DEBBYE

1 pound lump crabmeat
6 strips of crisp bacon
1 scant teaspoon dry mustard
½ teaspoon paprika
½ teaspoon celery salt

½ teaspoon Tabasco sauce
½ cup chili sauce
1 teaspoon tarragon vinegar
1½ cups mayonnaise

Divide crabmeat into 6 portions and generously fill individual ramekins. Heat in 400 degree oven and top with strips of crisp bacon. Blend together mustard, paprika, celery salt, and Tabasco. Add chili sauce and vinegar. Mix well and blend with mayonnaise. Spread the warm crabmeat with this sauce and glaze under the broiler flame. Serves 6.
Debbye Procter   *Lafayette, Louisiana*

LOBSTER-CRAB CASSEROLE

1 pound lobster tails
1 pound lump crabmeat
¼ cup butter
⅓ cup onion, minced
2 cloves garlic, minced
6 tablespoons flour
6 tablespoons butter
3 cups milk

¼ cup light, dry sherry
1¼ teaspoons salt
¼ teaspoon white pepper
6-8 drops hot pepper sauce
2 cups mild Cheddar cheese, shredded
1 cup lightly buttered bread or cracker crumbs

Cook lobster and remove meat from tails. Cut into bite-sized pieces. In a heavy skillet, sauté onion, garlic, and crabmeat in butter. Add lobster pieces and remove from heat. In a medium-sized saucepan, melt 6 tablespoons butter. Stir in flour and blend well over low heat. Add milk slowly. Cook and stir constantly until mixture boils and thickens. Pour sauce over lobster and crabmeat. Add cheese and cook over low heat until cheese melts. Add sherry and other seasonings. Pour into a lightly buttered casserole. Top with bread or cracker crumbs. Bake in 350 degree oven for 25-30 minutes. Serves 8.
Mrs. Philip H. Smith (Ann)

LOBSTER NEWBURG

¼ cup onion, chopped
3 tablespoons butter
1½ cups milk
8 ounces cream cheese
1½ cups cooked lobster, cubed
1 3-ounce can sliced mushrooms, drained

¼ cup Parmesan cheese
2 tablespoons parsley, snipped
¼ teaspoon salt
¼ cup white wine
Toasted English muffins

Sauté onion in butter. Gradually add milk to soften cream cheese, mixing until well blended. Add onions and remaining ingredients except wine. Heat until bubbly. Just before serving, add wine. Serve over English muffins. Serves 4.

Mrs. Michael Hauser (Ruthie)

COQUILLES SAINT JACQUES

2 pounds scallops
1 teaspoon lemon juice
1 cup water
½ teaspoon salt
4 tablespoons butter
¼ cup onion, finely chopped
¼ pound mushrooms, sliced
⅓ cup flour
Dash of pepper

1 cup light cream
½ cup milk
1 cup Gruyère cheese, grated
½ cup dry white wine
1 tablespoon lemon juice
1 tablespoon parsley, snipped
½ cup large bread crumbs
2 tablespoons butter, melted

Combine 1 cup water, lemon juice, and salt in a saucepan. Add scallops and simmer 3 minutes. Drain on paper towels. Sauté onion and mushrooms in 4 tablespoons butter until tender. Remove from heat and stir in flour and pepper. Gradually add milk and cream. Bring to a boil, stirring until thick. Reduce heat and add cheese; stir until melted. Remove from heat and add wine, lemon juice, parsley, and scallops. Turn into 8 ramekins or a casserole. Top with remaining butter and crumbs. Broil 4 inches from heat until brown, about 2 or 3 minutes.

Mrs. Warren Middlemas, Jr. (Martha)

BAKED SHRIMP OR SCALLOPS

3 cups shrimp or scallops
1 cup water chestnuts, sliced
½ pound butter
4 tablespoons flour
2 tablespoons green onions, minced
2 tablespoons celery, minced
1 tablespoon parsley, minced

1 teaspoon rosemary
½ teaspoon marjoram
½ cup water
¼ cup dry sherry
Salt
Pepper
1 cup bread crumbs

Melt butter in a saucepan and sauté green onions. Blend in flour and add water, celery, parsley, sherry, and seasonings. Bring to a boil, stirring slowly. Add seafood, water chestnuts, and bread crumbs. Remove from heat and place on a well-buttered sheet of aluminum foil and seal. Bake at 350 for 30 minutes.

Mrs. Sterrett Procter   Lafayette, Louisiana

SCALLOPED SCALLOPS

1 pound scallops
½ cup soft bread crumbs
1 cup crackers, crushed
½ cup butter, melted

½ teaspoon salt
Pepper
1 cup light cream

Butter an 8-inch square baking dish. Wash scallops and drain thoroughly. Combine crumbs, crackers, and butter. Place half of the scallops in dish. Sprinkle with half of the crumbs and spices. Add remaining scallops, crumbs, and spices. Pour cream over top and dot with butter. Bake at 350 degrees for 30 minutes. Serves 4.

Mrs. John Davidson (Judy)

SAUTÉED SCALLOPS
...quick, easy, and good...

3 tablespoons butter
1 clove garlic, minced
2 tablespoons chives or scallions

1 pound scallops
White wine

Melt butter in a skillet and add garlic and chives. Add scallops and toss lightly until opaque. DO NOT OVERCOOK! Serve on thinly sliced toast. Rinse pan out with a little white wine and pour over scallops. Serves 2 or 3.

Mrs. Jack Hamm (Jane)

SHRIMP AND CRABMEAT AU GRATIN

⅔ stick butter
3 heaping tablespoons flour
2 tablespoons sugar
1 teaspoon salt
½ teaspoon pepper
1 tablespoon paprika
2 cups milk

Sherry to taste
⅓ stick butter
½ pound crabmeat
½ pound shrimp, cooked
1 cup sharp cheese, grated
Slivered almonds

Melt ⅔ stick of butter in a saucepan and gradually add flour, milk, sherry, sugar, salt, and pepper. Allow it to come to a boil and keep warm. Grease a casserole dish with remaining butter. Place half of shrimp and crab in casserole and half of the cheese followed by a layer of sauce. Repeat layers and sprinkle top with paprika and almonds. Bake at 325 degrees for approximately 45 minutes.
Mrs. Jim Dunkerly (June)

SHRIMP-CRAB AU GRATIN

½ cup margarine, melted
½ cup flour
2 cups half and half
1½ teaspoons salt
1 pound select crabmeat
1 pound shrimp, cooked and
   deveined

1 teaspoon Worcestershire sauce
½ cup white wine
1 package sliced almonds
1 cup sharp cheese, grated
Buttered bread crumbs

Make a cream sauce with margarine, flour, and cream. Add salt, crabmeat, shrimp, Worcestershire, and wine. Mix well. Place in buttered casserole. Top with cheese and almonds or buttered bread crumbs. Bake at 350 degrees for 25-30 minutes. Serves 6-8.
Mrs. Dayton Logue (Ann)
Mrs. Malcolm M. Traxler (Martha Lee)

SHRIMP AND CRAB CASSEROLE

1 medium green pepper, chopped	½ teaspoon salt
1 medium onion, chopped	⅛ teaspoon pepper
1 cup celery, chopped	1 tablespoon Worcestershire sauce
½ pound shrimp, peeled and deveined	1 cup mayonnaise
½ pound crabmeat	1 cup buttered crumbs

Combine all ingredients except crumbs. Place in buttered casserole dish. Sprinkle top with crumbs. Bake at 350 degrees for 30 minutes. Serves 8.
Mrs. Stanley Worsham (Mildred)

GULF SHRIMP AND CRABMEAT AU GRATIN
...as featured in Ford Times Magazine...

1 pound lump crabmeat	Salt
1 pound shrimp, cooked	Pepper
3 tablespoons sherry	½ cup crushed cracker crumbs
3 tablespoons butter	½ cup Romano cheese
3 cups medium cream sauce	1 tablespoon paprika
3 ounces sharp cheese	

Medium Cream Sauce:
Melt 6 tablespoons butter in a saucepan. Stir in 6 tablespoons flour and cook for a minute. Add 3 cups milk or half and half and stir constantly until sauce thickens.

Saute shrimp and crabmeat in butter. Add sherry, sharp cheese, and hot cream sauce. Season with salt and pepper. Heat thoroughly and pour into a casserole or individual au gratins. Sprinkle top with cracker crumbs, Romano cheese, and paprika. Dot with butter and cook at 350 degrees until golden brown. Serves 6.
Seven Seas Restaurant

PARTY SEAFOOD

4 cups shrimp, cooked
1 7-ounce can lobster
1 7½-ounce can crabmeat
2½ cups celery, thinly sliced
⅔ cup onion, finely chopped
1 cup mayonnaise
2 teaspoons Worcestershire sauce
1 teaspoon salt
½ teaspoon pepper
1½ cups dry bread crumbs
⅓ cup margarine, melted
Lemon slices
Parsley

Peel shrimp and cut into halves. Flake lobster and crabmeat. Combine seafoods. Add celery, onion, mayonnaise, Worcestershire, salt, and pepper. Place in a 1½-quart casserole. Mix bread crumbs with margarine. Sprinkle over casserole. Bake at 350 degrees for 30-35 minutes or until lightly browned. Garnish with lemon slices and parsley. Serves 6-8.
Mrs. James W. Marshall, Jr. (Margie)
Mrs. Julian Bennett (Agatha)

SEAFOOD CASSEROLE

2 pounds shrimp, cooked and
  deveined
1 quart oysters, poached in their
  juice
1 pound scallops, cooked
1 pound crabmeat
¼ cup butter
¼ cup flour
1½ cups milk
½ teaspoon salt
¼ teaspoon dillweed
⅛ teaspoon pepper
⅛ teaspoon dry mustard
Pinch of thyme
2 cups cheese, grated
2 egg yolks
Juice of 1 lemon
1 pound mushrooms

Make cream sauce with butter, flour, and milk. Add spices, cheese, and salt. Heat until cheese melts. Add slightly beaten egg yolks. Cook 5 minutes over hot water. Mix seafood, sauce, and sautéed mushrooms. Add lemon juice and pour into a large casserole dish and garnish with additional cheese. Bake at 450 degrees for 15 minutes. Serves 12.
Mrs. James E. Lewis, Jr. (Lida)

SEAFOOD CASSEROLE SUPREME

1 pound cooked shrimp, cleaned
1 pound crabmeat
1 package frozen Alaskan king crab
3 tablespoons butter
½ pound sliced mushrooms
Cream Sauce:
4 tablespoons butter
6 tablespoons flour
2 cups half and half

1 green pepper, chopped
1 onion, diced
1 small jar pimiento, chopped
1 sprig of parsley, minced
Sherry to taste

Salt
Pepper

Saute´ mushrooms, onion, and pepper in butter about 10 minutes. Make cream sauce and add seafood, mushrooms, pepper, and onion. Add parsley, pimiento, and sherry. Place in a buttered casserole and bake at 350 degrees until bubbly. Serves 6-8.
Mrs. E. Clay Lewis, III (Marsha)

PAELLA

½ pound shrimp, cleaned
¼ cup butter
¼ cup oil
1 3-pound fryer
1 clove garlic, crushed
1 chorizo, sliced
2 cups rice
¼ teaspoon powdered saffron
4 cups hot chicken broth

1 teaspoon salt
Pepper
1 tablespoon pimiento, diced
2 lobster tails
12 clams in shells, if possible
1 10-ounce package frozen peas
1 9-ounce package frozen
  artichoke hearts
Pimiento strips

Heat butter and oil in a heavy flame-proof casserole or paella pan. Add chicken, which has been cut into pieces, and garlic and cook until chicken is lightly browned on all sides. Remove chicken and set aside. Add chorizo, brown lightly, and set aside. Drain off all but ¼ cup fat. Add rice and cook, stirring until golden. Stir saffron into broth and add to rice. Bring to a boil; add salt and pepper. Push chicken and sausage into rice mixture and add diced pimiento. Cover and bake at 350 degrees for 30 minutes. Cut lobster tails through shells into chunks, leaving meat in shells and add to rice mixture. Cover and bake 15 minutes longer. Fluff rice lightly with fork and add clams, shrimp, peas, and artichoke hearts. Cover and bake 15 minutes longer or until liquid is absorbed. Garnish with pimiento strips. Serves 6-8.
Charles W. Ireland

QUICK PAELLA

1 large onion, thinly sliced
4 tablespoons butter
2 tablespoons olive oil
1¾ cups rice, uncooked
3½ cups hot chicken broth
1 teaspoon powdered saffron
1 pound shrimp, peeled and
  deveined

1 can clams and juice
1 small can mushrooms
1 small can peas
1 small jar pimiento
2 chicken breasts, cooked

Bone cooked chicken breasts. Sauté onion in butter and oil for 5 minutes. Add rice and stir while cooking for 2 to 3 minutes. Stir in broth in which saffron has been dissolved. Blend in shrimp, clams, juice, chicken, and mushrooms. Cook 15-18 minutes covered, stirring occasionally. Add peas and pimiento. Cook until rice is tender. Serves 6-8.
Mrs. J. W. Herrington (Carolyn)

BAKED SCAMP WITH CREOLE SAUCE

Scamp is the fisherman's favorite.

3 pounds scamp fillets
Salt
Pepper
Flour
1 stick margarine
1 cup onions, chopped
1 cup celery, chopped
½ cup green pepper, chopped
1 clove garlic, minced
2 No. 2 cans Hunt's whole
  tomatoes, undrained

1 tablespoon Worcestershire sauce
1 tablespoon catsup
1 tablespoon chili powder
Juice of 1 lemon
1 teaspoon salt
1½ tablespoons sugar
1 tablespoon parsley flakes
1 6-ounce can sliced mushrooms,
  drained
Dash of Tabasco
1 BAY LEAF

Salt and pepper the fish and lightly dust with flour. Place fish in a large baking dish, being sure the fillets are not overlapping; set aside. Melt the butter and sauté onions, celery, green pepper, and garlic until tender. Cut the tomatoes into small pieces and add with juice to the sautéed vegetables. Add remaining ingredients, except mushrooms. Cover and cook for 1 hour. Discard BAY LEAF. Add mushrooms and stir. Pour sauce over scamp and cover casserole tightly with foil. Bake at 350 degrees for 1 hour, basting occasionally with sauce. Serves 6 adults generously.
Note: Red snapper or grouper may be substituted for the scamp, if desired.
Mrs. David J. Turner (Patty)

SAPPHIRE VALLEY SHRIMP

Boil any amount of shelled and deveined shrimp in water seasoned with nutmeg, allspice, BAY LEAVES, cayenne pepper, dillseed, and fennel seed. When shrimp turn pink, drain and dry on paper towel. Place in a casserole and cover with a mixture of garlic, butter, and fresh shallots. Bake in a hot oven until bubbly. Serve with French bread to dip in sauce.
Fairfield Inn Chef via
Ted Alford

KING MACKEREL STEAKS SUPREME

2 pounds king mackerel steaks
1 egg
1½ cups salad oil
Juice of 1 lemon
¼ cup vinegar
1½ teaspoons salt
1 tablespoon Worcestershire sauce

Dash of Tabasco
1 tablespoon Fish Garni Seasoning
½ teaspoon pepper
1 onion, thinly sliced
Paprika
Parsley

Place fish steaks in a single layer in a shallow baking dish. Blend egg and oil together in a blender until very thick. Add remaining ingredients except onion. Cover steaks with sauce and marinate for at least 30 minutes. Top with onion slices. Bake at 400 degrees for 25 minutes. Garnish with paprika and parsley. Also good with trout or snapper.
Mrs. A. V. Hooks (Mildred)

BAKED KING MACKEREL

1 large king mackerel, filleted
Salt
Pepper
2 cups packaged bread crumb
   dressing
1 large onion, chopped

3 ribs of celery, chopped
2 tablespoons butter
Parsley
Lemon
White wine
Garlic salt

Sauté chopped onion and celery in butter. Add bread crumb dressing and remaining seasonings. Mix well. Salt and pepper fillets. Place one fillet in a buttered baking dish and spread with dressing. Place other fillet on top of dressing, creating a sandwich effect. Bake at 325 degrees until done. Baste with additional butter during baking.
Note: You may use several small fillets or 2 large ones.
Mrs. Owen Reese (Anne)

CHEESE BAKED KING MACKEREL

2 large fillets
1 6-ounce package Kraft Swiss
cheese
1 4-ounce package mozzarella
cheese, shredded
2 tablespoons butter
2 rounded tablespoons flour
1 cup milk

White wine
Worcestershire sauce
Lemon juice
2 green onions, including
tops, chopped
Salt
Pepper
Paprika

Remove skin and dark streak from fillets; place fillets in a shallow baking dish. Squeeze a liberal amount of lemon juice over fish; sprinkle with wine and Worcestershire sauce to taste. Add salt, pepper, and paprika. Set aside. Make a cream sauce with the butter, flour, salt, pepper, and milk. Sauce should be smooth and thick. Place slices of Swiss cheese over fish; cover with white sauce, then with shredded mozzarella (about ¾ of the package). Sprinkle with paprika. Bake at 350 degrees for 40 minutes. Five minutes before fish is done, sprinkle with green onions.
Mrs. Ronald Groom (Harriett)

OVEN-FRIED FISH

2 pounds fish fillets
1 tablespoon salt
1 cup milk

1 cup bread crumbs
4 tablespoons butter

Cut fillets into serving size pieces. Add salt to milk and soak fish for a short time. Roll fillets in crumbs; place in well-buttered baking pan. Put butter on top of fish. Place pan on shelf near the top of a very hot oven (500 degrees) and bake 10-12 minutes or until fish flakes easily when tested with a fork.
Mrs. Edward A. Hutchison (Barbara)

CHEESE BAKED SNAPPER

1 3-pound snapper
1 13-ounce can evaporated milk

1 cup Cheddar cheese, grated

Have a 3-pound snapper prepared for baking, leaving head on fish. Salt and pepper the fish and place in a buttered dish. Pour the milk over the fish and bake at 350 degrees for 30 minutes. Sprinkle cheese over the fish and bake another 15 minutes. Serves 4 or 5.
Mrs. Rayford Jones (Frances)

FISH WITH WHITE WINE SAUCE

4 pounds scamp or snapper
  fillets
Salt
Paprika
1 stick butter
Juice of 1 lemon

¾ cup sauterne
8 ounces Velveeta cheese
1 clove garlic, finely chopped
2 pounds shrimp, cooked
Parsley

Salt fish, sprinkle with paprika, and place in a flat baking dish. In a saucepan, melt butter and combine with lemon juice. Baste fish with mixture and pour ½ cup of sauterne over all. Bake uncovered at 350 degrees for approximately 30 minutes or until fish is flaky. Baste often. In a double boiler place remaining sauterne and cheese. Continue stirring until cheese has melted. Add garlic and shrimp. Place fish on a large platter and pour sauce over all. Garnish with parsley. Serve immediately. Sauce may be thinned with additional sauterne. Serves 6.

Mrs. E. B. Daughtry (Myrle)
Mrs. Charles E. Lytle (Ann)

POMPANO EN PAPILLOTE

3 medium pompano
2 cups crabmeat
2 egg yolks
1 pint fish stock
1 stick butter
4 onions

1 cup fresh mushrooms, chopped
White wine
1 tablespoon flour
Salt
White pepper

Make fish stock by boiling the heads and bones. Cut the pompano into 6 fillets and poach for 5 minutes in salted water. Saute' crabmeat in ¼ cup butter with a dash of white wine for 3 minutes. Saute' onions and mushrooms in ¼ cup butter for about 5 minutes. Add fish stock, reserving a little to rub with the flour to make a smooth paste. When the stock has simmered with the onions and mushrooms about 10 minutes, slowly stir in the flour paste and cook down until thickened. Remove from heat and add egg yolks. Season with salt, pepper, and wine to taste. In the center of each fillet, place a generous spoonful of the sautéed crab. Place the fish on a piece of aluminum foil and slide into a paper bag. While fish is inside paper bag, cover the top of each fillet with remaining crabmeat and top with sauce. Securely fold bag and bake for 10 minutes in a hot oven. Serve piping hot in the bag which is cut open at the table.

Mrs. Dayton Logue (Ann)

BAKED SNAPPER IN A BAG

2 pounds red snapper fillets
1 cup celery, chopped
2 large tomatoes, peeled
   and chopped
1 small onion, chopped

Juice of 2 lemons
Salt
Pepper
1 "Brown-In-Bag"

Rinse fish and pat dry. Salt and pepper fish and sprinkle with the juice of one lemon. Place vegetables in a bag. Salt and pepper; squeeze juice of the other lemon over vegetables. Place fish on top of vegetables. Seal bag and puncture ten times. Bake at 350 degrees for 1 hour. Serve over rice.
Note: Be sure to place bag in a dish while baking.
Mrs. Charles F. Anderson (Janet)

BAKED FISH WITH EGG BREAD DRESSING

1 3-3½ pound red snapper
1 recipe Egg Bread
3 slices light bread
1 medium onion, chopped
Pepper

1 can chicken broth
Lemon slices
Juice of ½ lemon
¼ cup catsup
2 or 3 bacon slices

Make a dressing of crumbled Egg Bread, light bread, pepper, onion, and chicken broth. Add enough water to make a moist consistency. Make two slashes across the top of the fish. Place dressing in a well-greased 9x13 pan and put the fish in center of dressing. Place strips of bacon in the cross-cut slits, sprinkle with lemon juice, and place lemon slices over dressing and fish. Dilute catsup in a little water and drizzle it over all. Bake at 375 degrees for about 1 hour. Serves 6.

Egg Bread:
2 cups self-rising cornmeal
½ cup self-rising flour
½ teaspoon salt

2 eggs
½ cup oil
Milk

Combine dry ingredients; add eggs, oil, and enough milk to make a firm batter. Bake in an iron skillet in a 450 degree oven approximately 20 minutes, until golden brown. Cool.
Mrs. Rayford Jones (Frances)

POTATO DRESSING FOR BAKED FISH

4 pounds Irish potatoes
2 hard-cooked eggs, chopped
1 egg
2 ribs of celery, finely chopped
⅔ cup milk
1 tablespoon butter
2 tablespoons onion, minced

Salt
Pepper
3 pounds red snapper, filleted
  or whole
1 sprig of parsley, snipped
1 pimiento, chopped
Paprika

Boil potatoes; remove skins and cream with butter and milk. Beat egg and add to potatoes. Add salt, pepper, onion, hard-cooked eggs, and celery. Bake fish at 350 degrees until it is half done. Place dressing all around fish and finish cooking together until done. Sprinkle fish and dressing with paprika before serving. Serves 4.
Mrs. A. T. Fort   *Lumpkin, Georgia*

JANET'S RED SNAPPER AND DRESSING

1 package cornbread stuffing mix
8 small snappers, filleted
1 cup celery, chopped
½ cup green onions, chopped
1 stick butter

Milk
1½ cups sour cream
Salt
Pepper
Almonds, buttered and toasted

Sauté celery and onion in butter. Add stuffing and mix well. Add sour cream, salt, and pepper, adding enough milk until dressing sticks together. Place four fillets in a buttered baking dish. Cover with dressing and top with remaining fillets. Bake for 45 minutes at 325 degrees or until fish is done. Cover each fillet with almonds prior to serving. Serves 8.
Mrs. Charles F. Anderson (Janet)

FISH SUPREME

3 pounds fillet of flounder,
  pompano, or trout
1 cup stale bread crumbs
Juice of 1 lemon
2 cups sour cream

1 6-ounce package Swiss cheese
Salt
Freshly ground pepper
Worcestershire sauce

Place ⅓ of bread crumbs in the bottom of a buttered oblong baking dish and add a layer of fish. Sprinkle with lemon juice, salt, Worcestershire sauce, and pepper; cover with layer of cheese. Cover all with 1 cup of the sour cream. Repeat layers. Cover top with buttered crumbs and bake at 325 degrees for 40 minutes. Serves 6.
Connie Stone Thomas

GRAND LAGOON STUFFED FLOUNDER
. . .as served at Captain Anderson's. . .

5 medium-sized flounder
1 stick butter, melted

3 tablespoons lemon juice

Prepare flounder by cutting through the middle of the top side and removing bone. Place stuffing mixture in flounder. Combine butter and lemon juice and baste fish with this mixture. Bake for 25 minutes at 350 degrees.
Stuffing:

1 large onion, diced
2 green peppers, diced
½ rib of celery, diced
4 eggs
2 tablespoons salt
1 tablespoon pepper

½ cup prepared mustard
½ cup Worcestershire sauce
2 cups salad dressing
1 pound saltine crackers, crushed
1½ pounds claw crabmeat
Juice of 2 lemons

Combine ingredients and mix well. This dressing may be used to stuff shrimp.
Johnny and Jimmy Patronis

FRIED SHRIMP BATTER I

1 egg,beaten
¼ teaspoon sugar
3-4 tablespoons milk

Self-rising flour to thicken
Salt
Pepper

Beat egg, sugar, and milk together. Add self-rising flour until batter is of medium thickness. Add salt and pepper to taste.
Mrs. Buford Ennis (Dot)

FRIED SHRIMP BATTER II

1 cup ice water ·
1 cup plain flour

1 egg
¼ teaspoon soda

Combine ingredients and coat shrimp with batter. Fry in hot oil. Salt after cooking and serve immediately.
Mrs. Frank Sullivan (Jackie)

BATTER FOR FRYING SHRIMP OR VEAL

1 cup flour
1 teaspoon baking powder
½ teaspoon salt
2 eggs, separated

⅔ cup milk
1 teaspoon salad oil
1 teaspoon lemon juice
3 tablespoons white wine

Combine flour, baking powder, and egg yolks. Add salt, salad oil, and wine. Mix well. Add lemon juice if cooking seafood. Add just enough of the milk to make a thick batter and fold in the stiffly beaten egg whites. Batter should be thick. Coat meat with batter and fry in hot oil.
Mrs. Burns Collins (Paula)

DOTTIE'S HOT POTTED SHRIMP

1 tablespoon green onions, chopped
1 teaspoon garlic, minced
¼ cup butter
Dash of Worcestershire sauce
Dash of fresh lemon juice
Dash of white wine
Salt
Freshly ground pepper
5-6 jumbo shrimp
1 teaspoon parsley
½ teaspoon fresh dill, chopped
Toast points

Shell and devein shrimp. Saute'onions and garlic in butter until tender. Add shrimp, Worcestershire, lemon juice, wine, salt, and pepper. Cook the shrimp for 5 or 6 minutes, turning them occasionally. Add parsley and dill, blending well. Serve over toast points. Good served as a first course or use smaller shrimp and serve from chafing dish. Serves 1.
Mrs. T. L. Yarborough (Dorothy)

SHRIMP A LA JACQUE

2 pounds jumbo shrimp, boiled
   and deveined
1 stick butter, softened
1 clove garlic
3 tablespoons butter
2 tablespoons flour
¾ cup milk
Gouda cheese
3 egg yolks
⅓ cup white wine
Salt
Pepper

Mash clove of garlic into a stick of softened butter at least one hour before using.
Cheese Sauce:
Over medium heat melt 3 tablespoons butter and add flour. Add milk and small amount of grated Gouda cheese. Beat egg yolks. Combine with mixture, stirring rapidly. Add wine, salt, and pepper. Place 6-8 shrimp in baking shells and cover with sauce. Top each with garlic butter and cover with a generous amount of grated Gouda cheese. Bake for 3-4 minutes at 400 degrees and then broil until brown and crusty.
Mrs. C. S. Dresser (Lela)
Mrs. Herbert Mizell, III (Carol)

SHRIMP JAMBALAYA

3 tablespoons butter
½ cup onion, chopped
½ cup green onion, chopped
½ cup green pepper, chopped
½ cup celery, chopped
¼ pound cooked ham, diced
2 cloves garlic, crushed
2 cups chicken broth
3 large tomatoes, chopped
¼ cup parsley, minced

½ teaspoon salt
⅛ teaspoon black pepper
¼ teaspoon thyme
⅛ teaspoon cayenne pepper
1 BAY LEAF
1 cup rice, uncooked
2 pounds shrimp, cooked
   and cleaned
¼ cup green pepper, chopped

Melt butter in a large heavy skillet. Stir in next six ingredients. Cook over medium heat for about five minutes, stirring occasionally. Add broth and next seven ingredients. Cover and bring to a boil. Add rice and simmer 20 minutes. Blend in shrimp and remaining green pepper. Simmer uncovered 5 minutes longer. Serves 6.
Variation: Chicken and summer sausage are good in this.
C. Pannette

SNAPPER IN FOIL

1 4½ pound snapper, filleted
Seasoned salt
Pepper
2 thick onion slices

2 green peppers, quartered
1½ tablespoons butter
Fresh lemon juice

Place each fillet on a separate piece of heavy duty foil. Sprinkle each with seasoned salt, pepper, and lemon juice to taste. Top with onion slices, butter, and green pepper; seal foil leaving some room for expansion. Place each package on a baking sheet and bake at 375 degrees for 45 minutes. Slit foil at the table being careful not to let the juices escape. This may be prepared ahead of time and refrigerated until baking. Serves 4.
James I. Lark, Sr.

GREEN NOODLES AND SHRIMP

2½ pounds shrimp, cooked
1 8-ounce package green noodles
2 tablespoons olive oil
Salt
1 bunch scallions, finely chopped

1 cup mayonnaise
2 eggs
1 carton sour cream
1 can mushroom soup
Sharp cheese, grated

Boil noodles in salted water with oil. Toss hot noodles lightly with scallions. Blend mayonnaise, eggs, sour cream, and soup in blender until well mixed. Place noodles and shrimp in a casserole and cover with mixture. Sprinkle cheese on top. Bake at 350 degrees for 30 minutes.
Mrs. J. M. Ros, Jr. (Rachel)

SHRIMP THERMIDOR

¾ pound shrimp, cooked
½ cup mushrooms, sliced
¼ cup butter, melted
¼ cup flour
2 cups milk

1 teaspoon salt
½ teaspoon dry mustard
Pepper
Parmesan cheese
Paprika

Cut large shrimp in half. Saute´ mushrooms in butter. Blend flour, salt, mustard, and pepper. Add milk and cook until thickened. Stir in shrimp and place in 6 buttered baking shells. Sprinkle with cheese and paprika. Bake at 400 degrees for 10 minutes.
Mrs. James Nixon (Flo)

SHRIMP FRIED RICE

2 tablespoons salad oil
1 pound small shrimp, shelled and
    deveined
½ teaspoon salt
¼ teaspoon pepper

4 cups cold, cooked rice
2 eggs, slightly beaten
2 tablespoons soy sauce
2-3 green onions, chopped

Heat oil in skillet. Add shrimp, salt, and pepper. Cook until shrimp are pink. Stir in rice. Add eggs and stir 2-3 minutes. Add soy sauce and green onions. Serves 6.
Mrs. John Fishel (Louise)

SHRIMP WITH CRABMEAT STUFFING

1½ pounds large shrimp
½ pound crabmeat
4 tablespoons butter
⅓ cup onion, finely chopped
¼ cup green pepper, finely chopped
2 tablespoons flour
¾ teaspoon salt
⅛ teaspoon pepper

1 cup milk
1 teaspoon dry sherry
1 teaspoon dry mustard
1 teaspoon Worcestershire sauce
2 tablespoons mayonnaise
2 tablespoons butter
¼ cup Parmesan cheese
Paprika

Wash shrimp; shell and devein. Make a shallow cut lengthwise down the back of each shrimp. Drain crabmeat and remove any remaining shell. Cook onion and green pepper in butter until tender. Blend in flour, salt, and pepper. Stir in milk and cook until thickened, stirring constantly. Add sherry, mustard, Worcestershire, mayonnaise, and crabmeat; mix well. Stuff shrimp with crabmeat mixture. Dot with butter and place on a buttered baking sheet. Sprinkle with cheese and paprika. Bake at 350 degrees for 12 to 15 minutes. Serves 6.
Mrs. Edgar Daffin (Ann)

MARGOT'S SHRIMP AND WILD RICE

2 pounds shrimp
1 can cream of mushroom soup
2 tablespoons onion, chopped
2 tablespoons butter, melted
2 tablespoons lemon juice
½ teaspoon Worcestershire sauce
1 teaspoon dry mustard

¼ teaspoon pepper
½ cup sharp cheese, diced
1 box Uncle Ben's Wild Rice
   Mix, cooked
3 tablespoons pimiento
¼ cup almonds, chopped
3 tablespoons fresh parsley, snipped

Peel and devein the shrimp. Combine all ingredients and mix thoroughly. Pour into a greased 2-quart casserole and bake for 30 minutes at 375 degrees. Serves 8.
Variation: You may use 2 cups of cooked wild rice in place of Uncle Ben's.
Mrs. Don Barbour   *Mobile, Alabama*

SHRIMP CREOLE

½ lemon, sliced
4 whole peppercorns

2 pounds shrimp, shelled and
deveined

In a large pan bring 1 quart water to a boil. Add above ingredients; reduce heat and simmer for 3 minutes. Drain and reserve 1 cup liquid.

4 slices bacon, cut up
2 tablespoons butter
1 clove garlic, minced
1 cup onion, chopped
1½ cups green pepper, chopped
1½ cups celery, sliced
1 1-pound 12-ounce can tomatoes
  and juice
1 6-ounce can tomato paste

1 tablespoon lemon juice
1 tablespoon sugar
1 teaspoon salt
½ teaspoon pepper
1 BAY LEAF
¼ teaspoon Tabasco
½ teaspoon thyme
¼ teaspoon cayenne pepper
½ teaspoon filé powder

Sauté bacon in a Dutch oven. Remove bacon from pan and add butter, garlic, onion, celery, and green pepper. Cook about 5 minutes. Add 1 cup reserved shrimp liquid, tomatoes, tomato paste, bacon, and lemon juice. Add Tabasco, sugar, salt, pepper, BAY LEAF, and thyme. Bring to a boil, and simmer for 1½ hours. Add shrimp and filé powder. Remove BAY LEAF before serving. This is very good made the day before and refrigerated overnight. Serve over rice. Serves 6.
Mrs. Creed Greer (Selby)

QUICK CREOLE SHRIMP

1 pound shrimp, boiled
1 cup onion, chopped
1 cup green pepper, chopped
1 cup celery, chopped
2 tablespoons bacon drippings
1 tablespoon Worcestershire sauce

Hot sauce to taste
1 teaspoon salt
½ teaspoon pepper
1 quart fresh tomatoes, chopped
Rice

Shell and devein shrimp and cut in half if too large. Sauté shrimp, onion, pepper, and celery in bacon drippings. Add other ingredients except rice and put in a 2½-quart baking dish. Bake at 450 degrees for about 15 minutes. Yields 6 servings. Serve over cooked rice.
Mrs. John Moseley (Mavis)

SHRIMP-CRAB DIVINE

1 pound crabmeat
1 pound cooked shrimp
½ green pepper, finely chopped
½ cup onion, chopped
2 pimientos, chopped
1 tablespoon Worcestershire sauce
⅛ teaspoon pepper

3 cups cooked rice
1 cup celery, finely chopped
1 small can mushrooms, drained
1 cup mayonnaise
½ teaspoon salt
¾ cup light cream
Buttered bread crumbs

Pick over crabmeat removing any shell. Combine all ingredients. Pour into a large casserole and bake at 375 degrees for 30 minutes or individual casseroles for 20 minutes. Sprinkle with buttered bread crumbs, if you wish. Serves 8-10.
Note: One package frozen peas and ⅓ cup snipped fresh parsley may be added to this.
Mrs. John Fishel (Louise)
Mrs. D. E. McCloy   *Monticello, Arkansas*

SHRIMP AND RICE SUPERB

2 12-ounce packages white and wild
   rice frozen in pouch
2 tablespoons butter
1 cup bias-cut celery
2 2½-ounce jars sliced
   mushrooms, drained
½ cup green onions, sliced

2 tablespoons pimiento, chopped
2 cups cooked shrimp (reserve
   6 for garnish)
⅛ teaspoon pepper
½ teaspoon salt
½ teaspoon Accent

Cook rice according to package directions. In butter, sauté celery and green onions until tender. Stir in mushrooms, pimiento, seasonings, and shrimp. Fold this mixture into cooked rice. Carefully blend. Turn into a buttered 2-quart shallow casserole.
Topping:
1 can cream of mushroom soup
1⅓ cups sour cream
2 tablespoons butter, melted

⅔ cup bread crumbs
2 tablespoons fresh parsley, snipped

Combine soup and sour cream and mix well. Spoon over shrimp and rice mixture. Toss bread crumbs with butter. Add fresh parsley. Sprinkle over casserole. Bake at 325 degrees for 30 minutes. Top with remaining shrimp and bake an additional 5-10 minutes. Serves 8-10.
Mrs. Norman Bailey (Hoyle)

CURRIED SHRIMP

3 pounds shrimp
3 cups shrimp stock
3 tablespoons butter
3 tablespoons flour
Sambals:
Toasted, slivered almonds
Toasted coconut

3 chicken bouillon cubes
1½ tablespoons curry powder
McCormick's Shrimp Boil in bag
Rice

Chutney

Cook shrimp in shrimp boil, using about ⅓ of the amount called for in the directions. Reserve 3 cups of stock. Melt butter in a large saucepan, adding flour and curry powder; stir. Add stock and bouillon cubes. Continue to cook until desired thickness. Add peeled and cleaned shrimp. Season to taste. Serve over rice and top with sambals, if desired. Serves 8-10.
Mrs. Cleve Stokes (Lucy Ellen)

MARIE'S CURRIED SHRIMP

1½ pounds shrimp
1 stick oleo
¼ cup flour
½ teaspoon salt
Dash of paprika

1 teaspoon curry powder
1½ cups milk
3 tablespoons catsup
¼ cup sherry

Blend oleo, flour, salt, paprika, and curry powder. Gradually stir in milk, cooking until smooth. Before serving, add catsup, sherry, and shrimp. Heat and serve over rice. Garnish with the following sambals: chopped nuts, coconut, chopped eggs, chopped onion, crisp crumbled bacon, or chutney.
Mrs. Eugene J. Bazemore (Marie)

SHRIMP ORLEANS

1 medium onion, diced
1 tablespoon butter
1 clove garlic, crushed
1 can cream of mushroom soup

2 cups cooked shrimp, cleaned
1 cup sour cream
¼ cup catsup
1 3-ounce can mushrooms, drained

Melt butter in a skillet. Add onions and garlic and cook until tender. Combine soup, sour cream, and catsup; stir into onions. Add mushrooms and shrimp. Heat slowly. Serve over rice.
Mrs. Charles Helms (Leah)

SHRIMP STROGANOFF

2 pounds shrimp, shelled and
  deveined
8 tablespoons butter, melted
1½ cups mushrooms, sliced
3 tablespoons onion, chopped
1 clove garlic, minced
3 tablespoons flour

½ cup chicken consommé
½ cup milk
½ cup white wine
1 teaspoon catsup
½ teaspoon Worcestershire sauce
1 cup sour cream
1 tablespoon dillweed

Cook shrimp in half the butter for 5-7 minutes. Use more butter, if desired. Remove from heat and keep warm. Saute mushrooms in remaining butter. Add onion and garlic and stir until tender. Add flour, consommé, milk, and wine. Cook until thickened. Add catsup and Worcestershire. Remove from heat and blend in sour cream and dill. Season to taste. Add shrimp to the mixture. Serve over rice. Serves 4-6.
Mrs. William E. Holland, III (Hannelore)

CHINESE SHRIMP

1 pound shrimp
1 tablespoon cornstarch
¼ cup vinegar
Salt
2 tablespoons soy sauce
5 teaspoons sugar

¼ teaspoon monosodium glutamate
4 cloves garlic, finely minced
2 tablespoons scallions, chopped
1½ tablespoons fresh ginger,
  finely chopped
3 cups oil

Shell, devein, and rinse shrimp. Pat dry and place in a small bowl with cornstarch. Work with fingers until all shrimp are lightly coated. Set aside. In another bowl, combine vinegar, salt, soy sauce, sugar, and monosodium glutamate. Combine garlic, scallions, and ginger and set aside. Heat oil in a wok or skillet. When hot, add shrimp. Cook, stirring about 1½ minutes. Drain and discard all but about 1½ tablespoons of the oil. Heat and add ginger mixture; stir. Add the vinegar sauce and when it boils, add shrimp and stir. Serve immediately.
Mrs. Nelson Cole   *Birmingham, Alabama*

SEAFOOD KEBOBS YARBOROUGH

48 large shrimp
48 large bay scallops
24 bacon slices
24 mushroom caps
Marinade:
⅓ cup peanut oil
⅓ cup soy sauce
⅓ cup dry white wine
¼ cup Worcestershire sauce
¼ cup liquid smoke
2 tablespoons dark brown sugar

Pineapple chunks
Green pepper pieces
Onion wedges
12 skewers

1 tablespoon ground ginger
2 teaspoons garlic powder
Tabasco to taste
1 teaspoon dry mustard
Lemon and Pepper Seasoning
Juice of 1 lemon

Cut bacon strips in half and partially cook in oven. Shell and devein shrimp, leaving on tails. Mix marinade in pint jar; shake well and pour over shrimp and scallops. Let marinate for at least 2 hours. Thread ingredients alternately on 12 skewers. Shrimp should be skewered through the fat end and again near the tail. Grill over charcoal with plenty of hickory chips, brushing once on each side with marinade. Pour remaining marinade into saucepan and boil rapidly until reduced to a thick glaze. When done, remove kebobs from skewers and place over rice on heated platters. Ladle sauce over kebobs, if desired.
Mrs. T. L. Yarborough (Dorothy)

SWEET AND SOUR ROCK SHRIMP TAILS

¾ pound rock shrimp tails
¼ cup margarine
1 cup onions, sliced
1 small green pepper, cut into
1-inch squares
1 1-pound 4-ounce can
pineapple (heavy syrup)

½ cup sugar
2 tablespoons cornstarch
½ teaspoon dry mustard
¼ teaspoon salt
½ cup white vinegar
1 tablespoon soy sauce
⅔ cup small tomato wedges

Boil shrimp in shells; peel and devein. Cut large shrimp in half. Saute onions and pepper in margarine until pepper is tender but not browned. Drain pineapple and reserve syrup. Combine sugar, cornstarch, mustard, and salt. Stir in syrup from pineapple; add vinegar and soy sauce. Mix well and add to onion mixture. Cook, stirring constantly, until thick and clear. Fold in pineapple, shrimp, and tomatoes. Heat and serve over rice.
The Editors

SHRIMP PIRLEAU

1½ pounds shrimp
2 cups cooked rice
1 cup onion, chopped
½ cup green pepper, chopped
1 6-ounce can tomato paste
1 8-ounce can tomato sauce
½ cup water

1 tablespoon Worcestershire sauce
1 teaspoon Tabasco
8 slices of bacon
6 tablespoons bacon drippings
Salt
Coarsely ground pepper

Fry bacon until crisp; drain, and set aside. Saute onions and peppers in drippings until tender. Add shrimp and saute just until they turn pink. Add tomato paste, tomato sauce, ½ cup water, and rice. Season with Worcestershire, Tabasco, salt, and pepper. Cover and cook over low heat for approximately 20 minutes. Top with crumbled bacon and serve hot.
Benjamin White Redding

SPICY SHRIMP

4 pounds shrimp, cooked and
    peeled
¼ cup parsley, snipped
3 green onions, chopped
1 pint mayonnaise
¼ cup vinegar
½ cup Mazola Oil

Juice of ½ lemon
3 tablespoons capers (in tarragon)
1 tablespoon white onion, grated
Salt
2 tablespoons Creole mustard
Green Food Coloring

Chill shrimp. Mix remaining ingredients in blender until creamy. At serving time, place shrimp on a plate of crisp lettuce and top with sauce. Serves 8.
Mrs. Harvey Mathis (Marge)

SHRIMP WITH HOLLANDAISE SAUCE

1 pound large shrimp, peeled and
    deveined
½ lemon
2 tablespoons olive oil

½ teaspoon salt
¼ teaspoon pepper
1 cup Hollandaise sauce

Arrange the shrimp in a shallow au gratin dish. Sprinkle with lemon juice, olive oil, salt, and pepper. Broil for 3 or 4 minutes. Turn shrimp and broil 3 or 4 minutes longer. Spoon Hollandaise sauce over shrimp. Return to oven and brown lightly for 2 or 3 minutes. Serves 2.
Mrs. Sterrett Procter   *Lafayette, Louisiana*

SHRIMP VERONIQUE

2 cups shrimp, cooked and
  cleaned
3 tablespoons white wine
1 meduim onion, finely chopped
1 clove garlic, minced
¼ teaspoon salt
1 can cream of mushroom soup
3 tablespoons butter

1 teaspoon curry powder
¼ cup fresh, green, seedless
  grapes
4 tablespoons sour cream
1 teaspoon lemon juice
Dash of pepper
¾ cup fresh mushrooms, chopped

Melt butter in a saucepan. Add onion, mushrooms, garlic, salt, and pepper. Cook until onions are clear but not brown. Add soup, curry, grapes, sour cream, lemon juice, and wine. Stir. Add shrimp, mixing well. Serve as a casserole or in individual baking shells. Serves 4.

Note: I serve this with French-cut green beans which have been finely chopped and mixed with 2 cups cooked rice.

Mrs J. C. Harris (Ruby)   *Cove Hotel*

BOILED SHRIMP AND COCKTAIL SAUCE

1 quart water
1 carrot
1 small onion
Juice of ½ lemon

1 teaspoon salt
½ teaspoon pepper
1 pound shrimp

Combine all ingredients except shrimp in pot. Bring to a boil. Add shrimp and cover. Simmer for 5 minutes. Drain and cool. Shell and devein shrimp. Place in a covered bowl and chill.

Sauce:

1 tablespoon horseradish
1 cup catsup
3 tablespoons chili sauce

2 tablespoons lemon juice
Salt
Tabasco

Combine all ingredients and chill.

Mrs. Lamar Sikes (Patty)

BUTTER FRIED SHRIMP

2 pounds large shrimp
Salt
¼ cup olive oil
1 cup sifted all-purpose flour

4 tablespoons butter
Lemon juice
Parsley
Garlic salt

Shell and devein shrimp. Salt and let stand a few minutes. Rinse in cold water and pat dry with paper towels. Salt again and dredge in flour, shaking off excess. Heat butter and oil in skillet until hot. Place half of shrimp in skillet and cook until brown on one side; turn and brown on the other. Remove to platter and keep warm while cooking remaining shrimp. You may need to add more butter and oil. Before serving, sprinkle with lemon juice, parsley, and garlic salt.
Mrs. E. Clay Lewis, III (Marsha)

MARY ANN'S TUNA CASSEROLE

1 8-ounce package egg noodles
1 can Le Sueur peas, drained
2 cans cream of mushroom or
  celery soup
2 large cans Albacore tuna, drained
Seasoned Salt
Pepper
1 cup green onions, chopped

1 cup celery, chopped
1 cup sharp Cheddar cheese,
  grated
½ stick butter
½-1 cup milk
1 can water chestnuts, chopped
1 can onion rings

Cook noodles al dente. Drain. Combine noodles with all ingredients except onion rings and cheese. Place in a buttered casserole. Top with onion rings and cheese. Cover and bake at 325 degrees for 20-30 minutes.
Mrs. Tim Smith (Mary Ann)

PEPPER PAN ROAST

½ cup onions, minced
½ cup green pepper, minced
1 clove garlic, crushed
1 cup butter

1 quart oysters, drained
Salt
Pepper
Toast points

Saute' onion, green pepper, and garlic in butter for 2 to 3 minutes. Remove garlic. Add oysters and cook until plump. Add salt and pepper. Serve on toast points.
Mrs. James E. Carter (Jeri)

SALMON LOAF

1 1-pound can salmon (reserve juice)
1 tablespoon onion, grated
1 tablespoon lemon juice
½ teaspoon celery salt
¼ teaspoon garlic salt
1 cup cracker crumbs

4 drops Tabasco
½ cup milk
1 egg, beaten
2 tablespoons oleo, melted
Salt
Pepper

Put milk, onion, lemon juice, Tabasco, celery salt, garlic salt, salt, pepper, and egg in a bowl. Add salmon that has been boned and dark skin removed. Flake with a fork. Add oleo and crumbs. If dry, add salmon juice. Pour into a buttered casserole and bake uncovered at 350 degrees for 45 minutes. Serves 4-6.

Mrs. E. R. Bane   *Clay Center, Kansas*

ESCALLOPED OYSTERS

1½ cups cracker crumbs
½ cup butter
1 pint oysters

4 teaspoons oyster liquor
2 teaspoons milk

Pick over oysters removing any particles of shell. Melt butter and mix with cracker crumbs. In a well-buttered baking dish, layer crumbs, half of the oysters, salt, pepper, and some of oyster liquor which has been mixed with the milk. Continue layering until dish is filled. Pour rest of liquid on top layer of crumbs and dot with additional butter. Cover dish and bake at 375 to 400 degrees for 30 minutes. Remove cover and brown.

Elizabeth Wing Byrd

PETE'S OYSTERS

...a variation of an old custom in oyster country...

Make a sauce of melted butter and Worcestershire sauce. Open oysters and place half-shells over fire on charcoal grill. Add one teaspoon of sauce and a sprinkling of Parmesan cheese to each oyster. Cook until edges of oysters begin to curl. Let each guest eat from the grill with fondue forks. Add new oysters to the shells as cooked ones disappear.

Mrs. Peter Brower (Judy)

PERFECT SCALLOPED OYSTERS

1 pint oysters
2 cups medium-coarse cracker crumbs
½ cup butter, melted
¾ cup light cream

¼ cup oyster liquor
¼ teaspoon Worcestershire sauce
½ teaspoon salt
Pepper

Drain oysters, reserving liquor. Combine crumbs and butter. Spread ⅓ of crumbs in a buttered casserole. Cover with half the oysters. Sprinkle with pepper. Using another third of the crumbs, spread a second layer; cover with remaining oysters. Sprinkle with pepper. Combine cream, oyster liquor, Worcestershire, and salt. Pour over the oysters and top with remaining crumbs. Bake for 40 minutes at 350 degrees. Serves 4-6.
Mrs. George Logue, Jr. (Alice)

SCALLOPED OYSTERS

1 pint oysters
1 cup water
1 small can evaporated milk
1 can mushroom soup
1 cup milk

½ stick butter
Salt
Pepper
Dash of Worcestershire sauce
½ pound saltine crackers

Combine oysters with water. Heat until edges curl. Do not drain. Add evaporated milk, mushroom soup, milk, butter, salt, pepper, and Worcestershire sauce. Add coarsley crushed crackers. Put into buttered casserole. Bake at 400 degrees for 30-40 minutes. Serves 10.
Mrs. W. E. Middleton

OYSTERS FLORENTINE

3 10-ounce packages chopped spinach
1½ cups sharp Cheddar cheese, grated

3 cups medium white sauce
1½ pints oysters
Cracker crumbs
Additional grated cheese for top

Cook spinach according to package directions and drain. Make white sauce and add cheese. To sauce add oysters which have been drained and chopped. Salt to taste. Put spinach in a buttered casserole and cover with cream sauce. Sprinkle top with crumbs and additional cheese. Bake at 300 degrees for 20-30 minutes. Serves 12.
Mrs. K. E. Padgett (Sarah)

OYSTERS HOLLANDAISE AU GRATIN

24 oysters and liquor
4 egg yolks, beaten
1 cup butter, softened
Salt
Cayenne pepper

Parmesan cheese
Lemon juice to taste
Rock salt
Oyster shells

Bring oysters and liquor to a boil and poach until edges curl. Remove oysters and set aside. Reduce the liquor over high heat to one-fourth cup. Cool. Place pan over low heat and stir in egg yolks. Cook until thickened. Stir in butter adding seasonings and oysters. Divide mixture among half shells that have been previously boiled to remove any sand. Sprinkle mixture with cheese. Place filled shells on a bed of rock salt in a shallow baking dish. Broil until hot. Serves 4-6.

Mrs. Warren Middlemas, Jr. (Martha)

ANTOINE'S OYSTERS ROCKEFELLER

3 green onions
½ cup parsley leaves, tightly
    packed
1 cup spinach leaves, tightly
    packed
1 tablespoon aniseed
1 cup water
¼ teaspoon hot pepper sauce

½ teaspoon salt
½ teaspoon ground thyme
1 tablespoon anchovy paste
½ cup butter
½ cup toasted bread crumbs
24 oysters, reserve liquor
Rock salt

Grind parsley, spinach, and onions together. Simmer aniseed in water for 10 minutes. Strain out the seed. Add ground vegetables to anise-flavored liquid (this approximates the flavor of absinthe, which was in the original formula). Simmer covered for 10 minutes. Season with hot pepper sauce, salt, thyme, and anchovy paste. Add butter and bread crumbs. If sauce is too thick to spread easily, thin it with a little of the oyster liquor. Open oysters. Place oysters in the half shell on a bed of rock salt in a shallow baking dish. Bake in a preheated 350 degree oven for about 6 minutes or broil them for 5 minutes only, until the edges curl. Spread each oyster with a spoon of the sauce and return to broiler for 5 minutes longer. Serves 4.

Mrs. Ray Wagner (Nancy)

ESCALLOPED OYSTERS-A LA HUTCHISON

4 12-ounce cans fresh oysters
½ pound crackers
1 pint half and half
2 tablespoons plain flour

2 sticks butter
Salt and pepper to taste
Paprika

Add flour to cream and stir until well dissolved. Grease casserole well (bottom and sides) with one-half stick soft butter. Cover bottom of casserole with crackers which have been crumbled by hand. Add one layer of oysters. Pour half of the cream mixture over oysters. Add salt, pepper, and sliced butter. Repeat process by making another layer as above. Cover well with a layer of crumbled crackers, sliced butter, salt, and pepper. (You should judge the amount of salt by the saltiness of the oysters.) Sprinkle with paprika and bake in a 375 degree oven for about 40 minutes. Let cool for a few minutes before serving. Serves 6.
Mrs. Ira Hutchison (Allene)

OYSTER AND ARTICHOKE CASSEROLE

1 cup flour
1 quart milk
2 sticks butter
½ pint light cream
6 dozen oysters (reserve liquor)
2 teaspoons salt
1 teaspoon black pepper

Dash of Tabasco
2 teaspoons Worcestershire sauce
½ cup sherry
8 fresh artichoke hearts
Artichoke leaves
Bread crumbs

Cook and finely chop artichoke hearts. Melt butter and blend in flour. Remove from heat, adding a little cream and milk (which has been combined and heated). Heat oysters; skim off excess liquid and reserve. Add oysters to cream sauce. Simmer for about 5 minutes, adding seasonings, artichoke hearts, and sherry. If too thick, add a little of the reserved oyster liquor. Pour into casserole and arrange leaves slightly overlapping around the edge of the dish. Sprinkle with buttered bread crumbs. Bake 10 minutes at 350 degrees. Serves 8.
Mrs. Sterrett Procter   *Lafayette, Louisiana*

Game & Poultry

STUFFED CORNISH GAME HENS

6 whole Cornish game hens
Butter

Stuffing:

2 cups celery, diced
1 stick margarine
2 small cans mushrooms
2 chicken bouillon cubes
2 cups rice
1½ cups water

Salt
Pepper

2 teaspoons salt
½ teaspoon pepper
1 onion, chopped
¼ cup celery leaves, chopped
1 teaspoon poultry seasoning
1 cup walnuts, chopped

Combine all ingredients except walnuts. Cover and cook until rice is tender. Remove from heat; stir in walnuts. Season birds, stuff, dot with butter, and bake at 350 degrees about 2 hours or until done.

Mrs. Henry Dusseault (Lillian)

CORNISH GAME HENS MADEIRA

8 Cornish hens, split
½ cup water
Juice of 3 oranges
Juice of 1 lemon
1 teaspoon orange bits
1 teaspoon lemon bits
1 tablespoon dry mustard
1 teaspoon ginger

Pinch of cayenne pepper
½ teaspoon salt
1 cup Madeira
2 cups currant jelly
2 tablespoons cornstarch
Currants (optional)
Green grapes (optional)
Mandarin oranges (optional)

Place hens in a shallow baking dish. Add ½ cup water. Bake at 350 degrees until done, basting frequently. Mix juices, bits, mustard, ginger, salt, cayenne pepper, Madeira, and currant jelly in a saucepan. Heat until jelly is dissolved. Add ½ cup sauce to cornstarch. Stir until completely dissolved. Return to saucepan. Stir until thickened. When hens are done, add pan juices to sauce. Pour sauce over hens. Garnish with optionals, if desired. Serves 16.

Note: Grated rind may be used instead of the bits.

Mrs. B. Philip Cotton (Salie)

CORNISH GAME HENS

2 game hens, halved
3 tablespoons butter
½ cup onion, minced
1 6-ounce can sliced Broiled-In-
Butter mushrooms

¾ cup white wine
2 tablespoons cornstarch
¼ cup cold water
1 teaspoon gravy color enhancer
1 cup sour cream

Melt butter in skillet. Saute' onions slightly, add hens, skin side down, and brown about 10 minutes. Turn hens. Drain mushrooms and reserve liquid. Add wine and mushroom liquid to hens. Lower heat, cover, and simmer 30 minutes. Remove hens and place on heated platter. Combine cornstarch, water, and color enhancer. Stir into pan drippings until thickened. Stir in sour cream and mushrooms. Heat, but do not boil. Pour sauce over hens and serve hot. Serves 4.
Mrs. James E. Preston (Sandra)

STUFFED CORNISH HENS

4 Cornish hens
2 sticks butter
1 large onion, finely chopped

1 cup cooked rice
1 cup sherry
1 can mushrooms

Boil livers and gizzards until tender and cut into small pieces. Saute' onion in 1 stick of butter until golden brown. Add livers, gizzards, and rice. Season to taste and stuff hens. Melt the other stick of butter. Add sherry and mushrooms and baste it over hens as they bake in a 350 degree oven. Serve on a bed of wild rice. Serves 4.
Mrs. James D. Nixon (Flo)

WILD DOVE

Doves, 2 per serving
Salt
Pepper
Flour

Butter
Grape or currant jelly
Toast points

Clean doves and split them down the back. Dust each bird lightly with flour, salt, and pepper. Brown in plenty of butter. When brown, add 1 tablespoon of jelly per bird. Cover and simmer 20 minutes. Serve on toast points.
Mrs. Clark Whitehorn (Ginny)

FRIED DOVE OR QUAIL WITH GIBLET GRAVY

Dove or quail, 2 per serving
Pet Milk
Flour
Salt

Pepper
Cooking oil
Livers and gizzards from birds

Salt and pepper birds. Make paste of flour and milk and coat birds. Heat cooking oil to medium heat. Put flour in a paper bag; add birds and shake. Brown birds on each side and drain. Parboil livers and gizzards in a small amount of salted water. When tender, remove and cut into small pieces. Reserve broth. Pour out oil, leaving only the bottom drippings. Sprinkle flour in drippings and stir until dark brown. Add livers, gizzards, salt, pepper, and enough broth to make gravy into desired thickness. Let come to a full boil, reduce heat, and simmer until ready to serve. Serve over rice.
Mrs. John R. Arnold (Helen)

QUAIL WITH MUSHROOM SAUCE

6 to 8 quail
Flour
2 eggs, beaten

1½ to 2 cups fine, dry bread crumbs
Cooking oil
Wild rice

Skin and clean birds. Dust quail with flour; dip into eggs and then roll in bread crumbs. Chill thoroughly, at least one hour. Fry in deep fat about 15 minutes. Serve with wild rice and mushroom sauce.
Mushroom Sauce:

3 tablespoons butter
½ pound mushrooms, sliced
1 tablespoon flour

1 teaspoon soy sauce
¾ cup whipping cream

Melt butter and add mushrooms. Sprinkle with flour; sauté for 5 minutes. Add soy sauce and cream. Cook over medium heat, stirring until bubbly and thick.
Mrs. Robert A. Cogburn (Louise)

HUNTER'S CHOICE

Dove or quail, 2 per serving
Salt
Pepper
Bacon drippings

½ stick butter
Juice of ½ lemon
1 tablespoon Worcestershire sauce
Toast points

Season each bird well with salt and pepper. Barely cover the bottom of a large heavy skillet with water. Simmer birds 10 minutes in a tightly covered skillet. Remove birds and pour off liquid. Fry birds in bacon drippings. Pour off grease. Stir in butter, lemon juice, and Worcestershire sauce. Serve birds with sauce over toast points.
Mrs. John Christo, Jr. (Mary Lee)

TO BAKE A DUCK

4 small or 2 large ducks
1 bottle Italian salad dressing
⅓ bottle sauterne
⅓ bottle wine vinegar
Bacon slices

1 apple, quartered
1 onion, quartered
1 rib of celery, quartered
1 green pepper, quartered

Combine salad dressing, sauterne, and wine vinegar. Marinate ducks in mixture at least two hours. Stuff cavity of each duck with apple, onion, green pepper, and celery. Spoon 2 tablespoons marinade into each cavity. Salt and pepper ducks and place a slice of bacon over each one. Wrap each duck in foil. Bake at 275 degrees for 4-5 hours. Serves approximately 8.
Mrs. Jack Dyer (Jill)

MEXICAN STYLE QUAIL

12 quail
3 tablespoons flour
1 No. 2 can tomatoes
½ cup onions, chopped
3 cloves garlic, crushed
1 can Ro-Tel tomatoes

1 cup rice, uncooked
½ teaspoon oregano
Salt
Pepper
Butter
Bacon drippings

Salt and pepper quail and shake in flour. Brown in butter. Set aside. Place rice in skillet with bacon drippings. Stir in onion and garlic. Cook until brown. Pour in tomatoes and oregano, mixing well. Add browned quail. Cover and cook on low heat for 1 hour. Serves 6.
Mrs. Benjamin W. Redding (Dee)

132

SOUPER DUCK

2 small ducks	1 can onion soup
Lawry's Seasoned Salt	1 roasting bag

Clean ducks well and coat each, including cavity, with seasoned salt. Grill over charcoal for about 30-40 minutes or until done. Remove ducks from grill and place them in a roasting bag. Pour onion soup over ducks and place the bag in a warm oven until ready to serve.
Mrs. Henry Smallwood (Hanna)

ORANGE GLAZED DUCK

1 5-pound Long Island Duck	½ teaspoon ground ginger
3 tablespoons butter	½ cup currant jelly
1 cup fresh orange juice	½ cup Cognac
1 large orange, sliced	Orange slices
1 teaspoon paprika	Green grapes

Cut duck in half and remove excess fat. Brown in butter; remove from skillet and add orange juice, sliced orange, paprika, ginger, currant jelly, and Cognac. Simmer sauce over low heat for 10-15 minutes. Pour over duck, cover, and bake at 400 degrees for 1 hour. Baste occasionally with sauce. Bake uncovered for 30 minutes longer, or until duck is tender. Garnish with orange slices and grapes.
Mrs. William E. Holland, Jr. (Iris Lee)

FRIED TURKEY BREAST

1 large turkey breast	Cooking oil
Buttermilk	Salt
Flour	Pepper

Chill turkey breast to make meat firm. With a sharp knife remove meat from bone, making two large pieces. Slice through the two sections across the grain into half-inch thick slices. Salt, pepper, and soak in buttermilk one hour. Roll in flour; deep fry quickly in cooking oil.
Note: This method is equally suitable for cooking wild or domestic turkey.
Mark Thomas

BROILED CHICKEN

½ chicken, per serving
Lemon and Pepper Seasoning
½ cup water

1 teaspoon cornstarch
Paprika

Remove wings and split chicken in half. Wash and pat dry with paper towels. Wings may be broiled but place them beside the chicken so they will not overcook. Season. Broil 6 inches from heat in pan without rack. Place cut side of chicken up and broil 10 minutes or until brown. Turn and repeat. Add cornstarch dissolved in water to pan. Turn skin side down, cover with foil, and cook 30-45 minutes at very low heat. Serve with its own delicious gravy.
Mrs. Earle Thompson (Nadine)

CHICKEN-ARTICHOKE CASSEROLE

1 14-ounce can artichokes, drained
Italian dressing
1 hen or 2 large fryers
2 sprigs of parsley
Celery leaves

1 BAY LEAF
1 teaspoon thyme
Salt
Pepper

Marinate artichokes in Italian dressing for several hours. Cook chicken with seasonings until tender. Cut into bite-sized pieces. Layer in a 3-quart casserole along with marinated artichokes. Cover with sauce and topping. Bake at 350 degrees until lightly browned and bubbly.
Sauce:

¼ cup butter
¼ cup flour
2 cups chicken stock

3 cups mild cheese,
    shredded
½ teaspoon nutmeg

Melt butter. Add flour and cook slightly. Do not brown. Add stock. Cook until thickened and add cheese and nutmeg.
Topping:

¼ cup dry bread crumbs
1 teaspoon savory

1 teaspoon thyme
2 tablespoons butter

Combine crumbs and herbs. Sprinkle over casserole and dot with butter. Serves 6.
Miss Elizabeth Knight

CHICKEN PIE SUPREME

1 6-pound roasting chicken, cut up	3 sprigs of parsley
3 ribs of celery, plus leaves	4 peppercorns
1 onion, quartered	2 cups chicken broth
1 BAY LEAF	1 cup dry white wine

Put vegetables, seasonings, wine, chicken broth, chicken, and enough water to barely cover in deep kettle. Bring to boil slowly. Lower heat and simmer for 1 hour. Do not overcook. Remove chicken. Strain broth. Pour a little broth over chicken. Cover both and refrigerate overnight. Skim fat from top of broth the next day.

Poached chicken, skinned	Pepper
4 tablespoons butter	1 can baby Belgian carrots, drained
3 tablespoons flour	¼ pound fresh mushrooms, sliced
2 cups strained broth	2 tablespoons parsley, snipped
⅔ cup heavy cream	Pastry for one crust pie
Salt	Parsley

Cut chicken into large pieces and set aside. Melt butter in a heavy skillet. Stir in flour until smooth. Stir constantly with a wooden spoon 3 or 4 minutes. Do not allow to brown. Heat broth with cream. Beat into butter mixture with wire whisk until smooth. Cook over moderate heat until slightly thickened. Season with salt and pepper. Add chicken pieces, carrots, mushrooms, and parsley. Pour into baking dish. Prepare crust and cover, crimping edges. Cut slits in crust to allow for steam. Bake at 425 degrees for 30 minutes until crust is golden. Garnish with parsley. Serves. 6.

Mrs. Charles Ireland (Caroline)

CHICKEN KIEV

3 chicken breasts	Pepper
⅓ cup butter, softened	2 eggs, slightly beaten
¼ cup onion, minced	Ritz cracker crumbs
¼ cup parsley, minced	Flour
Salt	

Split, skin, and bone breasts. Pound between two pieces of waxed paper. Salt and pepper breasts; set aside. Combine butter, onion, and parsley and put in freezer for 10 minutes. Divide butter mixture between breast halves. Roll up, tucking sides in, and securing with pick. Dip in flour, eggs, and roll in crumbs. Chill for 1 hour. Fry in hot oil until golden. Freezes well. Serves 6.

Mrs. Casper E. Harris (Sue)

ROLLED CHICKEN WASHINGTON

Cheese Filling:

½ cup mushrooms, finely chopped
2 tablespoons butter
2 tablespoons all-purpose flour
½ cup half and half

¼ teaspoon salt
Dash of cayenne pepper
1¼ cups sharp Cheddar cheese, shredded

Cook mushrooms in butter for 5 minutes. Blend in flour. Stir in cream. Add salt, cayenne, and cheese. Stir constantly over very low heat until cheese is melted. Turn into pie plate, cover, and chill thoroughly about 1 hour. When mixture is firm, cut into 6 or 7 equal portions. Shape into short sticks.

Cutlets:

6 or 7 whole chicken breasts, boned and skinned
All-purpose flour

2 eggs, slightly beaten
¾ cup fine, dry bread crumbs
Cooking oil

Place each breast, boned side up, between two pieces of Saran Wrap. Overlap meat where breast is split. Working out from the center, pound with a wooden mallet to form cutlets not quite ¼ inch thick. Peel off Saran. Sprinkle meat with salt. Place a cheese stick on each breast, tucking in the sides. Roll chicken, pressing to seal well. Dust rolls with flour, dip in egg, and roll in bread crumbs. Cover and chill thoroughly, at least one hour. This may be prepared the day before serving. One hour before serving, fry rolls in deep fat (375 degrees) for 5 minutes, or until crisp and golden brown. Drain on paper towels. Place rolls in shallow baking dish and bake at 325 degrees for 30 to 45 minutes. Serve on a warm platter. Serves 6 or 7.

Mrs. James A. Poyner (Nell)

CHICKEN AND HAM ROLLS

4 chicken breasts, halved and boned
1 chicken bouillon cube
1 can cream of chicken soup
½ cup sauterne

8 thin slices cooked ham
8 slices Swiss cheese
Flour
Butter

Flatten chicken with a mallet. Place a slice of ham and cheese on top; roll, tucking in the ends. Dredge each roll in flour and saute lightly in butter. Place in a buttered casserole. Dissolve bouillon cube in ¼ cup hot water. Combine soup, bouillon, and sauterne; pour over breasts. Bake covered at 350 degrees for 1 hour. Uncover and bake 30 minutes longer. Serves 8.

Mrs. Harvey Brewton (Lillie)

BALKAN CHICKEN

2 fryers
Salt
Pepper
1 clove garlic, minced
3 large onions, thinly sliced
3 tablespoons butter or olive oil

½ teaspoon monosodium glutamate
½ cup water
½ cup white wine
2 cups sour cream
1 cup ripe olives, sliced

Cut chicken into pieces and season to taste with salt and pepper. Sauté the chicken in butter until brown on all sides, removing the pieces as they brown. Sauté garlic and onions in the same pan. Return chicken to the pan; add the monosodium glutamate, wine, and water. Taste for seasoning. Cover and simmer for 1 hour. To serve, stir in sour cream and olives and simmer for 20 minutes. Do not boil, as it will curdle. Serve with hot fluffy rice. Serves 6.
Mrs. William J. Boyle (Marise)

BERTHA'S CRAB STUFFED CHICKEN BREASTS

6 whole chicken breasts, skinned
  and boned
½ cup onion, chopped
½ cup celery, chopped
5 tablespoons butter
3 tablespoons white wine
7 ounces crabmeat, drained

½ cup herb stuffing mix
½ teaspoon paprika
2 tablespoons all-purpose flour
1 envelope Hollandaise Sauce Mix
¾ cup milk
½ cup Swiss or Cheddar cheese,
  shredded

Flatten chicken breasts with mallet and season with salt and pepper. Sauté onion and celery in 3 tablespoons butter until tender. Remove from heat. Add wine, crab, and stuffing. Mix well. Divide mixture among chicken breasts. Roll and secure well. Combine flour and paprika. Roll breasts in mixture. Drizzle breasts with 2 tablespoons melted butter. Bake at 375 degrees for 1 hour. Combine Hollandaise Sauce with milk and cook until thickened. Add cheese. Pour over breasts and serve. Serves 6.
John Henry Sherman, Jr.

SUPRÊME FARCI

½ chicken breast, per serving
Salt
Pepper
Accent
Garlic salt
1 tablespoon butter
Pecans, chopped

Parsley, minced
Onion, minced
1 teaspoon flour
2 teaspoons sherry
Egg, beaten
Milk
Italian bread crumbs

Bone, skin, and pound chicken breast. Season with Accent, garlic salt, salt, and pepper. Top with butter and sprinkle onion, nuts, parsley, sherry, and flour over breast. Roll up, tuck in sides, and secure with skewer. Place rolled breast on a cooky sheet and freeze. Remove frozen breast from freezer and roll in additional flour. Dilute beaten egg with milk. Dip frozen breast in egg mixture and then in bread crumbs. Fry frozen breast in deep oil for a few seconds to seal. Drain, wrap, and refreeze breast. When ready to serve, thaw breast for 1 hour at room temperature and refrigerate the remainder of the day. Bake at 400 degrees for 15 to 20 minutes. Serve with sauce. Serves 1.

Sauce:

½ stick butter
1 onion, chopped
Garlic to taste
1 BAY LEAF
4 tablespoons flour
½ cup sherry or white wine

2 cups chicken stock
Salt
Pepper
1 tablespoon Worcestershire sauce
1 tablespoon parsley
½ cup sour cream

Saute onions in butter until tender. Blend in flour. Stir in remaining ingredients except sour cream and simmer for 15 minutes. To serve, remove BAY LEAF and stir in sour cream. Ladle over Suprême Farci. Serves 8.

Mrs. Chesley S. Fensom (Darlene)

PARTY CHICKEN

8 large chicken breasts, boned
8 slices of bacon
1 4-ounce package chipped beef

1 can cream of mushroom soup
½ pint sour cream

Wrap each chicken breast with a slice of bacon. Line a greased baking dish (8x12x2) with chipped beef. Place chicken breasts over beef. Combine soup and sour cream; pour over breasts. Refrigerate. When ready to serve, bake uncovered at 275 degrees for 2 to 3 hours. Serves 8.

Mrs. Jack Blackwell (Theola)

DELUXE CHICKEN A LA KING

3 tablespoons butter
1 green pepper, shredded
½ cup celery, chopped
1 small can mushrooms
1 small onion, grated
3 tablespoons flour
2 cups milk
1 small can green peas

1 small jar pimiento (optional)
2 cups cold chicken, diced
2 egg yolks
Lemon juice
Salt
Pepper
Paprika

Melt butter in a pan and add green pepper, celery, and mushrooms. Sauté about 5 minutes. Add onion and flour mixed with part of the milk. Add the remaining milk with the egg yolks beaten in. Stir until thickened. Add the chicken and cook a few minutes longer, stirring constantly. Add lemon juice and seasonings. Stir in peas and pimiento. Serve in patty shells or on toast points. Serves 8.
Mrs. Charles Helms (Leah)

COUNTRY CAPTAIN

3 pounds chicken breasts
Flour

Paprika
Cooking oil

Dredge breasts in flour and paprika; brown in hot oil. Place chicken in a casserole dish.
Sauce:

1 No. 2 can tomatoes
1 large green pepper, chopped
1 large onion, chopped
2 cloves garlic, crushed
1 cup parsley, snipped
1 tablespoon Worcestershire
   sauce
1 tablespoon curry powder

1 cup chicken broth
1 tablespoon vinegar
2 tablespoons dry mustard
1 teaspoon thyme
1 cup currants
1 teaspoon salt
1 teaspoon pepper
¼ pound butter

Sauté onion and garlic in butter. Add remaining ingredients and simmer for 2 hours. Pour sauce over chicken in casserole and bake at 325 degrees for 1 hour. Serve over rice with almonds, if desired.
Mrs. Troy Barker (Theo)
Mrs. Merritt Pope (Edna)

CHICKEN AND DRESSING

2 large fryers
1 small package Pepperidge Farm
  Herb Seasoned Stuffing
4 cups broth
1 stick butter
½ cup flour
6 eggs, beaten
Salt
Pepper
1 can cream of mushroom soup

¼ cup milk
1 cup sour cream
¼ cup chopped pimientos
1 tablespoon salt
8 peppercorns
4 whole cloves
1 rib of celery
1 carrot
1 onion, quartered

Place salt, peppercorns, cloves, celery, carrot, and onion in a large pot. Add chickens and enough water to cover. Cook until chicken is done. Remove chickens to cool. Reserve broth. Place dry stuffing mix in a large bowl. In a saucepan, melt butter; add flour and stir until smooth. Add broth and eggs, stirring well. Remove chicken from bones; cut into bite-sized pieces and add to stuffing. Pour broth mixture over stuffing; mix well until wet. Bake in a 9x13-inch pan at 325 degrees for 1 hour. Combine soup, milk, sour cream, and pimientos in a saucepan. Heat and spoon sauce over chicken when served. Serves 6-8.
Mrs. Wilton Duncan   *Tallahassee, Florida*

FOIL BAKED BARBECUED CHICKEN

1 3-pound chicken, cut up
½ cup water
⅓ cup catsup
⅓ cup vinegar
¼ cup brown sugar
2 tablespoons Worcestershire
  sauce

4 tablespoons margarine, melted
2 tablespoons lemon juice
2 teaspoons salt
2 teaspoons paprika
2 teaspoons chili powder
2 teaspoons dry mustard

Salt and pepper chicken pieces. Combine above ingredients. Dip chicken pieces into mixture. Seal tightly with aluminum foil. Bake covered for 45 minutes at 400 degrees. Uncover and bake 15 minutes more, basting with remaining sauce. This may be cooked in the oven or on the grill. Serves 4.
Mrs. Ronald B. Hamlin (Dottie)

DURKEE CHICKEN

2 2-pound fryers, split in half   Lemon and Pepper Seasoning
Durkee Sauce   Seasoned salt
    Paprika

Arrange chicken in baking dish, breast side down. Cover each piece with Durkee Sauce and sprinkle with remaining ingredients. Cover tightly with foil and bake 45 minutes at 325 degrees. Remove foil and place under broiler a few minutes to brown. Turn chicken pieces breast side up again covering with dressing, salt, Lemon and Pepper Seasoning, and paprika. Replace foil and bake another 45 minutes. Uncover and brown under broiler. This is an easy but very good chicken dish! The gravy is delicious with rice. This chicken is also good served cold. Serves 4.
Mrs. John Robert Middlemas (Kendall)

YELLOW RICE AND CHICKEN

1 fryer, quartered   1 green pepper, chopped
1 onion, chopped   2 tablespoons salt
½ clove garlic, minced   1 15-ounce can tomatoes
1 BAY LEAF   1 quart water
Pinch of saffron   2 pimientos, sliced
2 cups rice, uncooked   1 small can Le Sueur peas
½ pint olive oil

Cut fryer in quarters and fry in oil with onion and garlic. Add tomatoes and water. Boil 5 minutes. Add BAY LEAF, salt, rice, saffron, and green pepper. Stir thoroughly. Place in 350 degree oven for 20 minutes. Garnish with peas and pimientos. Serves 4 with plenty of rice.
Note: If you wish to serve 8, add another chicken and brown in the original oil. Do not double anything else. It is best to brown onion and garlic with second chicken.
Mrs. Jack N. Segler (Patty)

PANHANDLE FRIED CHICKEN

1 fryer	Salt
1 egg	Pepper
⅓ cup milk	Vegetable oil
Flour	

Cut up chicken. Combine egg and milk in a flat bowl. Salt, pepper, and then flour each piece of chicken. Dip into egg mixture and back into flour. Pour oil into skillet to a depth of 2 inches. Heat to medium-high and add chicken pieces. Watch carefully and turn each piece with tongs when brown. When browned completely, cover, and reduce heat to low for 10-15 minutes. Remove cover and cook about 5 minutes more until crisp. Drain on paper. Serves 4-5.

Mrs. Rex Rowell, Sr. (Nannie)

POULTRY STUFFED PEPPERS

4 firm green peppers	1 teaspoon parsley flakes
2 eggs, beaten	½ teaspoon curry powder
1 cup milk	1½ cups cooked chicken, diced
1 teaspoon salt	4 tablespoons American cheese, shredded
Dash of pepper	1 cup Cheddar cheese croutons
1 small onion, grated	

Cut tops from peppers. Remove all seeds and fibers. Boil 5 minutes in 1 cup of water. Drain well upside down. Combine eggs, milk, salt, pepper, onion, parsley flakes, and curry powder. Add chicken and croutons. Stuff peppers and sprinkle with cheese. Place in a baking dish with 1 cup boiling water. Bake at 350 degrees for 35 minutes. Serves 4.

Mrs. Ray W. Moorman (Irene)

CHICKEN CASSEROLE

1½ cups cooked chicken, diced	1 teaspoon onion, grated
½ cup mayonnaise	½ cup cracker crumbs
1 can cream of chicken soup	2 tablespoons Worcestershire sauce
2 hard-cooked eggs, diced	
1 cup celery, chopped	¼ teaspoon curry powder
½ cup slivered almonds	1 cup crushed potato chips

Combine all ingredients except potato chips. Pour into a baking dish. Sprinkle with potato chips. Bake at 350 degrees for 30 minutes. Serves 6-8.

Mrs. Lester C. Brock (Martha)
Mrs. William J. Parish, Jr. (Nancy)

PAPRIKAS CSIRKE
(CHICKEN PAPRIKA)

1 3-pound fryer, cut up	1½ tablespoons paprika
Salt	1 cup chicken stock
4-5 tablespoons cooking oil	2 tablespoons flour
1 cup onion, finely chopped	1½ cups sour cream
½ teaspoon garlic, minced	Spaghetti or rice
2 cups mushrooms	

Pat chicken dry with paper towels and salt generously. In a 10-inch skillet, heat oil until light haze forms. Brown chicken pieces until golden on both sides. Pour off fat, leaving thin film. Add onion, garlic, and mushrooms. Saute over medium heat for 10 minutes. Remove from heat and add paprika, stirring to coat onions well. Return to heat; add stock and bring to a boil, stirring until well blended. Return chicken to skillet. Bring back to a boil; simmer for 40 minutes. Remove chicken to platter. Combine flour and sour cream in a bowl, using a wire whisk. Pour into pan juices and stir until thickened. Return chicken and simmer 5 minutes to heat throughout. Serve with rice or spaghetti. Serves 6.
Mrs. Spencer Lloyd (Romana)
Mrs. Troy Barker (Theo)

RACHEL'S CHICKEN CASSEROLE

1 chicken, cooked and diced	½ teaspoon salt
1 cup rice, cooked in chicken broth	½ cup mayonnaise
¼ cup slivered almonds	1 teaspoon lemon juice
1 can mushroom soup	¼ cup celery, diced
2 hard-cooked eggs, thinly sliced	Crushed potato chips or bread
1 small onion, diced	crumbs

Combine all ingredients except potato chips or bread crumbs in a buttered casserole. Refrigerate overnight. Remove 1 hour before cooking. Sprinkle with potato chips or bread crumbs. Bake uncovered for 30 minutes at 375 degrees. Serves 6.
Mrs. J. M. Ros, Jr. (Rachel)

CHICKEN CURRY

4 chicken breasts
¼ cup butter

1 can chicken broth

Brown chicken in hot butter 5 minutes per side. Add broth and bring to a boil. Reduce heat, cover, and simmer for 20 minutes. Remove chicken and cut into pieces; keep warm. Measure liquid in skillet and add water to make 3 cups. Reserve for curry sauce.

Sauce:

3 tablespoons butter
1 clove garlic, crushed
1 cup onion, chopped
3 teaspoons curry powder
¼ cup flour
¼ teaspoon cardamon

1 teaspoon ginger
1 teaspon salt
¼ teaspoon pepper
2 teaspoons lime peel
2 tablespoons lime juice
¼ cup chutney

In a skillet melt butter and saute' garlic, onion, and curry powder. Remove from heat and stir in flour, cardamon, ginger, salt, and pepper. Gradually stir in the reserved broth, lime peel, and lime juice. Bring to a boil. Reduce heat and simmer for 20 minutes. Stir in cooked chicken and chutney. Heat gently just to boiling point. Serve with sambals, if desired.
Mrs. Larry Smith (Lyn)

CURRIED CHICKEN

⅓ cup butter
1 tablespoon onion, finely chopped
⅓ cup flour
1 teaspoon salt
2 teaspoons curry powder
¼ teaspoon pepper

½ teaspoon Worcestershire sauce
2 cups chicken stock
1 cup half and half
2½ cups cooked chicken, diced
   (about 4 breasts)

Melt butter, add onion, and saute' until clear. Add flour, mixing well. Stir in seasonings. Slowly add stock, stirring to eliminate lumps. Add cream and chicken. Simmer 30-40 minutes covered. Serve over hot rice. Surround serving dish with little bowls filled with the following sambals: Major Grey's Chutney, peanuts, grated egg yolks, coconut, and golden raisins.
Mrs. John Fishel (Louise)

OVEN CHICKEN SUPREME

8 pieces chicken
1 envelope onion salad dressing
  mix

1 stick margarine, softened
1 teaspoon paprika
Fine, dry bread crumbs

Combine salad dressing mix, margarine, and paprika. With a spatula spread mixture on chicken pieces. Roll in bread crumbs; place skin side up (sides not touching) in a greased jelly roll pan. Sprinkle with additional paprika for color. Bake at 375 degrees for 50 minutes. Do not turn.
Mrs. Dixon R. McCloy (Hodge)

CURRY CHICKEN LOAF OR RING

1 6-pound hen
1 onion, chopped
Celery leaves
1 teaspoon oregano
2 teaspoons curry powder
2 cups soft bread crumbs
2 cups cooked rice
¼ cup pimientos, diced

4 eggs, beaten
1 teaspoon salt
¼ teaspoon white pepper
½ stick butter
3 cups chicken broth
½ cup celery, diced
¼ cup green pepper, diced
2 teaspoons curry powder

Cook hen in water with onion, celery leaves, oregano, and curry powder. Bone and dice meat, reserving 4 cups broth. Combine remaining ingredients and add chicken. Bake at 350 degrees in a greased loaf pan or ring which has been placed in a pan of water for 35 minutes, or until firm. Let stand for 10 minutes.

Mushroom Curry Sauce:

2 scallions, chopped
6 tablespoons butter
5 tablespoons flour
2 teaspoons curry powder
1 cup chicken broth

1 cup heavy cream
2 egg yolks, beaten
2 tablespoons parsley, snipped
½ pound fresh mushrooms

Sauté scallions in butter. Add flour, broth, cream, curry powder, and egg yolks. Sauté mushrooms in butter. Just before serving, add parsley and mushrooms. Serve over loaf or in a small bowl in the center of the ring. Serves 10 to 12.
Mrs. H. Mack Lewis (Eleanor)

CREAMED CHICKEN WITH GRAPES AND ALMONDS

4 chicken breasts
1 cup celery, chopped
1 cup onion, chopped
1 can cream of mushroom soup
1 cup seedless, green grapes

1 cup cheese, grated
Half and half
Salt
Pepper
Almonds

Place chicken breast, onion, celery, salt, and pepper in a kettle with water to cover. Simmer until done. Bone chicken and cut into small pieces. Place chicken in casserole. Add soup, grapes, and enough half and half to moisten. Top with almonds and cheese. Bake at 300 degrees for 20 minutes.
Note: Spoon into patty shells for a pretty luncheon dish.
Mrs. Malcolm M. Traxler (Martha Lee)

TAHITIAN CHICKEN

4 whole chicken breasts, split
    and boned
¾ cup bottled oil and vinegar
    salad dressing
2 teaspoons curry powder

2 large limes
1 can pineapple chunks, drained
2 medium bananas
½ cup honey
Skewers

Bone chicken breasts and cut each into four pieces. Combine dressing and curry powder in a bowl; add chicken and marinate in refrigerator for 2 hours. Just before cooking; peel bananas, and cut into 2-inch pieces. Cut limes into wedges. Drain chicken, reserving marinade. Thread chicken, pineapple, banana, and limes alternately on 8 long skewers. Stir honey into remaining marinade and brush generously over kebobs. Broil or grill, turning, and basting often until chicken is golden, about 10 minutes. Serves 6-8.
Mrs. James Mullins (Jean)

CHICKEN BREASTS SUPREME

8 chicken breasts, skinned
½ pint sour cream
1 can cream of mushroom soup

½-1 cup sherry
Paprika
Toasted almond slices

Preheat oven to 350 degrees. Salt chicken and place in an oblong baking dish. Combine sour cream, soup, and sherry and pour over chicken. Sprinkle generously with paprika. Bake 1 hour and 15 minutes. Top with almonds. Serve with rice seasoned with ginger and more almonds. Serves 8.
Mrs. Gordon Hill (Mary)

CHICKEN SPAGHETTI SUPREME

2 4-pound chickens
2 onions, quartered
1 large carrot cut into 1-inch lengths
2 ribs of celery plus leaves
10 peppercorns
3 sprigs of parsley
2 cups green pepper, chopped
3 cups onion, finely chopped
1 2-pound 3-ounce can Italian
   plum tomatoes
1½ sticks butter
2 cups celery, finely chopped
6 cloves garlic, minced

1 pound mushrooms, thinly sliced
1 pound round steak, ground
1 BAY LEAF
¼ teaspoon thyme
1 cup flour
6 cups chicken stock
½ cup whipping cream
2 pounds vermicelli
1 pound sharp Cheddar cheese,
   shredded
2 cups Parmesan cheese, grated
Salt
Pepper

Place chickens in deep kettle. Add quartered onions, carrot pieces, celery ribs and leaves, parsley, peppercorns, and salt to taste. Add cold water to just cover; bring to a boil, reduce heat, and simmer until tender. Allow chicken to remain in stock until ready to use. Place tomatoes in a large kettle. In a skillet, sauté mushrooms, chopped celery, onion, green pepper, and garlic in ½ stick of butter until onions are translucent. Add to tomatoes. Brown ground round steak in same skillet. Add BAY LEAF, thyme, and salt and pepper to taste. Add to tomatoes and simmer for 20-30 minutes, stirring from the bottom occasionally. Melt 1 stick of butter in a saucepan; add flour and stir with wire whisk. Add stock, stirring until thickened. Stir in cream and combine with tomato mixture. Remove skin from chicken and cut into large, bite-sized pieces. Cook vermicelli al dente; rinse well. Place a little sauce in the bottom of a casserole dish. Add a layer of vermicelli, then chicken, Cheddar cheese, and more sauce. Continue to layer, ending with cheese. Add a little more stock if dry before baking. Sauce should be a bit soupy. Bake casserole uncovered, until just heated through, in a 400 degree oven. Serve with Parmesan cheese. Serves 16.

Mrs. Charles Ireland (Caroline)

CHICKEN ELEGANTE

3 fryers, cut up
4 teaspoons salt
½ cup butter
2 large cans peach halves and syrup
2 medium onions, cut into rings

2 teaspoons lemon juice
1 teaspoon ginger
4 teaspoons cornstarch
¼ cup water
2 green peppers, cut into strips

Sprinkle chicken with 3 teaspoons salt. Brown in butter. Drain peach syrup into skillet. Add onions, lemon juice, ginger, and 1 teaspoon salt. Cover and simmer for 30 minutes. Add green pepper and simmer 10 minutes longer. Blend cornstarch with water; stir into chicken mixture. Add peaches and simmer 5 minutes longer. Serve with cooked rice. Serves 12.
Mrs. William F. Harrison, Jr. (Ruth)

CHICKEN WIGGLE

5-6 pound hen
1 large green pepper, diced
1 large jar pimiento, undrained
1 large can Le Sueur peas,
   drained

1 large can mushrooms, drained
1 16-ounce package very thin
   noodles
Hen stock
Salt

Salt hen and simmer until tender. Cool and cut into bite-sized pieces. Sauté green pepper and combine with hen. Add peas, chopped pimiento, mushrooms, salt, pepper, and ½ cup barbecue sauce. Boil noodles in stock until tender. Drain and add to hen mixture. Serve hot and top each serving with a little barbecue sauce. Serves 6 to 8.

Barbecue Sauce:

1 stick butter, melted
1 cup vinegar

1 tablespoon red pepper
1 tablespoon black pepper

Melt butter in a saucepan; add remaining ingredients and blend well. This makes a hot sauce.
Mrs. Samuel C. Rowe, Sr. (Nelle)

CHICKEN SPAGHETTI

1 hen
1 8-ounce package spaghetti
1 quart chicken broth
2 16-ounce cans tomatoes
1 clove garlic, pressed

1 pound mild cheese, grated
1 4-ounce can mushrooms, sliced
½ pint heavy cream
Parmesan cheese

Stew hen; cut into bite-sized pieces. Cook spaghetti in broth with tomatoes and garlic on low heat for 45 minutes, stirring occasionally from the bottom. Do not drain. Add mushrooms and chicken. Set aside for 30 minutes. Stir in mild cheese and cream. Heat thoroughly. Sprinkle with Parmesan cheese. Serves 8.

Mrs. Kent Hall (Isabel)

COVE BOULEVARD CHICKEN TETRAZZINI

4½ pounds roasting chicken, cut up
Salt
1 teaspoon onion salt
½ teaspoon celery salt
Chicken broth
1 8-ounce package spaghetti
6 tablespoons butter
½ pound fresh mushrooms, sliced

1 tablespoon lemon juice
2 tablespoons flour
¼ teaspoon paprika
¼ teaspoon pepper
⅛ teaspoon nutmeg
¼ cup sherry
1 cup heavy cream
⅔ cup Parmesan cheese, grated

Place chicken in kettle with enough water to cover. Add salt, pepper, onion salt, and celery salt. Simmer until tender. Remove chicken and reserve two cups of broth. To remaining broth, add 3 quarts of water, 2 tablespoons of salt, spaghetti, and cook al dente. Place spaghetti in a 2-quart casserole. In a skillet, melt 3 tablespoons butter. Add mushrooms, lemon juice, and ½ teaspoon salt. Sauté until mushrooms are soft. Toss with spaghetti. Cover and refrigerate. In a saucepan, melt 3 tablespoons butter; stir in flour, paprika, salt, pepper, and nutmeg. Slowly stir in 2 cups broth and sherry. Cook until thickened. Add cream and pour over chicken. Refrigerate. Before serving, pour chicken mixture over spaghetti, reserving some chicken pieces for garnish. Toss well; top with Parmesan cheese and paprika. Bake at 400 degrees for 25 minutes. Serves 12.

Mrs. Clell C. Warriner, Jr. (Jean Ann)

CHICKEN CACCIATORI

1 4-pound chicken, cut up
Salt
Pepper
Flour
5 or 6 ounces olive oil
4 medium onions, diced
1 cup mushrooms
1 green pepper, chopped

1 BAY LEAF
4 tablespoons parsley, snipped
1 clove garlic, minced
2 ribs of celery, chopped
1 cup tomatoes
1 can tomato paste
¾ cup vermouth
Spaghetti

Season and flour chicken. Brown in oil. Add onions, mushrooms, garlic, green pepper, BAY LEAF, parsley, and celery. Cook for 5 minutes over low heat. Add tomatoes, tomato paste, and vermouth. Cover and simmer until chicken is tender, at least 45 minutes. Place chicken over cooked spaghetti; pour sauce over all. Serves 6.
Mrs. Spencer Lloyd (Romana)

CHICKEN ALMOND CASSEROLE

6 chicken breasts, boned
Salt
Pepper
¼ cup butter
1 can cream of chicken soup
¾ cup sauterne

1 5-ounce can water chestnuts, drained and sliced
1 3-ounce can sliced mushrooms
2 tablespoons green pepper, chopped
¼ teaspoon crushed thyme
¼ cup slivered almonds

Salt and pepper chicken; brown in butter until golden. Remove chicken and add soup to drippings. Heat to boiling. Add all other ingredients. Place chicken in a casserole dish and top with sauce. Cover with foil; bake at 350 degrees for 30 minutes. Uncover and bake 20 minutes more. Serve with rice. Serves 6.
Mrs. Dennis Whittaker   *Cupertino, California*

CHICKEN TORTILLA CASSEROLE

4 or 5 whole chicken breasts	1 onion, grated
1 dozen corn tortillas	1 can Chili Salsa (Old El Paso)
1 can cream of chicken soup	½-¾ pound Cheddar cheese, grated
1 can cream of mushroom soup	

Boil chicken until tender. Bone and cut into large pieces. Cut tortillas into 1-inch strips. Mix soups, Salsa, and onion together. In a large casserole, layer tortillas, chicken, and soup mixture. Refrigerate for 24 hours. Bake at 300 degrees for 1 to 1½ hours. Top with cheese and return to oven to melt. Serves 6.

Mrs. Carolyn Mann Lark　　　*San Diego, California*
Mrs. Robert Hill

BAKED CHICKEN BREASTS

Chicken breasts (one per serving, skinned and boned)	Oleo
Meat tenderizer	Flour
Lemon and Pepper Seasoning	London bread crumbs
Parsley, snipped	Sour cream
	1 egg, beaten

Sprinkle inside of each breast with tenderizer; set aside a few minutes (or refrigerate overnight). Sprinkle each breast on inside with seasoning; add 1 teaspoon parsley and 1 tablespoon oleo. Roll each breast into a ball; secure with skewer or picks. Roll in flour until well coated, then into egg, then bread crumbs. In a buttered shallow casserole dish, place 1 tablespoon sour cream for each breast and place breasts on top. Cover tightly with foil. Bake at 300 degrees for 2 hours.

Mrs. John Fore (Natalie)
Mrs. M. P. Lockhart　　　*Birmingham, Alabama*

CHICKEN IN WINE SAUCE

2 fryers, cut up
Salt
Flour
½ stick oleo

1 can cream of chicken soup
1 4-ounce can chopped mushrooms
   (reserve juice)
2 tablespoons sherry

Skin chicken pieces; salt and flour lightly and brown in oleo in an electric skillet at 350 degrees. Heat soup in saucepan with mushrooms and juice. Bring to a boil; remove from heat. Add sherry. Place chicken pieces top side up in a 2-inch deep pan. Spoon sauce over chicken and cover pan well with heavy foil. Bake at 400 degrees for 40-60 minutes. Serve over rice. Serves 6.
Mrs. Howard Langston (Irene)

CHICKEN BREASTS SAUTERNE

3 tablespoons olive oil
2 tablespoons butter
Salt
Pepper
3 whole chicken breasts, split
   and boned

1 pound fresh mushrooms,
   sliced
1 cup sauterne
2 tablespoons cornstarch
½ cup water

In a skillet combine oil and butter; heat until melted. Season chicken and brown lightly (about 20 minutes) in oil mixture. Add mushrooms and cook 15 minutes. Cover skillet and steam 15 minutes more. Remove chicken and mushrooms to heated platter and keep warm. Add cornstarch to water, stirring until completely dissolved. Add sauterne to skillet, blend in cornstarch mixture, and stir constantly until thickened. Pour sauce over chicken. Serves 6.
Mrs. Ronald G. Groom (Harriett)

CHICKEN DIVAN

2 10-ounce packages frozen broccoli
   or 1 can Le Sueur peas
2 cups cooked chicken, diced
2 cans cream of chicken soup
1 cup mayonnaise

1 teaspoon lemon juice
½ teaspoon curry powder
½ cup cheese, shredded
½ cup bread crumbs
1 tablespoon butter

Cook broccoli in salted water until tender. Drain. Place broccoli and chicken in a casserole dish. Combine mayonnaise, lemon juice, curry powder, and soup. Pour over chicken. Melt butter; pour over crumbs and toss well. Spread crumbs and cheese evenly on top. Bake at 375 degrees for 20-25 minutes.
Mrs. John R. Arnold (Helen)
Mrs. Reynolds E. Pitts (Jean)

HERBED TURKEY LOAF

1 teaspoon instant chicken
  bouillon granules
½ cup hot water
2 eggs, slightly beaten
½ cup milk
2 cups soft bread crumbs
½ cup celery, finely chopped

2 tablespoons pimiento, chopped
⅛ teaspoon dried rosemary, crushed
⅛ teaspoon dried marjoram, crushed
¼ teaspoon salt
Pepper
4 cups cooked turkey, finely
  chopped

Dissolve chicken granules in hot water. In a medium-sized bowl, combine eggs, milk, bread crumbs, celery, and pimiento. Add turkey, seasonings, and mix well. Bake in 8x8x2-inch pan in a 350 degree oven for 45 minutes or until center of loaf is firm. Cut in squares and serve with cream sauce.

Cream sauce:

2 tablespoons sliced green onions
  with tops
1 tablespoon butter
1 tablespoon flour
½ teaspoon instant chicken
  bouillon granules

¼ teaspoon salt
⅔ cup milk
3 tablespoons sour cream
Paprika

In a small saucepan, saute' green onions in butter. Blend in flour, granules, salt, and milk slowly. Stir until thick. Just before serving, add sour cream. Pour sauce over loaf and sprinkle with paprika. Serves 6.

Mrs. Ray W. Moorman (Irene)

MANDARIN CHICKEN

4 cups cooked chicken, diced
½ cup barbecue sauce
½ cup orange juice
2 tablespoons oil
¼ cup brown sugar
½ cup water chestnuts, sliced
½ cup pineapple tidbits

2 tablespoons flour
1 teaspoon salt
1 teaspoon candied ginger, finely
  chopped
Macadamia nuts or almonds
Rice

Combine oil, flour, barbecue sauce, orange juice, brown sugar, and salt. Cook, stirring constantly until thickened. Add chicken, pineapple, water chestnuts, and ginger. Cover and simmer 10 minutes. Serve over rice and sprinkle with nuts. Serves 8.

Mrs. Richard Erickson (Diane)
Mrs. Tom Holman (June)

PATIO CASSOULET

1 medium onion, diced	½ teaspoon salt
½ pound sweet Italian link sausage	1 green pepper, cut into rings
2 tablespoons vegetable oil	1 1-pound 4-ounce can white kidney beans
1 4-pound fryer, cut up	¼ teaspoon hot pepper sauce
1 pound can Italian plum tomatoes	1 teaspoon Worcestershire sauce

Cut sausage into chunks. Cook onion and sausage in oil in a large skillet until sausage is brown. Push to one side. Brown chicken pieces in the same skillet. Remove chicken. Add salt, tomatoes, and green peppers to skillet, mixing with onion and sausage. Cook for 5 minutes. Place in a casserole. Add beans, hot pepper sauce, and Worcestershire. Stir to mix well. Add chicken pieces. Cover and bake at 350 degrees for 45-60 minutes, or until chicken is done. Serves 4.
Note: You may substitute cooked white navy beans if white kidney beans are unavailable.
Mrs. Robert H. Fackelman (Ann)

MOTHER ANN'S CHICKEN AND DUMPLINGS

1 large hen	Salt
2 tablespoons butter	Pepper

Cut up hen and cover with water in kettle. Add butter, salt, and pepper to taste. Simmer until tender. Remove hen and reserve stock.
Dumplings:

2 cups plain flour	1 teaspoon salt
¾ cup warm water	

Combine flour, salt, and water. Roll dough on floured, waxed paper as thin as possible, a little at a time. Cut into dumplings 1-inch wide by 4-inches long. Add a few at a time to boiling hen stock. Continue until all dumplings have been dropped into kettle. Cover and cook over low heat for 15 minutes. Serves 6.
Mrs. Alex Mathis, Sr. (Anne)

Meats

BEEF WELLINGTON

1 beef fillet (6-8 pounds)	2 tablespoons tomato paste
Melted butter or margarine	2 cups sifted all-purpose flour
½ pound mushrooms, chopped	½ teaspoon salt
3 tablespoons butter or margarine	¾ cup shortening
1 pound cooked ham, ground	10 tablespoons water
¼ cup sherry or white wine	2 egg yolks

Set oven at 425 degrees. Trim fat from fillet; place on rack in roasting pan and brush well with melted butter or margarine. Roast 20 to 25 minutes; remove from pan and cool. Sauté mushrooms until soft in 3 tablespoons butter or margarine. Combine mushrooms, ham, wine, and tomato paste; set aside. Sift flour and salt into mixing bowl; cut in shortening until mixture is like cornmeal. Sprinkle 6 tablespoons water over mixture, 1 tablespoon at a time. Toss with fork until mixture clings together. Roll out on floured board to a rectangle 3 inches longer than fillet and wide enough to encase it. Set oven at 450 degrees. Place fillet on pastry 2 inches in from one long side. Press mushroom mixture firmly onto fillet. Bring pastry up and over fillet to cover it; press well to seal. Moisten ends, fold in, and seal. Beat egg yolks with 4 tablespoons water and brush over pastry. Cut designs from pastry scraps and arrange on pastry roll. Brush with egg mixture. Transfer carefully to a baking sheet. Bake 20-25 minutes or until golden brown. Serves 12-14.
Mrs. Dayton Logue (Ann)

MARINATED ROAST

1 4-pound eye of the round	½ cup dry red wine
Salt	1 4½-ounce jar sliced mushrooms
Lemon and Pepper Seasoning	

Season roast with salt and Lemon and Pepper Seasoning. Let roast stand at room temperature for 1 hour. Place roast in a shallow pan and cook at 325 degrees for 2½ hours. During the last hour of cooking, baste the roast with the wine. Add mushrooms and make gravy with pan drippings.
Mrs. Philip H. Smith (Ann)
Mrs. N. J. Glisson   *Marianna, Florida*

FILET DE BOEUF

1 4-5pound fillet roast
1 stick butter, melted
3 tablespoons Worcestershire
  sauce
Salt
Pepper

Salt and pepper fillet and marinate in butter and Worcestershire sauce for 2 hours. Bake at 400 degrees for 45 minutes, basting with marinade. Roast will be rare.
Mrs. Harry A. Smith (Mable)

MANZO ALLA GRECO

(Beef Greek Style)

1 6-8 pound top round of beef
1 2-ounce can mushrooms
2 slices of bacon, chopped
½ cup onion, chopped
½ cup carrots, chopped
½ cup celery, chopped

1 tablespoon parsley, minced
1 tablespoon shortening
1 teaspoon salt
1 teaspoon pepper
¾ cup dry red wine
1½ pints soup stock or bouillon

Place meat in large pan with shortening, vegetables, bacon, mushrooms, and ½ cup wine. Cook slowly until wine has evaporated. Add remaining wine, salt, and pepper. Cook slowly until meat and vegetables have browned. Add stock and continue cooking until meat is tender. Serve sliced meat with gravy. Yields 10-12 generous servings. Better than ever if cooked the day before.
Mrs. Paul Gilardi (Mary)

SPICY POT ROAST

1 3-pound pot roast
¼ cup wine vinegar
¼ cup catsup
¼ cup oil
2 tablespoons soy sauce

2 tablespoons Worcestershire
  sauce
½ teaspoon garlic salt
½ teaspoon dry mustard

Brown roast on all sides. Combine all ingredients and pour over meat. Cover and cook at 325-350 degrees for 2 hours or until done.
Mrs. Raymond Syfrett (Ann)

KOREAN PULGOGI

...Better Homes and Gardens Prize Winner...

1 cup salad oil
⅔ cup sugar
6 tablespoons soy sauce
1 small onion, chopped
1 clove garlic, chopped

1 tablespoon flour
1-4 pounds beef, cut into
  cubes
Sesame seeds, toasted

Place the first 6 ingredients in a blender. Blend and store in refrigerator at least 12 hours. Pour marinade over meat and marinate in refrigerator at least 8 hours or prepare 2 or 3 days in advance. Place meat on skewers and grill over hot charcoal. Sprinkle with toasted sesame seeds.
Mrs. Ronald Hall   *Stillwater, Oklahoma*

BEEF KEBOBS

¼ cup salad oil
2 tablespoons cider vinegar
1 teaspoon onion salt
1 teaspoon celery salt
¾ teaspoon garlic salt
½ teaspoon salt
1 teaspoon oregano
½ teaspoon pepper

1 tablespoon prepared mustard
1 small BAY LEAF
2 pounds sirloin
16 green pepper squares
16 mushroom caps
16 tomato wedges
16 onion wedges

Cut sirloin into cubes. Combine first 10 ingredients in a saucepan. Heat to boiling and cool. Add meat and pepper squares to mixture. Stir. Cover and let stand in refrigerator 6 hours or overnight. Alternate meat, green pepper, onions, mushrooms, and tomatoes on skewers. Cook over slow burning charcoal fire 20 to 25 minutes, basting often with marinade. Serves 8.
Mrs. James E. Lewis (Lida)

GLAZED CORNED BEEF

Boil corned beef 30 minutes per pound or until tender. Remove from water and place in a pan. Stud with whole cloves. Sprinkle generously with brown sugar. Bake at 475 degrees for 30 minutes. Slice and serve.
John Henry Sherman, Jr.

BOEUF MARCHAND DE VIN

1 4-pound tenderloin	Pepper
Salt	6 slices of bacon

Salt and pepper tenderloin. Completely cover surface with bacon. Bake at 350 degrees for 45 minutes for a rare roast. Turn oven to broil to crisp bacon. Serve with sauce.

Marchand De Vin Sauce:

¾ cup butter	2 tablespoons flour
½ cup onions, finely chopped	½ teaspoon salt
5 cloves garlic, minced	⅛ teaspoon pepper
⅓ cup shallots, finely chopped	Dash of Tabasco
½ cup cooked ham, minced	¾ cup beef stock
½ cup fresh mushrooms, finely chopped	½ cup dry wine
	1 tablespoon Maggi sauce

The day before, saute' onion, garlic, shallots, ham, and mushrooms in butter. When onions are brown, stir in flour, salt, pepper, and Tabasco. Continue to simmer about 10 minutes until well browned. Add beef stock, wine, and Maggi. Simmer over medium-low heat for 40 minutes. Refrigerate overnight. Heat when ready to use.

Mrs. Benjamin W. Redding (Dee)
Mrs. Warren Middlemas, Jr. (Martha)

ENGLISH RIB ROAST

1 4-rib roast	Rosemary
Salt	½ of lemon
Pepper	

Have butcher crack the bones and tie roast so that the roast is round. Rub lemon juice directly from the lemon into the sides of the roast. Let the roast stand for ½ hour. Rub salt, pepper, and dried rosemary into the roast. Skewer the roast to the rotisserie and cook 15 minutes to the pound. The roast may be placed directly on the grill with a heavy foil pan to catch the drippings, cooking 20 minutes to the pound. Serve roast with pan gravy.

Mrs. Dayton Logue (Ann)

STUFFED SIRLOIN ROAST

1 3-pound sirloin tip roast	1 or 2 cans mushrooms,
1 clove garlic, minced	sliced
1 onion, thinly sliced	2 tablespoons stuffed olives, sliced
1 green pepper, slivered	½ cup bread stuffing
2 tablespoons butter	1 tablespoon pimiento, minced
1 can cream of celery soup	Pepper

Cut a large pocket in roast with a small opening. Saute' onions, garlic, and green pepper in butter until tender. Stir in soup, mushrooms, olives, bread stuffing, pimiento, and season with pepper. Bring to a boil and remove from heat. Fill pocket and place in a shallow roasting pan. Bake at 450 degrees for 15 minutes; reduce heat to 350 degrees and bake 30 minutes longer. Roast will be medium rare. Serves 6.
Mrs. Robert Hughes (Judy)

SUNDAY ROAST

1 5-pound rump roast	5 tablespoons oil
1 large yellow onion, chopped	¼ cup flour
1 clove garlic (optional)	Salt
1 tablespoon Worcestershire sauce	Pepper

If using garlic cut into 3 pieces lengthwise. With a sharp knife make 3 deep slits in the roast. Insert garlic and close slits. Heat 2 tablespoons of oil in an iron skillet until very hot. Place roast in the skillet and brown well on all sides. Remove roast and place in a roasting pan which has a tight fitting cover. Salt and pepper roast on all sides. Return skillet to medium heat and add 3 tablespoons of oil. Sauté onion until brown, stirring well to loosen browned meat bits on bottom of skillet. Add the flour, stirring constantly as if making a roux. When the flour is a light brown, add 4 cups warm water. Bring this to a boil and stir being sure that all flour is absorbed. Do not worry about lumps as they will dissolve. Add Worcestershire sauce, salt, and pepper to taste. Continue to boil gravy gently for 5 minutes and then pour over roast. Cover and bake at 350 degrees for 30 minutes; remove cover and baste with gravy. Cover and return to oven for 15 minutes longer. The roast will be well done on the outside and rare on the inside. Remove roast to platter and let stand for 15 minutes before carving. (Do not let roast stand in gravy or it will continue to cook.) Serve gravy over sliced roast and rice.
Note: This method of cooking may be used for any beef roast. If using less than a 5-pound roast, reduce cooking time.
Mrs. David J. Turner (Patty)
Mrs. Robert S. Clayton   *Mobile, Alabama*

SHERRIED BEEF

2 pounds stew beef
1 small onion, chopped
Garlic salt
Pepper
Flour

1 6-ounce can mushrooms
4 tablespoons sherry
1 can beef bouillon
½ cup butter

Season and flour beef. Saute' beef and onion in butter. Add mushrooms, bouillon, and sherry. Cook over low heat until meat is very tender. Serve over yellow rice. Serves 4-6.
Mrs. James E. Preston (Sandra)

EASY BEEF BURGUNDY

2 pounds top round steak
Meat tenderizer
4 medium onions, sliced
1 clove garlic
¼ cup butter
2 cans beef gravy
½ cup Burgundy

Salt
Pepper
¼ teaspoon thyme
¼ teaspoon marjoram
¼ teaspoon oregano
1 small can mushrooms

Cut meat into cubes and sprinkle with meat tenderizer. Saute' sliced onions and garlic in butter until tender. Discard garlic and remove onions. Brown meat in drippings. Add gravy, wine, and spices. Add onions and drained mushrooms. Simmer covered for 2 hours or until tender. Serve over rice or noodles. Serves 6.
Mrs. John Davidson (Judy)
Mrs. Emerson Sweat (Sara)

BEEF BURGUNDY

1 pound round steak
2 tablespoons margarine
1 can golden mushroom soup
⅛ teaspoon pepper

¼ cup Burgundy
1 medium onion, sliced
Wide noodles

Cut steak into 1-inch cubes and brown in margarine. Add remaining ingredients, except noodles. Cover and simmer for 1 hour. Serve over hot noodles.
Mrs. Hugh V. Roche (Carla)
Mrs. W. Steve Southerland (Mary Sue)

BEEF INTERNATIONALE

2 pounds round steak, cut in thin strips
2 tablespoons margarine
2 medium onions, thinly sliced
2 green peppers, cut in strips
½ cup water
1 can cream of celery soup
½ cup Miracle Whip
1 can sliced mushrooms, drained
Salt
Pepper
Paprika

Brown meat in margarine. Add onions, green pepper, and water. Cover and simmer 30 minutes, adding more water if necessary. Combine soup with Miracle Whip and mushrooms; add to meat mixture and season to taste. Heat, stirring occasionally. Serve over noodles sprinkled with paprika. Serves 6-8.
Betty Boone Ereckson

SCANDINAVIAN NOODLES WITH MEAT SAUCE

1 8-ounce package egg noodles
1 pound ground beef
¼ cup onions, chopped
½ teaspoon dillweed
1 can mushroom soup
½ cup sour cream
½ teaspoon salt
Dash of pepper

Cook noodles according to package directions. In a 10-inch skillet, brown meat and onions. Stir in soup, sour cream, salt, pepper, and dillweed; cook until heated. Serve over hot noodles. Makes 4 servings.
Mrs. Reynolds E. Pitts (Jean)

ROUND STEAK IN RED DEVIL GRAVY

1½ pounds round steak
Flour
¼ cup shortening
2 onions, sliced
1 cup catsup
1 cup water
1 teaspoon beef extract
1 tablespoon Worcestershire sauce
1 teaspoon salt
¼ teaspoon pepper

Roll steak in flour which has been seasoned with salt and pepper, and pound thin. Cut into serving pieces. Brown in hot shortening. Remove steak and brown onions. Add remaining ingredients. Mix well and return steak to sauce. Cover and cook 1½ hours until tender. Add a little water if gravy is too thick. Serve with rice.
Mrs. Albert M. Lewis, Jr. (Jean)

BEEF STROGANOFF I

1½ pounds beef sirloin
4 tablespoons butter
1 cup mushrooms, sliced
½ cup onions, chopped
1 clove garlic, minced
3 tablespoons flour

1 tablespoon tomato paste
1¼ cups beef stock or
    bouillon
1 cup sour cream
3 tablespoons sherry

Have butcher slice a piece of sirloin tip very thin and cut it into ¼-inch strips. Dredge the strips in salt to taste and approximately 1 tablespoon flour. In a heavy skillet, add 2 tablespoons of butter. When melted, add the sirloin strips and brown quickly, turning the meat to brown all sides. Add the mushrooms, onion, and garlic. Cook 3 or 4 minutes or until onion is barely tender. Remove the meat and vegetables from the skillet. Add the remaining 2 tablespoons of butter and blend in the flour. Add the tomato paste and stir well. Stir in the cold meat stock and stir constantly until mixture thickens and the browned pieces have loosened from bottom of pan and sauce is smooth. Return browned meat and vegetables to sauce in skillet; stir in sour cream and sherry. Heat briefly but do not boil. Serve with parsleyed rice. Serves 6.
Mrs. William Boyle (Marise)

BEEF STROGANOFF II

1 pound top sirloin
½ teaspoon salt
4 tablespoons flour
½ cup butter
1 cup fresh mushrooms, sliced
½ cup onion, chopped

1 clove garlic, crushed
1 tablespoon tomato paste
1 can beef consomme´
1 cup sour cream
2 tablespoons sherry

Cut sirloin into ½-inch strips. Combine salt and 1 tablespoon flour. Roll meat strips in flour mixture. Melt 2 tablespoons of butter in a skillet. Add sirloin and brown on all sides. Add mushrooms, onion, and garlic. Cook until onion is tender, about 15 minutes. Remove meat and mushrooms from skillet. Melt 2 tablespoons of butter in pan drippings. Add remaining flour, stirring to avoid lumps. Add tomato paste and consomme´. Cook, stirring constantly until mixture thickens. Return meat and mushrooms to skillet. Stir in sour cream and sherry. Serves 4.
Mrs. J. M. Ros, Jr. (Rachel)

CARBONNADES DE BOEUF

¼ cup salad oil
2 pounds round steak
2 medium onions, thinly sliced
¼ cup flour
1½ cups hot water
1 cup beer
1 clove garlic, minced
1 BAY LEAF

2 teaspoons salt
½ teaspoon sugar
1½ teaspoons vinegar
⅛ teaspoon nutmeg
Sprig of parsley
¼ teaspoon oregano
6-8 2-inch bread squares
Prepared mustard

Cut steak into 1-inch cubes. In a large skillet, heat 2 tablespoons salad oil. Add beef, a few pieces at a time, and brown quickly on all sides. Remove steak and add remaining salad oil and onions. Sauté until tender. Stir in remaining ingredients except bread squares. Return meat to skillet and bring to a boil. Place mixture into a 2½-quart casserole. Cover and bake in a preheated 325 degree oven for 2 hours or until tender. About 20 minutes before meat is done, remove carbonnades from oven, and skim all fat from surface. Spread the bread squares generously with the mustard and place on top of casserole. Spoon a little of the gravy over the bread and return uncovered casserole to a 350 degree oven. Bake until bread has browned and is crisp. Serves 4-5.
Mrs. James A. Poyner (Nell)

CHINESE PEPPER STEAK

1½ pounds sirloin, 1-inch thick
¼ cup Crisco Oil
1 clove garlic, crushed
1 teaspoon salt
1 teaspoon ginger
½ teaspoon pepper
3 large green peppers, sliced
2 large onions, sliced

¼ cup soy sauce
½ teaspoon sugar
½ cup beef bouillon
1 can water chestnuts, sliced
1 tablespoon cornstarch
¼ cup cold water
4 green onions, cut into
   1-inch pieces

Cut steak into 1-inch strips and season with salt and pepper. Heat oil in skillet; add garlic and ginger. Sauté until garlic is golden. Add steak slices and brown for 2 minutes. Remove meat from skillet; add peppers and onions and sauté until tender. Place meat back in skillet, add all other ingredients, and heat. Serve immediately over fluffy rice or noodles.
Mrs. William H. Chatoney (Billy Kay)

STUFFED STEAK

1 flank steak
Red wine vinegar
Salt
Pepper
⅓ cup celery, chopped
1 small onion, chopped
1 clove garlic
Polyunsaturated oil

2 large apples, cored and
  chopped
2 cups bread cubes
¼ teaspoon nutmeg
1 tablespoon brown sugar
3 tablespoons polyunsaturated
  margarine
1 10-ounce package frozen peas

Flatten a flank steak on a board and trim all excess fat. Marinate in vinegar for an hour. Drain; salt and pepper lightly. Saute celery, onion, and garlic in oil until tender. Remove garlic and add apples. Mix lightly with bread cubes and remaining ingredients except peas. Place stuffing in center of steak. Roll and tie with string. Brown steak carefully on all sides in a Dutch oven. Cover tightly and bake in a 350 degree oven until tender. Add peas 10 minutes before serving.

Note: This recipe was tested by the Massachusetts Heart Association. It points the way to good heart health.

Mrs. R. H. Fackelman (Ann)

CALIFORNIA CASSEROLE

2 pounds round steak
⅓ cup flour
1 teaspoon paprika
¼ cup Crisco

1 medium onion, finely chopped
2 cans cream of chicken soup
1 package frozen dumplings
2-4 tablespoons butter

Cut steak into bite-sized pieces. Combine flour and paprika; roll steak in mixture. Brown steak in Crisco; add onion. Transfer to a casserole dish with 2-4 tablespoons butter in it. Heat soup and pour over meat. Bake uncovered in moderate oven at 350 degrees for 45 minutes or until tender. Top with dumplings. Increase temperature to 425 degrees and bake casserole for 20-25 minutes or until golden brown. Serves 6-8.

Mrs. Robert Schultz

CASSEROLE SHORT RIBS

2 pounds beef short ribs
1 20-ounce can tomatoes
1 cup water
3 tablespoons onion, chopped
1 tablespoon horseradish

1½ teaspoons salt
½ teaspoon pepper
⅛ teaspoon ground ginger
2 BAY LEAVES

Cut ribs into serving pieces. Melt a small piece of fat in a heavy skillet and brown ribs on all sides. Place meat in a 2-quart casserole. Combine remaining ingredients and pour mixture over meat. Bake covered at 350 degrees for 1½-2 hours or until ribs are very tender. Serves 4.
Mrs. John Fishel (Louise)

BARBECUE STEW

1½ pounds stew beef
2 tablespoons shortening
1 cup beef broth
½ cup water
¼ cup catsup
1 tablespoon prepared mustard
1 large clove garlic
Dash of Tabasco

½ teaspoon salt
Pepper
2 large onions
1 small green pepper
1½ cups mushrooms
Rice
2 tablespoons flour

Brown beef in hot shortening. Drain fat. Add beef broth, ¼ cup water, catsup, mustard, garlic, Tabasco, salt, and pepper. Cover and simmer for 1½ hours. Add quartered onions and cook for 40 minutes more. Add mushrooms and green pepper which has been cut into strips. Cook for an additional 20 minutes, stirring occasionally. Blend flour into ¼ cup of water making a smooth paste. Slowly stir into the stew and cook until thickened. Serve over rice. Serves 6.
Mrs. Julian Pierson   *Severna Park, Maryland*

ROULADEN

Steak cutlets, ¼-inch thick
Meat tenderizer
Salt
Pepper
Paprika
Garlic salt
Mustard

Bacon
Onion
Dill pickles
Flour
Margarine
Sour cream

Slice steak into individual serving portions. Sprinkle meat slices with tenderizer, salt, pepper, paprika, and garlic salt. Spread each slice with mustard and top with uncooked bacon and a thin slice of onion and dill pickle. Roll and tie with cord. Dust with flour and brown in butter. Add a small amount of water, cover, and simmer for 1 to 1½ hours. Serve with gravy made with sour cream and the drippings.
Mrs. Joe M. Keller (Jane)

ENCHILADAS

1 package French's Enchilada
   Sauce Mix
1 15-ounce can tomato sauce
1¾ cups water
1½ pounds ground beef
1 onion, diced

10-ounces Monterey Jack
   cheese, grated
1 can green chilies, diced
Jalapeños pepper (optional)
10-15 flour tortillas

Combine tomato sauce, water, and sauce mix following the package directions. Brown beef and onion. Drain fat. Add green chilies and Jalapeños peppers, if desired. Add cheese, reserving some for top and cook until melted. To assemble enchiladas, pour some of the sauce into a plate and dip each side of tortillas into sauce. Place several teaspoonfuls of meat mixture on tortilla. Roll tortilla around meat mixture. Place in baking dish. Pour sauce over enchiladas until dish is half full. Cover generously with remaining grated cheese. Bake at 350 degrees for 25 to 30 minutes or until cheese is hot and bubbly.
Miss Kathleen Pilcher   *Charleston, South Carolina*

WESTERN CHILI CASSEROLE

1 pound ground beef
1 cup onion, chopped
¼ cup celery, chopped
1 15-ounce can chili with beans

¼ teaspoon pepper
2 cups corn chips, slightly crushed
1 cup sharp cheese, grated

Brown meat, add celery, and ¾ cup of onion; saute until just tender. Drain off excess fat. Add chili and pepper and stir over heat. Place a layer of chips in an ungreased 1½-quart casserole. Alternate layers of chili mixture, chips, and cheese, reserving ½ cup chips and ¼ cup cheese for trim. Sprinkle center with remaining cheese and onion. Cover and bake at 350 degrees for 10 minutes, or until piping hot. To serve, border casserole with corn chips. Makes 6 servings.

Betty Boone Ereckson

BEEF TACOS

1 pound ground beef
¾ teaspoon salt
1 8-ounce can tomato sauce
¼ teaspoon Tabasco
1½ teaspoons chili powder

1 cup sharp Cheddar cheese,
  shredded
Lettuce, shredded
Tomatoes, chopped
6 taco shells

Brown beef. Drain. Sprinkle with salt. Combine tomato sauce and Tabasco. Add to beef with chili powder. Simmer until liquid evaporates (about 15 minutes). Add cheese; stir until melted. Fill taco shells and garnish with lettuce and tomato. Filled shells without garnish may be individually wrapped and frozen. When ready to serve, unwrap and place in baking dish. Bake at 400 degrees about 15 minutes or until hot throughout. Makes about 6 large tacos.

Mrs. Joe M. Keller (Jane)

TACOS

1 pound ground beef
1 can green chilies, chopped
1 can Austex chili with beans
Garlic salt to taste
Lettuce, shredded

Tomatoes, chopped
Onion, chopped
Cheese, shredded
Taco sauce
Tortillas

Brown beef and drain. Add green chilies, chili, and garlic salt. Simmer. Place meat mixture in tortillas which have already been fried. Top with lettuce, tomatoes, onion, cheese, and taco sauce.
Mrs. William E. Lark (Ruthie)

PACHONGAS

3 dozen large flour
  tortillas
6 pounds lean ground beef
4 large onions, chopped
4 green onions, including tops,
  chopped
4 green peppers, chopped

1 can chopped green chilies, drained
2 12-ounce packages Longhorn
  cheese, shredded
1 12-ounce package Cheddar
  cheese, shredded
Cooking oil

Brown meat slowly. Add onions, green onions, green pepper, and chilies. Saute until done. Drain in colander. Place heaping spoonful of meat mixture on tortilla. Top with spoonful of combined cheeses. Roll tortilla and fry in hot cooking oil to seal until golden. Drain. At this point, the Pachongas may be wrapped and frozen. Serves 36.
To Serve: If frozen, defrost, place in oven, and heat thoroughly. Place one Pachonga on dinner plate and top generously with the following.
Toppings:
Lettuce, shredded
Tomatoes, chopped
Onions, chopped

Cheese, grated
Green Chili Enchilada Sauce

Note: One Pachonga per serving is ample. Re-fried beans may be served on the side.
Mrs. Ronald Hall   *Stillwater, Oklahoma*

MEATLOAF WITH CHEESE SURPRISE

2 pounds ground chuck
2 cups soft bread crumbs
¾ cup milk
2 eggs, slightly beaten
½ cup onion, finely chopped
½ cup green pepper, chopped
2 tablespoons horseradish

2 teaspoons seasoned salt
Pepper
1 8-ounce package sharp Cheddar
  cheese, grated
½ cup parsley, minced
Paprika

Combine meat with next eight ingredients. Place half of this mixture in a loaf pan. Cover with half of cheese and top with half of the parsley. Repeat with the remaining meat, cheese, and parsley. Bake at 350 degrees for 1 hour or until done. Sprinkle with paprika and let stand 10 minutes before slicing. Serves 6-8.
Mrs. Tim Smith (Mary Ann)

GARDEN CLUB MEAT LOAF

3 pounds ground beef
2 cups bread crumbs
2 small onions, chopped
2 eggs, beaten

1 tablespoon salt
½ teaspoon pepper
½ cup tomato sauce

Combine ground beef, crumbs, onions, eggs, salt, pepper, and tomato sauce. Pat into a 13x9x2-inch pan.
Sauce:

2 small cans tomato sauce
½ cup water
3 tablespoons vinegar

3 tablespoons brown sugar
2 tablespoons mustard
2 teaspoons Worcestershire sauce

Mix sauce ingredients and pour over meat loaf. Bake at 350 degrees for 1 hour and 15 minutes. Baste occasionally during baking. Serves 16.
Mrs. Jesse Bealor (Cordelia)

SUMMER MEATLOAF

2 pounds ground chuck
½ cup Pepperidge Farm
　Dressing Mix
1 medium onion, chopped
4 sprigs parsley, minced
1 bouillon cube
1 tablespoon Parmesan cheese

1 egg, beaten
1 teaspoon salt
¼ teaspoon pepper
Margarine
1 teaspoon oregano
1 8-ounce can tomato sauce

Dissolve bouillon cube in ½ cup water. Combine meat, dressing mix, onion, parsley, bouillon, cheese, egg, salt, and pepper. Shape into a loaf and dot with margarine. Bake at 375 degrees for 30 minutes. Remove from oven and spread with tomato sauce and sprinkle with oregano. Bake an additional 20 minutes. This is great cubed (when cold) and added to spaghetti sauce like meatballs.
Mrs. Jake M. Eley

GROUND BEEF-CELERY CASSEROLE

1 pound ground beef
½ teaspoon celery salt
¼ teaspoon pepper
1 teaspoon dried parsley
½ cup rolled oats
1 cup rice

1½ cups celery, chopped
1 large onion, chopped
1 can cheese soup
4 beef bouillon cubes
3½ cups canned beef bouillon

Brown beef. Add pepper, celery salt, and parsley. Mix well. Transfer to a flat 3-quart casserole. Sprinkle with oats, rice, celery, and onion. Spread soup evenly over casserole. Dissolve bouillon cubes in beef broth. Pour over mixture and bake at 350 degrees for 1 hour.
Mrs. E. Clay Lewis, III (Marsha)

STUFFED CABBAGE

1½ pounds ground chuck
1 cup onions, finely chopped
2 cloves garlic, minced
⅓ cup rice
2 teaspoons salt

3 teaspoons chili powder
1 teaspoon pepper
1 No. 2 can tomatoes
1 cabbage

Cook rice until barely tender. Combine meat, onion, garlic, and rice. Boil cabbage leaves in salted water a few minutes to tenderize. Place 3 tablespoons of meat mixture on cabbage leaf. Tuck in sides, roll, and secure with picks. Place a layer of stuffed leaves in a Dutch oven; cover with half of the tomatoes and sprinkle with 1½ teaspoons chili powder. Make a second layer using remaining ingredients. Cover and cook over low heat for 1½ hours.
Mrs. Hertha Carter

CASSEROLE ITALIANO

1 pound ground beef
⅓ cup onion, chopped
1 clove garlic, minced
1 tablespoon oregano
½ teaspoon salt

1 can tomato soup
⅓ cup water
2 cups cooked noodles
1 cup cheese, shredded

Brown beef, onion, garlic, and seasonings. Combine in a 1½-quart casserole with soup, water, and noodles. Sprinkle with cheese. Bake at 350 degrees for 30 minutes.
The Editors

GROUND BEEF AND CABBAGE CASSEROLE

1 medium onion, chopped
2 tablespoons butter
1 pound ground beef
1 teaspoon salt
Pepper
1 head of cabbage

2 cups American cheese,
  grated
1½ cups sour cream
1 cup buttered bread crumbs,
  toasted

Brown onion in butter. Add ground beef and brown. Season. Cut cabbage into 1-inch squares and add to beef mixture. Cover and cook slowly until cabbage becomes translucent, about 10 minutes. Add sour cream and cheese. Mix thoroughly. Pour into buttered casserole. Top with buttered bread crumbs. Bake at 375 degrees for 45 minutes. Good reheated for second day.
Mrs. D. B. James (Gertie)

PASTITSO ME KIMA

(Baked macaroni and meat)

1 pound macaroni, cooked
2 pounds lean ground beef
6 tablespoons butter
1 cup onion, chopped
1 teaspoon salt

½ teaspoon pepper
½ teaspoon cinnamon
4 teaspoons tomato paste
2 eggs
½ cup Romano cheese, grated

Melt butter in pan and saute' onion 3 to 5 minutes. Add meat stirring well until slightly brown. Cover and cook for 15 minutes. Add salt, pepper, cinnamon, tomato paste, and cook 8 more minutes, stirring constantly. Combine with macaroni. Add cheese and unbeaten eggs. Blend well with your hands. Pour into a lightly greased 9x12-inch baking dish. Cover with cream sauce.

Cream Sauce:
8 tablespoons butter
¾ cup flour
1 quart warm milk

4 eggs
½ teaspoon salt

Melt butter and add flour. Remove from stove and slowly stir in warm milk. Beat eggs slightly and add the hot mixture to the eggs. Add salt and cook until thickened. Pour and spread evenly over meat and macaroni. Bake in a preheated 375 degree oven 30 to 40 minutes until custard is set. Do not brown too quickly! Cut into serving pieces and remove with spatula.
Mrs. Bill Janos (Cathy)

CHEROKEE CASSEROLE

1 pound ground beef
1 tablespoon olive oil
¾ cup Bermuda onion, chopped
1½ teaspoons salt
Pepper
1 BAY LEAF
⅛ teaspoon thyme
⅛ teaspoon garlic powder

⅛ teaspoon oregano
2 cups (1 pound can) tomatoes
1 can cream of mushroom soup
1 cup Minute Rice
6 stuffed olives, sliced
2 or 3 slices American cheese, cut in
  ½-inch strips

Brown meat in olive oil. Add onion; cook over medium heat until onion is tender. Stir in seasonings, soup, tomatoes, and rice. Add half of olives. Simmer 5 minutes, stirring occasionally. Spoon into a baking dish. Top with cheese. Broil until cheese is melted. Decorate with remaining olives. Serves 6.
Mrs. James Faircloth   *Americus, Georgia*

HAMBURGER-NOODLE BAKE

2 tablespoons butter
1 pound ground chuck
1 clove garlic, minced
1 teaspoon salt
Dash of pepper
1 teaspoon sugar
2 8-ounce cans tomato sauce

1 8-ounce package wide
noodles
6 medium green onions
1 3-ounce package cream cheese
½ pint sour cream
1 cup Cheddar cheese, grated

Melt butter in a large frying pan and brown meat. Add garlic, salt, pepper, sugar, and tomato sauce. Cover and simmer for 15-20 minutes. Cook noodles al dente. Blend onions, cream cheese, and sour cream in blender. Place ⅓ of the noodles in a 2-quart casserole dish. Top with ⅓ of the cheese mixture, followed by ⅓ of the meat mixture. Continue to alternate layers. Sprinkle cheese on top. Bake at 350 degrees for 20 minutes.
Mrs. Robert Gary Lee (Jean)

HAMBURGER CASSEROLE

3 tablespoons butter
1½ pounds ground beef
1 teaspoon salt
¼ teaspoon pepper
2 8-ounce cans tomato sauce
1 cup creamed cottage cheese

½ cup sour cream
1 8-ounce package cream cheese
1 tablespoon poppy seed
⅓ cup onions, chopped
⅓ cup green pepper, chopped
1 8-ounce package noodles

Melt butter in skillet and brown meat. Add green pepper and onion; cook until tender. Stir in tomato sauce, salt, and pepper. Remove from heat. Cook noodles al dente and drain. In a bowl combine cottage cheese, sour cream, cream cheese, poppy seed, and noodles. Pour noodle mixture in a buttered casserole, and spread meat mixture over top. Cover with foil and refrigerate overnight. Remove from refrigerator. Bake at 375 degrees for 30 minutes. Remove foil and toss. Bake 15 minutes longer.
Mrs. K. E. Padgett (Sarah)

ANTICUCHOS

This is a recipe from, A Night In Old San Antonio

4 cups red wine vinegar
4 cups water
1 teaspoon oregano
1 teaspoon comino
1 teaspoon garlic powder
2 tablespoons pepper

Scant ½ cup salt
½ cup whole Mexican peppers,
  drained
Cooking oil (optional)
10 pounds beef, elk, moose
  or vension

Combine first 8 ingredients. Cut meat into cubes and coat with oil, if desired. Pour marinade over meat; place in refrigerator for 8 hours or up to 2 weeks. (Meat is well preserved as it is pickled.) Grill over hot charcoal. Serve as shish kebob or serve on a bed of poppy seed noodles.
Mrs. Ronald R. Hall   *Stillwater, Oklahoma*

LYNN'S SPAGHETTI SAUCE

2 medium onions, chopped
1 rib of celery, chopped
¾ stick margarine
2½ pounds ground beef
1 large can mushrooms
1 6-ounce can tomato paste
1 15-ounce can tomato sauce
1 8-ounce can tomato sauce

¼ teaspoon garlic powder
5 BAY LEAVES
2 tablespoons brown sugar
Oregano
Thyme
Soy sauce
Pepper
Dash of chili powder

Saute' onions and celery in margarine. Drain and set aside. Brown ground beef; drain off grease. Place onion, celery, and meat in a large heavy saucepan. Add tomato paste, tomato sauce, mushrooms, garlic powder, BAY LEAVES, and brown sugar. Season to taste with other spices. Cover and simmer for 2 hours. Serves 6 to 8.
Lynn Higby

BAY LEAVES SPAGHETTI SAUCE

. . .equally as good for making lasagne. . .

2 pounds ground chuck
8 large yellow onions, chopped
5 cloves garlic, minced
2-3 ounces olive oil
2 No. 2 cans Italian peeled
   tomatoes
3 6-ounce cans Hunt's
   tomato paste

1 8-ounce can sliced mushrooms
1 tablespoon salt, or more
   to taste
1 tablespoon parsley flakes
1 tablespoon oregano
1 tablespoon crushed red pepper
2 or more BAY LEAVES

In a heavy 3-quart Dutch oven, saute onions and garlic in olive oil until they just begin to brown. Break up the meat with your hands and add to onions and garlic. Brown meat, stirring often so as not to burn the onions. Cut the tomatoes into small pieces, adding them and their juice to meat-onion mixture. Add remaining ingredients, except mushrooms and stir well. Simmer the sauce covered for 3 hours, stirring very often. Thirty minutes before completed cooking time, taste for additional seasonings and add drained mushrooms. Serves 8-10 generously.
Variation: When using this sauce in making lasagne, I add ½ cup of Burgundy and chopped ripe olives.
Mrs. David J. Turner (Patty)

LASAGNA

1½ pounds ground chuck
1 large onion, grated
1 clove garlic
1 14½-ounce can Italian style
   tomatoes
1 12-ounce can tomato paste
1¼ teaspoons salt
1¼ teaspoons garlic salt
½ teaspoon pepper

1 teaspoon basil
1 teaspoon oregano
1 BAY LEAF
½ package lasagna noodles
¼ cup Parmesan cheese
½ pound mozzarella cheese
1 pound cottage cheese
1 egg, beaten

Brown meat in oil and drain, discarding any liquid. Add other ingredients, except noodles and cheeses. Cover and simmer for one hour. Remove BAY LEAF. Boil noodles and drain. Stir beaten egg into the cottage cheese. Layer ingredients alternating meat sauce, noodles, cottage cheese and Parmesan, ending with noodles and mozzarella cheese on top. Bake at 350 degrees for 30 minutes. Let stand for 15 minutes before serving.
Mrs. Steve Wilson (Sandra)

EAT MORE

3 pounds lean ground chuck
3 ribs of celery and leaves, chopped
1 large onion, chopped
1 large green pepper, chopped
Garlic salt to taste
1 teaspoon oregano
1 teaspoon basil
1 teaspoon dry mustard
3 tablespoons catsup
2 8-ounce packages Swiss cheese
1 teaspoon chili powder
1 capful liquid smoke
1 1-pound can tomatoes
2 cartons cottage cheese
2 8-ounce packages mozzarella cheese
2 4-ounce cans mushrooms
Pinch of salt
Parmesan cheese
1 8-ounce package egg noodles

Brown meat in a large skillet using a small amount of oil. Stir to prevent sticking. Add onion, celery, and pepper. Cook until tender. Add tomatoes and mushrooms. Cook until almost dry. Add seasonings. Cook noodles al dente and drain. In three 1½-quart casserole dishes, arrange in the following order: Layer of sauce, layer of cottage cheese, sprinkle with Parmesan cheese, layer of noodles, slices of Swiss and mozzarella cheeses. End with a layer of sauce on top. Sprinkle again with Parmesan cheese. Cook at 350 degrees until bubbly. Casseroles may be frozen. Serves 12.

Mrs. G. B. Adams　　　　　*Charlotte, North Carolina*

LIVER LOAF

1 pound beef liver
2 cups ground beef or ham
2 eggs
1 cup cooked rice
1 cup chili sauce
½ cup tomato soup
1 package dehydrated onion soup

Boil liver in water until tender. Do not overcook. Cool and grind, reserving broth. Slightly brown beef or ham. Combine all ingredients and put in a loaf pan. Bake at 325 degrees about 45 minutes. Serve with noodles which have been cooked in reserved broth.

Mrs. Harold L. Ross (Sarah)

JOHNNIE MOSSETTI

2 pounds ground beef
1 clove garlic
1 green pepper, chopped
1 onion, chopped
1 rib of celery, chopped
1 4-ounce can mushrooms
1 5-ounce bottle olives, chopped
½ pound Cheddar cheese

1 can tomato soup
1 6-ounce can tomato paste
1 8-ounce can tomato sauce
1 can Arturo Sauce (optional)
1 8-ounce package noodles
Cooking oil
Salt
Pepper

Cook onions and garlic in a small amount of oil until tender. Add ground beef and brown. Drain. Add soup, tomato paste, sauces, pepper, celery, mushrooms, and olives; season with salt and pepper to taste. Cook for one hour. Combine meat mixture with cooked, drained noodles, and stir in ¼ pound cheese. Place in casserole and grate remaining cheese on top. Bake for 30 minutes before serving.
Mrs. George Gore (Madelyn)

DRESSED UP LIVER

1 pound sliced calves' liver
⅔ cup plain flour
¼ teaspoon onion salt
½ teaspoon salt

⅛ teaspoon pepper
Kraft French dressing
Butter

Dip liver slices in dressing. Combine flour, salt, onion salt, and pepper. Dredge liver slices in flour mixture. Cook slowly in butter. *Do not overcook.*
Mrs. Casper E. Harris (Sue)

WIENER SCHNITZEL

4 veal cutlets
1 egg, slightly beaten
2 tablespoons flour
1 cup cracker meal
Salt

Pepper
Dash of paprika
½ stick margarine
2 tablespoons butter

Pound veal cutlets. Salt and pepper each side and dip each cutlet in flour, egg, and cracker meal. Sprinkle with paprika. Brown in margarine. Add butter, cover, and simmer over low heat for 15 minutes. Serve with lemon slices on top. May use pork chops if veal is not available.
Mrs. William E. Holland, III (Hannelore)

VEAL SCALLOPINI

1½ pounds veal cutlets
¼ cup flour
1 teaspoon salt
¼ teaspoon pepper
¼ cup oil
1 clove garlic
1 tablespoon lemon juice

1 medium onion, sliced
1 small BAY LEAF
1 teaspoon salt
¼ teaspoon pepper
3 whole cloves
1 can sliced mushrooms, (reserve liquid)

Cutlets should be ½ inch thick. Wipe meat with damp cloth and rub with flour that has been seasoned with 1 teaspoon salt and ¼ teaspoon pepper. Heat oil in a heavy skillet. Add veal and garlic. Cook veal until brown and remove garlic. Stir in mushrooms, mushroom liquid, and enough water to make ½ cup. Add remaining ingredients. Cover and simmer 45 to 50 minutes or until tender. Serve with pan gravy adding a little water if too thick.
The Editors

CORDON BLEU

8 veal cutlets
4 slices ham, halved
4 slices Swiss cheese, halved
Salt
Pepper
3 tablespoons flour

1 cup cracker meal
1 egg, slightly beaten
¾ stick margarine
2 tablespoons butter
4 lemon slices

Pound cutlets very thin. Season with salt and pepper. Between 2 cutlets place 1 slice of ham and 1 slice of cheese. Roll up and secure with picks. Dip in flour, egg, and cracker meal. Brown in margarine, add butter, cover, and simmer over low heat for 15-20 minutes. Garnish with lemon slices. If veal is not available, boned pork chops or pork tenderloin may be used.
Mrs. William E. Holland, III (Hannelore)

ITALIAN VEAL

6-8 veal cutlets, ¼ inch thick
½ cup milk
1 egg
Salt
Pepper
Fine bread crumbs
Olive oil
¾ cup onion, chopped
½ cup green pepper, chopped

1 small jar sliced mushrooms
  and liquid
1 6-ounce can tomato paste
3 8-ounce cans tomato sauce
Garlic powder
3 BAY LEAVES, crushed
1 tablespoon Italian Seasoning
½ teaspoon ground oregano
¼ pound mozzarella cheese, sliced

Beat together egg and milk. Salt and pepper each cutlet. Dip each into egg mixture and bread crumbs. In a heavy skillet brown cutlets in olive oil. Place cutlets in a baking dish. Saute´ onion and pepper in olive oil and add mushrooms and liquid and remaining ingredients, except cheese. Simmer about 30 minutes. Pour sauce over cutlets and bake at 350 degrees for 35 minutes. Place cheese over top and bake a little longer until cheese melts. *Note:* Pork cutlets may be substituted if veal is unavailable.
Mrs. Philip H. Smith (Ann)

ROAST LEG OF LAMB

1 5-pound leg of lamb
1 lemon
3 cloves garlic
Salt

Oregano
4 tablespoons butter melted
Potatoes, if desired
Pepper

Wash the meat well and place in a roasting pan. Cut slits in the meat close to the bone and insert garlic cloves. Squeeze juice of the lemon over meat. Sprinkle with salt, pepper, and oregano. Allow meat to stand about 30 minutes before beginning to bake or overnight in the refrigerator. Bake in a slow oven 250-300 degrees, 30 minutes per pound. Baste with melted butter. Add a little water to roasting pan, if needed, in the beginning. Add potatoes when roast is half done. Cover and continue to cook until done. When ready to serve, remove fat from pan drippings and serve au jus or thicken with cornstarch.
Mrs. Theodore G. Elchos (Jimmie)

LAMB AND BEANS

2 pounds lamb
½ stick butter
1 No. 2 can tomatoes *or* 1 8-ounce can tomato sauce
1 large onion, chopped

½ rib of celery, chopped
2 pounds string beans, cooked
Salt
Pepper
Potatoes (optional)

Have meat cut into serving pieces. Sauté for 5 minutes in a large skillet. Add butter and brown well. Place meat in a saucepan. Set aside. In the same skillet cook onion and celery until soft and brown. Add tomatoes, salt, and pepper and cook 5 to 10 minutes. Pour over meat, cover, and cook until meat is barely tender. Add prepared string beans and continue cooking until meat is done.
Mrs. Jimmy Patronis (Helen)

SUGAR GLAZED HAM

1 whole ham
1 cup brown sugar

1 Coca Cola
Cloves

Place ham in a 350 degree oven and cook until skin begins to brown. Remove skin and score fat into diamond shapes. Stud ham with whole cloves. Mix brown sugar together with enough Coca Cola to make a thick paste. Cover top of ham with brown sugar paste and return to oven. Baste ham occasionally with remaining Coca Cola. Then baste ham with drippings in pan until done. Bake 30 minutes per pound.
Mrs. Roy Groom (Ethel)

BAKED HAM WITH RAISIN SAUCE

Thick slice of ham
½ cup brown sugar
1 tablespoon mustard
¼ teaspoon ginger
¼ cup vinegar

1¼ cups water
2 sticks cinnamon
2 whole cloves
½ cup raisins
⅓ cup dry sherry

Score fat edges of ham and place in a shallow baking dish. In a saucepan mix sugar, mustard, ginger, vinegar, water, cinnamon, and cloves. Simmer for 10 minutes. Strain sauce and pour over ham. Cook uncovered until ham is done. Remove ham to a warm platter. Add raisins and sherry to sauce in pan. Serve over ham.
Mrs. Joe Cornett (Marianne)

HAM LOAF

¾ pound lean pork, ground
1 pound smoked ham, ground
½ cup milk

½ cup dry bread crumbs
1 egg, slightly beaten

Thoroughly combine all ingredients. Shape into loaf and place in a shallow baking pan. Score top of loaf with the handle of a wooden spoon. Bake at 350 degrees for 45-60 minutes. Baste occasionally with Brown Sugar Glaze. Serve with Horseradish Sauce.

Brown Sugar Glaze:
6 tablespoons brown sugar
2 tablespoons water

2 tablespoons vinegar
1 teaspoon dry mustard

Combine all ingredients and mix well.

Horseradish Sauce:
2 tablespoons horseradish
2 teaspoons vinegar
1½ teaspoons prepared mustard
¼ teaspoon salt

Few drops of Worcestershire sauce
Dash of cayenne pepper
Dash of paprika
¼ cup heavy cream, whipped

Combine the first 7 ingredients and fold into whipped cream. Chill. Makes 2 cups.

Mrs. Albert M. Lewis, Jr. (Jean)

HAM, RICE, AND BROCCOLI CASSEROLE

4 ounces Cheez-Whiz
1 can cream of chicken soup
¼ cup milk
¼ cup onion, chopped
2 tablespoons butter

1 10-ounce package frozen, chopped broccoli
2 cups cooked ham, diced
1 cup Minute Rice
½ teaspoon Worestershire sauce

Blend cheese, soup, and milk in a large bowl. Sauté onion in butter until clear. Cook broccoli according to package directions until almost tender; drain. Add onion, broccoli, ham, rice, and Worcestershire sauce to soup mixture. Pour into a 1½-quart casserole and bake at 350 degrees for 35 to 40 minutes. Serves 4 to 6.

Mrs. Foster Kruse (Helen)
Mrs. John Davidson (Judy)

HAM-CELERY-CHEESE STRATA

2 cups celery
8 slices white bread, trimmed
1 cup Cheddar cheese, grated
2 cups cooked ham, diced
4 eggs, slightly beaten

2 cups milk
2 tablespoons onion, chopped
½ teaspoon salt
⅛ teaspoon pepper

Cut celery into ½-inch slices and cook in small amount of boiling salted water 8-10 minutes. Drain. Cut 2-inch rounds from bread slices. Crumble remainder of bread in a shallow 1½-quart baking dish. Sprinkle with cheese, celery, ham, and onion. Top with bread circles. Combine remaining ingredients and pour over top. Cover and refrigerate at least 1 hour or overnight. Remove cover and bake at 350 degrees for 1 hour. Serves 4-6.
Mrs. Bill Marter   Manchester, Missouri

DEVILED CREAMED HAM

2 tablespoons onion, minced
3 tablespoons butter
3 tablespoons flour
2 teaspoons dry mustard
Dash of cayenne pepper

2 cups hot milk
1 teaspoon Worcestershire sauce
2 cups cooked ham, diced
Parsley

Cook onion in butter until tender. Stir in flour, mustard, and cayenne pepper. Add hot milk, stirring continuously, and cook until thickened. Add remaining ingredients.
Mrs. H. Lamar Sikes (Patty)

STUFFED BAKED PORK CHOPS

6 double pork chops
2 cups bread crumbs
4 tablespoons butter
1 small onion, minced
½ teaspoon Worcestershire sauce

¼ teaspoon salt
Pepper
1½ cups water
3 tablespoons catsup

Cut pocket in pork chops. Combine remaining ingredients except water and catsup to make stuffing and fill each pork chop. Brown chops and place in roasting pan. Make sauce of catsup and water and pour over chops. Bake at 400 degrees for 45 minutes.
Mrs. Albert M. Lewis, Jr. (Jean)

STUFFED PORK CHOPS, ITALIAN STYLE

6 double rib chops
  (with pockets)
½ cup onion, chopped
2 tablespoons butter
½ cup water

½ teaspoon oregano
1 cup packaged herb stuffing mix
2 8-ounce cans tomato sauce
  with cheese
6 slices mozzarella cheese

Heat oven to 350 degrees. Saute onion in butter; add water. Stir in stuffing and oregano; mix thoroughly. Loosely stuff pockets of pork chops with mix. Fasten pocket securely with wooden picks and tie with string. Place in shallow baking pan, pour tomato sauce over chops, and cover pan tightly with aluminum foil. Bake 1¼ hours; uncover. Top each chop with a slice of cheese. Bake for 15 minutes or until cheese is melted.
Mrs. Jim Riggan (Karen)

SMOTHERED PORK CHOPS

6 center-cut pork chops,
  1-inch thick
1 teaspoon salt
¼ teaspoon white pepper
Gravy:
1 teaspoon salt
¼ teaspoon white pepper
1 tablespoon sugar

¼ cup pancake mix
2 tablespoons shortening
3 medium onions, sliced

¼ cup flour
2 cups boiling water

Sprinkle chops with 1 teaspoon salt and ¼ teaspoon white pepper. Coat with pancake mix. Heat shortening in large skillet; brown chops well. Remove from skillet to shallow roasting pan. In the same skillet, add sugar and saute onions with remaining salt and pepper until lightly browned. Stir in flour; cook until well-blended. Gradually add boiling water. Cook over medium heat stirring constantly until sauce thickens and boils. Pour over chops. Cover pan tightly with aluminum foil. Bake in 350 degree oven for 1 hour and 20 minutes. Remove chops to serving platter. Skim fat from surface of gravy. Serve each chop with a generous portion of gravy.
Mrs. Reynolds E. Pitts (Jean)

FARMER PORK CHOPS

4 loin or shoulder pork chops
Flour
1 clove garlic, minced
Salt
Pepper
4 Irish potatoes, peeled and sliced

2 large onions, sliced
1½ cups sour cream
½ teaspoon dry mustard
1½ teaspoons salt
Cooking oil

Preheat oven to 350 degrees. Trim excess fat from chops and roll chops in flour. Brown chops and garlic in hot fat over medium heat. Season with salt and pepper. Place potatoes in casserole. Top with browned chops. Separate onion slices into rings and arrange over chops. Blend sour cream, salt, and mustard. Pour over potatoes, chops, and onions. Bake 1 hour and 30 minutes.
Mrs. George Logue, Jr. (Alice)

PORK CHOPS NEILL

1 pound pork chops
Flour
Salt
Pepper

1 can chicken gumbo soup
½ cup Burgundy
¼ teaspoon lemon peel, grated

Salt and pepper chops. Dredge in flour and brown in a small amount of oil. Pour off remaining oil and stir in soup, Burgundy, and lemon peel. Simmer about 1 hour.
Mrs. Stephen M. Smith (Saralee)

CHERRY SAUCED PORK CHOPS

6 ribs or loin pork chops,
   ¾-1-inch thick
1 teaspoon salt
¼ teaspoon pepper

1 pound can tart, red cherries
1 tablespoon cornstarch
¼ cup brown sugar

Brown chops in oil or bacon drippings. Drain. Season with salt and pepper. Drain cherries, reserving liquid. Add enough water to cherry juice to make 1 cup liquid. Combine cornstarch and sugar; add cherry juice. Cook, stirring constantly, until thickened and clear. Add cherries to sauce. Pour over pork chops. Cover tightly and simmer for 45 minutes. Serves 6.
Mrs. Curtis Bane (Ann)

ORANGE BAKED PORK CHOPS

6 thick pork chops
½ cup orange juice
1 teaspoon salt

¼ teaspoon pepper
½ teaspoon dry mustard
¼ cup brown sugar

Cut fat from pork chops and place in a large, shallow dish. Do not brown. Combine remaining ingredients and pour over chops. Bake at 350 degrees for approximately 1 hour depending on thickness. Baste occasionally during baking.
Mrs. Jesse Bealor (Cordelia)

PORK CHOPS WITH AMBER RICE

6 chops ¾-inch thick
1⅓ cups Minute Rice
1 cup orange juice

1 can chicken and rice soup
Salt
Pepper

Brown chops in pan. Season with salt and pepper. Place rice in a 12x10x2-inch baking dish. Pour juice over rice. Arrange chops on rice. Pour chicken and rice soup over all. Cover with foil and bake at 350 degrees for 45 minutes. Uncover and bake for 10 minutes longer. Serves 6.
Mrs. R. William Lawrence (Linda)

ORANGE-GLAZED PORK ROAST
WITH RAISIN RICE

1 3-pound pork loin
1 cup orange juice
½ cup brown sugar, firmly packed
½ cup onion, chopped
⅓ cup celery, chopped
2 tablespoons butter

1½ cups Minute Rice
1 cup hot water
½ cup raisins
½ cup nuts, chopped
1½ teaspoons salt
⅛ teaspoon pepper

Bake pork at 350 degrees about 2½ hours. Combine orange juice and sugar. Baste roast with 1 cup of the mixture. Saute onion and celery in butter. Mix with remaining ingredients; add juice mixture. Stir well and pour over loin. Cover and bake last 20 minutes of roasting time. Serves 4-6.
Mrs. James Marshall, Jr. (Margie)

PORK LOIN ROAST

1 6-pound pork loin
1 6-ounce can frozen orange juice
¼ cup brown sugar
½ cup water

½ teaspoon dry mustard
Orange slices
Parsley, snipped

Place roast in a shallow open roasting pan and bake at 325 degrees until surface is brown. Combine thawed orange juice, brown sugar, water, and dry mustard. Baste meat with this mixture. Allow 35-40 minutes per pound total roasting time. Garnish with parsley and orange slices. Serves 10.
The Editors

MOSTACCIOLI
(Large Macaroni)

1 pound pork sausage
½ cup onion, chopped
¼ cup celery, chopped
3 tablespoons butter
1 6-ounce can tomato paste
½ cup water
1 No. 2 can tomatoes
¼ teaspoon garlic powder

¼ teaspoon oregano leaves
2 BAY LEAVES
1 teaspoon salt
⅛ teaspoon red pepper
1 tablespoon sugar
1 8-ounce package Mostaccioli
Parmesan cheese

Fry pork sausage loosely in skillet until lightly browned. Drain off excess fat. Saute' onions and celery in butter in a large cooking pan. Add tomato paste and water. Add tomatoes and remaining seasonings, and cook on low heat for 1 hour. Cook macaroni al dente. Drain well. Add macaroni and sausage to sauce mix. Pour into a baking dish. Sprinkle with Parmesan cheese. Bake at 400 degrees for 20 minutes.
Mrs. Holdman DeSear (Ruth)

SAUSAGE-RICE CASSEROLE

1 1-pound package sausage	1 can mushroom soup
1 onion, chopped	1 cup celery, diced
½ cup water	⅓ cup green pepper, diced
1 can cream of chicken soup	Salt
1 teaspoon Worcestershire sauce	Pepper
¾ cup Minute Rice	

Break sausage into chunks; brown and drain. In sausage drippings, saute celery, onion, and green pepper. Remove from heat and combine all ingredients. Pour into a casserole dish. Bake at 350 degrees for 45 minutes.
Mrs. M. F. Martin   Birmingham, Alabama
Mrs. R. William Lawrence (Linda)

MEXICAN MEDLEY

1 pound pork sausage	1 cup sour cream
1 cup onion, chopped	¾ cup water
1 cup green pepper, chopped	1 tablespoon sugar
1 8-ounce package wide noodles, uncooked	2 teaspoons salt
1 pound can tomatoes	1-2 teaspoons chili powder

In a heavy skillet cook and stir sausage, onion, and pepper until tender. Drain excess grease and add other ingredients; stir. Cover and simmer for 30 minutes or until noodles are tender. Add more water if needed. Serve 4 to 6.
Mrs. Edward A. Hutchison (Barbara)

GRILLED SMOKED COUNTRY SAUSAGE

Smoked country sausage	Bread slices
Barbecue sauce	
Barbecue Sauce:	
1 bottle catsup	1 can tomato sauce
1 bottle A.1. sauce	1 stick oleo
1 bottle Worcestershire sauce	Juice of 1 lemon

Mix all ingredients for sauce and simmer for 15 minutes. Grill sausage and cut into 2-3 inch lengths. Dip each piece in barbecue sauce and roll in a slice of fresh bread.
Mrs. Warren Middlemas, Sr. (Emaline)

SWEET AND SOUR PORK I

1½ to 2 pounds boneless, lean pork
2 tablespoons shortening
1 1-pound 4½-ounce can pineapple chunks
½ cup water
¼ cup vinegar
1 tablespoon soy sauce

¼ cup dark brown sugar, firmly packed
½ teaspoon salt
2 tablespoons cornstarch
2 tablespoons water
⅓ cup onions, thinly sliced
¾ cup green pepper, cut into thin strips

Cut pork into strips about 3 to 4 inches long and 1-inch wide. Melt shortening and add meat. Cook over moderate heat until lightly browned. Drain pineapple and mix juice with water, vinegar, soy sauce, brown sugar, and salt. Pour over meat; cover and simmer for 1 hour or until tender. Combine cornstarch with 2 tablespoons water. Add to meat and cook over low heat stirring constantly until thickened. Add pineapple, onions, and green pepper. Cover and simmer 10 to 15 minutes. Serve over rice. Serves 4-6.
Mrs. Wes Zuber (Bea)

SWEET AND SOUR PORK II

4 pounds pork spareribs
1 20½-ounce can pineapple tidbits
⅓ cup celery, chopped
⅓ cup green pepper, chopped
⅓ cup vinegar
Salt
Pepper

½ teaspoon ground ginger
2 tablespoons oleo
2 tablespoons cornstarch
1 clove garlic, minced
2 tablespoons soy sauce
1 tablespoon sugar

Cut spareribs into serving pieces. Place ribs, meaty side down, in baking pan. Season with salt and pepper. Bake at 450 degrees for 30 minutes. Drain excess fat. Turn ribs over. Reduce oven heat to 350 degrees and bake for 1 hour. Drain pineapple, reserving syrup. Cook celery and green pepper in oleo until tender. Combine cornstarch and pineapple syrup and add to celery and green pepper mixture. Cook until thickened. Stir in pineapple, garlic, vinegar, soy sauce, sugar, ginger, and ½ teaspoon salt. Pour over ribs. Bake 30 minutes longer, basting occasionally. Serves 6.
Mrs. James R. Patterson (Wanda)

ORIENTAL RIBS

3 pounds lean pork ribs
1 7¾-ounce jar strained peaches
  (Junior baby food)
⅓ cup catsup
⅓ cup vinegar
2 tablespoons soy sauce

Dash of pepper sauce
½ cup brown sugar
2 teaspoons ground ginger
1 teaspoon salt
Dash of coarsely ground
  black pepper

Rub ribs on both sides with salt and pepper. Place meat side up in a foil-lined shallow pan and bake at 400 degrees for 45 minutes. Combine other ingredients to make sauce. At end of the 45-minute baking period, spoon off excess fat and cover ribs with half the sauce. Lower temperature to 325 degrees and bake for 1¾ hours, spooning additional sauce on ribs from time to time until all sauce has been used. Cut ribs into serving size pieces. Serves 4.

Mrs. John Moseley (Mavis)

BARBECUED PORK

Cook Boston butt in small amount of water on top of stove until well done. Cool and slice. Reheat with the following sauce.

Barbecue Sauce:
1 cup catsup
½ cup vinegar
½ cup Worcestershire sauce
1 stick oleo

1 tablespoon sugar
1 teaspoon salt
1 medium onion, grated

Combine all ingredients. Simmer sauce about 15 minutes. Add meat slices. Can be served as main dish or on heated buttered buns.

Mrs. Aubrey Teel (Leah)

Vegetables

ARTICHOKE HEARTS SURPRISE

2 packages frozen artichoke hearts
2 tablespoons lemon juice
1 tablespoon butter
½ teaspoon salt
¼ teaspoon pepper

1 package frozen, chopped broccoli
1 medium onion, diced
1 cup medium white sauce
2 tablespoons Parmesan cheese

Lightly butter a 1-quart shallow casserole. Cook artichoke hearts. Drain and toss with lemon juice, butter, salt, and pepper. Place in casserole. Cook broccoli with onion and drain. In blender, combine broccoli, white sauce, and cheese. Spread broccoli pureé evenly over the artichoke hearts. Bake at 375 degrees for 10 minutes. This may be prepared the day before. If it comes directly from the refrigerator, add 5 or 10 minutes to the cooking time. Serves 6-8.
Mrs. Donald H. Anderson (Doris)

ARTICHOKE CASSEROLE

1 large can artichoke hearts
⅓ cup Parmesan cheese
2 cups Italian bread crumbs

2 cloves garlic, minced
1 teaspoon onion, minced
½ cup olive oil

Drain hearts, reserve liquid, and thinly slice. Combine all other ingredients, including liquid. Alternate layers of artichoke hearts and bread crumb mixture ending with bread crumbs. Bake at 325 degrees for 20 minutes.
Mrs. Glyn Strickland   *New Orleans, Louisiana*

FRESH ASPARAGUS

Wash asparagus well and cut off tough lower portion. Soak in cold water. Tie together and place standing in a deep pot. Fill pot ⅓ full with water; add salt. Turn on heat to high until water boils; reduce heat to medium. Cover and steam until tender. One pound serves two people.
The Editors

ASPARAGUS-ENGLISH PEA CASSEROLE

1 can English peas, reserve juice
2 cans asparagus, reserve juice
Velveeta cheese to taste
½ stick butter

Salt
Pepper
3 heaping tablespoons flour
Buttered bread crumbs

Make a cream sauce with butter, flour, and vegetable juices. When sauce is thick, add cheese. Layer peas and asparagus in casserole; salt and pepper. Cover with cream sauce. Top with bread crumbs and bake at 350 degrees for 20-30 minutes.
Mrs. Charles E. Mathis (Beth)

ASPARAGUS ORIENTALE

2 tablespoons butter
1 bunch fresh asparagus
   (about 3 cups)

½ teaspoon salt
½ teaspoon Accent
⅛ teaspoon pepper

Melt butter in a large skillet. Bias cut asparagus into bite-sized pieces and add to hot butter. Season with salt, pepper, and Accent. Stir-cook asparagus for 4 or 5 minutes over high heat, shaking skillet often. Cook until crispy tender. Serves 6.
Mrs. Richard Clayton (Phyllis)

BARLEY CASSEROLE

1¾ cups barley
½ pound mushrooms
1 stick butter
3 onions, chopped
1 quart chicken stock (6
   bouillon cubes)

Pepper
Parsley
Pimiento

Saute sliced mushrooms in 2 tablespoons butter until tender. Remove. Add remaining butter and saute onion and barley until golden. Add mushrooms to barley and put into a casserole. Stir in 1¾ cups stock. Cover tightly and bake at 350 degrees for 30 minutes. Taste for seasonings and add 1¾ cups more stock. Bake 45 minutes longer. If too dry, add a little more stock. Garnish with pimiento and parsley.
Mrs. Ed Lee   Mobile, Alabama

BAKED BEAN CASSEROLE

2 or 3 medium onions, chopped	1 stick butter, divided
1 large green pepper, diced	¾ pound sharp cheese,
6 slices bread	grated
2 cans pork and beans	Bacon slices

Toast and crumb bread. Saute' onion and pepper in ½ stick butter until tender. Combine with beans. Place ½ mixture in a buttered casserole. Top with grated cheese and the remaining bean mixture. Cover with bread crumbs which have been tossed with remaining melted butter. Top with uncooked bacon slices. Bake for 1 hour at 350 degrees.
Mrs. Donald Craft (Loyce)

SPECIAL BAKED BEANS

...as served at Hearth 'n Garden...

3 pounds ground beef	3 10-ounce can pinto beans,
2-3 cups onions, chopped	drained
1 pound bacon, chopped	½ cup brown sugar
1 7-pound can pork and beans	Dash of liquid smoke
½ 7-pound can lima beans,	Dash of vinegar
drained	3 cups catsup

Brown ground beef and drain well. Saute' onions and bacon together; drain. Combine all ingredients and place in a large casserole and bake at 250 degrees for 3 hours. Serves 40-50.
Hearth 'n Garden Restaurant

BLACK BEANS ON RICE

1 12-ounce package black beans	2 BAY LEAVES
2 green peppers, chopped	¼ cup vinegar
1 large onion, chopped	⅔ cup safflower oil
1 clove garlic	Salt

Clean and wash beans. Soak overnight and reserve water. Add all ingredients and cook covered until beans are tender. During cooking, crush some of the beans and garlic on the side of the pot. When done, add an additional tablespoon of vinegar; remove from stove and let sit several hours. Mash more beans to make a thicker gravy, if desired. Serve over rice and sprinkle with chopped onions.
Mrs. J. R. Moody, III (Joyce)

LIMA BEAN CASSEROLE

2 medium onions, sliced
1 tablespoon butter or margarine
1 4-ounce can sliced mushrooms,
    drained
½ can cream of mushroom soup
1½ packages frozen, baby Lima
    beans

¼ teaspoon salt
Dash of pepper
½ teaspoon dillseed
½ cup whipping cream
½ cup Parmesan cheese,
    grated

Saute' sliced onions in butter until tender. Stir in drained mushrooms and soup. Cook Lima beans in boiling water with salt, pepper, and dillseed for 5 minutes. Drain. Combine Lima beans and onion mixture. Place in buttered shallow baking dish. Pour cream over mixture and sprinkle with cheese. Bake at 300 degrees for 30 minutes; increase temperature to 350 degrees and bake 20-30 minutes longer. (Do not overheat or the cream will separate.) This casserole may be assembled a day ahead and baked when ready to serve.
Mrs. Theodore G. Elchos (Jimmie)

BUFFET GREEN BEANS

2 pounds frozen, French-style
    green beans
1 can bean sprouts
1 8-ounce can water chestnuts,
    sliced
½ cup Parmesan cheese
2 tablespoons flour
6 tablespoons butter

1½ teaspoons salt
¼ teaspoon Worcestershire sauce
¼ teaspoon pepper
Dash of cayenne pepper
1 pint heavy cream
1 cup unblanched almonds,
    finely chopped

Cook beans in boiling water for 5 minutes and drain. Place in a 2-quart casserole in alternating layers with bean sprouts and water chestnuts.
Sauce: Melt 4 tablespoons butter. Blend in flour. Add cream and cook until thickened, stirring constantly. Add salt, peppers, cheese, and Worcestershire. Pour over vegetables to coat well. Melt remaining butter and add almonds. Bake at 400 degrees for 15-20 minutes. Serves 8-10.
Mrs. Harry Edwards (Mary)

SNAPPY GREEN BEANS

2 No. 2 cans Blue Lake green beans	2 tablespoons red wine vinegar
	½ teaspoon sugar
4 strips of bacon	1 tablespoon Worcestershire sauce
2 tablespoons pimiento, diced	¼ teaspoon dry mustard

Simmer beans 15 minutes in a saucepan. Cut bacon into ½-inch strips. Fry until crisp. Add bacon to beans. Add pimiento to bacon pan. Add vinegar, sugar, Worcestershire sauce, and mustard. Boil, stirring constantly. Pour over beans and mix well.

Mrs. Richard Laird (Judi)
Mrs. George J. Dudley (Ruth)
Mrs. E. R. Bane   Clay Center, Kansas

DILL GREEN BEAN CASSEROLE

3 cans cut green beans	1½ teaspoons dillweed or
Bacon drippings	dillseed

Put beans and their liquid in a saucepan. Season with bacon drippings; add dill and simmer for 45 minutes. Let cool in liquid 3 or 4 hours.
Sauce:

6 tablespoons margarine	Salt to taste
6 tablespoons flour	1 teaspoon pepper
½ cup milk	2½ teaspoons Accent
1 cup bean juice	Dash of Tabasco
3 teaspoons onion, grated	Cheese, grated

Melt margarine in double boiler. Remove from heat and add flour. Blend well. Replace on medium heat, adding remaining ingredients, except cheese. Stir until sauce begins to thicken. Pour sauce over drained beans. Sprinkle with grated cheese. Bake at 350 degrees for 35 minutes.

Mrs. Ronald B. Hamlin (Dottie)
Mrs. James A. Poyner (Nell)

BROCCOLI-PEAS CASSEROLE

2 10-ounce packages frozen, chopped broccoli
1 No. 303 can green peas
1 can cream of mushroom soup
1 cup mayonnaise
1 teaspoon salt

½ teaspoon pepper
1 cup sharp cheese, grated
1 medium onion, chopped
2 eggs, beaten
½ cup crushed round crackers

Cook broccoli according to package directions. Drain. Arrange half of cooked broccoli in a 2-quart casserole. Cover with peas. Mix soup, mayonnaise, salt, pepper, cheese, onion, and eggs to make sauce. Pour half of sauce over broccoli and peas. Add rest of broccoli and top with remaining sauce. Sprinkle crushed crackers on top. Bake at 350 degrees for 30 minutes. Serves 8.
Mrs. Gordon Hindsman (Helen)

BROCCOLI SOUFFLÉ

3 tablespoons butter
3 tablespoons flour
1 cup milk
¼ teaspoon salt
⅛ teaspoon pepper
2½ cups Cheddar cheese, grated

1 10-ounce package frozen, chopped broccoli
½ cup onion, finely chopped
3 eggs, separated

Make a white sauce with butter, flour, milk, salt, and pepper. Add cheese. Stir until melted. Fold in partially thawed broccoli and onion. Fold in beaten egg yolks. Beat egg whites until stiff and lightly fold into broccoli mixture. Pour into a foil lined 2-quart soufflé dish. Freeze. Remove foil. Bake in same dish. Set baking dish in a shallow pan filled with ½ inch hot water. Bake at 350 degrees for 45 minutes covered with foil; uncover and bake 1 hour until puffy and brown. To cook unfrozen, bake in an unlined dish set in a pan of hot water at 350 degrees for 1 hour. Serve immediately.
Miss Carol Jean Lewis
Mrs. Lee S. Huoni (Betty)

BROCCOLI CASSEROLE

2 packages frozen, chopped
   broccoli, thawed
2 cans cream of celery soup
2 cups Minute Rice, uncooked

1 8-ounce jar Cheez Whiz
¾ cup celery, chopped
¾ cup onion, chopped
1 stick margarine, melted

Combine all ingredients. Place in a buttered baking dish. Bake at 325 degrees for 1 hour. Serves 12.

Mrs. Walton B. Walters (Marge)
Mrs. James W. Marshall, Sr. (Dot)
Mrs. Robert Schultz

CABBAGE PIE

Oddly enough, this tastes not unlike oysters.

1 medium-sized cabbage,
   shredded
16 soda crackers
White Sauce:
¼ pound butter
4 tablespoons flour

½ teaspoon pepper
¼ teaspoon celery seed
1 teaspoon salt

2 cups milk

Fill a baking dish with alternating layers of crumbled crackers and shredded cabbage, starting with a layer of cabbage and ending with a layer of crackers, three layers of each. Make white sauce adding salt, pepper, and celery seed. Pour over the cabbage. Bake at 350 degrees for 1 hour. Serves 8.

Mrs. Arthur A. Shawkey (Lalia)
Mrs. Walter D. Merriam (Jo Ann)

CREAMED HORSERADISH BEETS

3 cups diced beets
2 tablespoons butter
2 tablespoons flour

½ teaspoon salt
1 cup milk
1 tablespoon prepared horseradish

Melt butter in a saucepan. Stir in flour and salt. Gradually add milk, cook until thick. Add horseradish. Pour sauce over hot beets. Good with pork. Serves 4.

The Editors

CARROTS AND GRAND MARNIER

2 bunches very small carrots
½ cup butter
¾ teaspoon sugar (I like a
  little more.)

½ teaspoon salt
¼ cup Grand Marnier

Melt butter in baking dish and stir in sugar and salt. Add very thinly sliced carrots and Grand Marnier. Cover and bake for 45 to 50 minutes at 350 degrees or until tender, but not brown. Serves 6.
Mrs. Florence Hood   Moultrie, Georgia

COPPER PENNIES

2 pounds carrots, sliced
1 medium green pepper
1 medium onion
1 can tomato soup
½ cup salad oil
1 cup sugar

¾ cup vinegar
1 teaspoon prepared mustard
1 teaspoon Worcestershire sauce
1 teaspoon salt
½ teaspoon pepper

Cook carrots. Drain. Cut onion and green pepper into rings. Make marinade with soup, oil, vinegar, sugar, mustard, Worcestershire, salt, and pepper. Pour this mixture over carrots, onion, and green pepper. Let stand over-night. Serve cold. Keeps 2-3 weeks in refrigerator.
Mrs. Edward L. Pipkin (Shirley)
Mrs. Robert Woods (Tootsie)
Mrs. E. H. Vallee   Beaumont, Texas

GLAZED CARROTS

¼ cup butter
½ cup brown sugar, firmly packed
½ cup cranberry-orange relish
2 tablespoons brandy or rum

3 1-pound cans carrots, well drained
  (fresh or frozen may be used)
Parsley, to garnish

Melt butter. Add sugar, relish, and brandy. Stir to blend. Add carrots and place over medium heat. Cook about 10 minutes or until carrots are well coated. Garnish with parsley. Serves 6-7.
Mrs. James E. Preston (Sandra)
Mrs. Bill Marter   Manchester, Missouri

CAULIFLOWER WITH GREEN GRAPES

1 large head cauliflower
1½ cups water
1 tablespoon salt

½ cup slivered almonds
1 cup seedless, green grapes
2 tablespoons butter

Break off each floret of cauliflower, then slice lengthwise into slices ¼ inch thick. In salted water, simmer cauliflower covered for 5 minutes or until tender. Drain. Fold in butter, grapes, and almonds. Serves 6.
Mrs. J. R. Moody, III (Joyce)

SWEET CORN PUDDING

3 eggs
3 tablespoons sugar
¼ cup butter, melted

½ cup milk
1 1-pound can whole kernel corn,
drained

Beat eggs. Add sugar, butter, and milk, beating well after each addition. Stir in corn. Refrigerate for 30 minutes. Mix again and turn into a buttered 1-quart casserole. Bake at 350 degrees for 30 minutes. Serves 4-6.
Mrs. Larry J. Weas   Jacksonville, Florida

CORN CASSEROLE

3 16-ounce cans cream-style
   corn
2 12-ounce cans whole kernel corn
1 pound bacon
1½ cups onion, chopped
1 large green pepper, chopped

1 cup celery, chopped
1 cup cracker crumbs
1 small jar pimiento
Salt
Pepper

Fry bacon and drain. Using small amount of the drippings, sauté onions, pepper, and celery until tender. Combine cream-style corn with whole kernel corn. Add crumbled bacon, sautéed vegetables, and half of the cracker crumbs. Salt and pepper to taste. Pour into a buttered 3-quart casserole. Top with remainder of crumbs. Garnish top with pimiento. Bake at 350 degrees until bubbly. Serves 18-20.
Mrs. Walton B. Walters (Marge)

GOOD CORN

*This is an old Wilmington, North Carolina, recipe that my wife
and I had the pleasure of being introduced to many years ago.*

2 cans Green Giant Mexicorn,
  well drained
1 can sliced mushrooms, drained
2 cans cream of mushroom soup

4 ounces Cracker Barrel sharp
  cheese, grated
Plenty of black pepper

Slowly heat all ingredients until cheese melts and is hot. Delicious!
David J. Turner

STUFFED MUSHROOMS

Herb seasoned stuffing mix
Sharp Cheddar cheese, grated
Mushrooms

Sherry
Butter

Sauté mushroom caps in butter. Mix equal parts of cheese with stuffing mix.
Dampen with enough sherry to moisten. Bake in preheated 400 degree oven
for 5 minutes or until heated throughout.
Mrs. Lynn C. Higby (Dedee)

HUNGARIAN MACARONI

1 can cream of mushroom soup
1 cup mayonnaise or Miracle Whip
1 medium onion, chopped
1 medium green pepper, chopped
1 small can mushrooms and juice
1 pound New York State cheese,
  grated

1 small jar pimiento, chopped
  (reserve juice)
1 8-ounce package macaroni
Bread crumbs

Cook macaroni al dente; drain. Combine soup, mayonnaise, mushroom juice,
and pimiento juice. Toss macaroni with onion, green pepper, mushrooms,
and pimiento. Arrange in two layers with cheese in the middle. Pour sauce
over and top with bread crumbs. Bake in a buttered casserole at 350 degrees
for 20-30 minutes. Serves 8-10.
Mrs. John Colmery (Maxine)
Mrs. Sam Ridley (Marge)
Mrs. C. T. Clayton, Sr.   *Birmingham, Alabama*

AUNT MARTHA'S RING OF PLENTY

This is great with fowl—Thanksgiving tradition in my family.

1½ cups cooked macaroni
1 cup cheese, diced
1 cup soft bread crumbs
1 tablespoon parsley, minced
3 tablespoons pimiento, minced
5 tablespoons butter, melted

2 tablespoons onion, grated
1 cup milk, scalded
2 eggs, well beaten
1 teaspoon salt
Red pepper to taste

Cut macaroni into short pieces. Combine ingredients in order given. Transfer to a well-buttered ring mold and place in a pan of hot water. Bake at 350 degrees until firm. Unmold and fill with creamed mushrooms or mushroom gravy of whatever meat is served.

Mrs. A. T. Fort   Lumpkin, Georgia

EGGPLANT PARMESAN

1 large eggplant
3 eggs, beaten
1 cup dried bread crumbs
¾ cup salad oil
½ cup Parmesan cheese, grated
1 teaspoon oregano

1 teaspoon thyme
Salt
½ pound mozzarella cheese,
   sliced
3 8-ounce cans tomato sauce

Pare eggplant, if desired. Cut into ¼ inch-thick slices. Dip each slice into beaten eggs, then into crumbs. Sauté in hot oil until golden brown on both sides. Place a layer of eggplant in a 2-quart casserole; sprinkle with some of the thyme, salt, Parmesan, oregano, and mozzarella. Then cover with some of the tomato sauce. Repeat until all eggplant is used, topping the last layer of sauce with several slices of mozzarella. Bake uncovered at 350 degrees for ½ hour or until sauce is bubbly. Serves 4-6.

Mrs. J. R. Moody, III (Joyce)

EGGPLANT SOUFFLÉ

1 medium eggplant	1 cup milk
2 tablespoons flour	3 eggs, separated
1 cup cheese, grated	1 teaspoon salt
2 tablespoons butter	1 teaspoon pepper

Peel and slice eggplant. Boil until tender, about 10 minutes. Add salt and pepper. Mash until fine. Make a cream sauce with butter, flour, milk, and cheese. Cool slightly and pour over well-beaten egg yolks. Slowly add eggplant. Beat egg whites until stiff and slowly add cooled cream sauce to which eggplant has been added. Place this in a buttered 2-quart casserole and bake at 350 degrees for 30 to 45 minutes. Serves 6-8.
Mrs. J. C. Watson (Edna)

EGGPLANT PARMIGIANA

1 large eggplant	¼ teaspoon crushed oregano
1 1-pound can tomatoes	1 BAY LEAF
1 6-ounce can tomato paste	½ cup Romano cheese, grated
¼ teaspoon garlic powder	2 cups soft bread crumbs
1½ teaspoons Season-All	½ pound sliced mozzarella
⅛ teaspoon black pepper	cheese
1 tablespoon parsley flakes	

Cut eggplant into ½-inch slices and peel. Parboil in small amount of salted water until barely tender. Remove and keep warm. In a skillet combine tomatoes, tomato paste, and seasonings. Cover and simmer 15 minutes. Remove BAY LEAF. Add Romano cheese and bread crumbs, mixing well. Place a layer of eggplant in a buttered, shallow 2-quart casserole. Cover with half the sauce, then half the mozzarella cheese. Repeat layers. Bake at 350 degrees for 20 minutes or until cheese melts and is lightly browned.
Mrs. Harry A. Smith (Mable)

CREAMED ONIONS

3-4 cups small white onions
3 tablespoons butter
3 tablespoons all-purpose flour
2 cups heavy cream
1 cup Cheddar cheese, shredded

½ teaspoon salt
¼ teaspoon ground nutmeg
¼ teaspoon paprika
1 teaspoon curry powder
Dash of Tabasco

Cook onions in boiling salted water for 8 minutes or until tender. Make a cream sauce of butter, flour, cream, and cheese. Add seasonings and onions. Heat and serve. Serves 6-8.
Mrs. Benjamin W. Redding (Dee)

OKRA AND TOMATOES

1 1-pound can tomatoes
1 large onion, chopped
½ pound fresh okra
½ teaspoon salt

Pepper
3 tablespoons bacon drippings
1 BAY LEAF

Wash okra and cut into small pieces. Sauté onion in drippings until clear. Cut tomatoes into small pieces. Add the undrained tomatoes and the okra to the onion mixture. Season with salt, pepper, and the BAY LEAF. Simmer over low heat for about 1 hour, stirring frequently. Especially good with fried chicken or pork.
Mrs. William E. Lark (Ruthie)

BAKED ONION

1 large onion, per serving
1 tablespoon brown sugar
1 teaspoon salt
½ teaspoon pepper

1 strip of bacon, cut in half
12x12-inch sheet of aluminum
   foil
4 pats butter

Peel onion and cut ¼ inch from top and bottom; place on foil. Cut onion almost through in quarters and place a pat of butter in each cut. Hold together with hands and place brown sugar, salt, and pepper on top. Crisscross with bacon strips; wrap individually in foil. Bake at 400 degrees for 1 hour.
Ellis Fowhand

ONION PIE
. . .something different to serve with steak. . .

1¼ cups Ritz cracker crumbs
6 tablespoons butter, melted
2 cups onions, thinly sliced
2 eggs

¾ cup milk
¾ teaspoon salt
Dash of pepper
¼-½ cup sharp cheese, grated

Mix together cracker crumbs and ½ stick butter. Press into an 8-inch pie plate. Chill. Saute´onions in 2 tablespoons butter. Spoon into crust. Mix lightly beaten eggs with milk, salt, and pepper and pour over onions. Sprinkle with cheese. Bake at 350 degrees for 30 minutes. Serves 4-6.
Mrs. Lynn Higby (Dedee)

GREEN PEAS AND MUSHROOMS

2 cans Le Sueur peas
1 garlic cheese roll
1 can mushroom soup
1 can mushrooms

1 jar pimiento
Toasted almonds
Butter

In a saucepan melt soup and cheese. Stir in drained peas, mushrooms, and pimiento. Place in a buttered casserole and sprinkle with almonds and bake at 350 degrees for 20 minutes.
Mrs. Philip H. Smith (Ann)

HOT POTATO CASSEROLE

1 large can milk
2 8-ounce packages Velveeta
  cheese
1 teaspoon Tabasco
1 stick oleo

1 teaspoon Worcestershire sauce
3 pimientos, chopped
3 teaspoons lemon juice
2 cans small, Irish potatoes, heated

Melt first five ingredients in double boiler. Cook slowly until thick like cream. Place drained potatoes in casserole and sprinkle with lemon juice. Add pimiento and pour sauce over potatoes. Cook only over water or in a chafing dish.
Mrs. J. C. Harris (Ruby)   *Cove Hotel*

SWISS POTATO CASSEROLE

3 cups milk
4 pounds Irish potatoes
1 egg
¾ pound Swiss cheese, grated
Salt
Pepper
Nutmeg
Garlic
Butter

Scald milk. Cool. Peel and slice potatoes. Beat egg, salt, pepper, and nutmeg together. Combine egg, milk, potatoes, and ½ of the cheese. Rub a casserole dish well with garlic and butter. Pour potatoes into dish and top with remaining cheese. Bake at 350 degrees for 1 hour. Serves 8.
Mrs. Abbott L. Browne (Mary Belle)

SWEET POTATO CASSEROLE

3 cups mashed, cooked, sweet
   potatoes
1 cup sugar
½ cup milk
⅓ cup butter
2 eggs
1 teaspoon vanilla

Combine above ingredients in a shallow baking dish.
Topping:
1 cup coconut
1 cup pecans, chopped
1 cup brown sugar
⅓ cup flour
⅓ cup butter, melted

Mix above ingredients well and sprinkle over sweet potatoes. Bake at 350 degrees until brown.
Mrs. Robert Woods (Tootsie)

SHREDDED SWEET POTATOES

6 large, sweet potatoes
1 cup orange juice
¼ pound butter, melted
½ cup sugar
½ cup white Karo syrup
2 tablespoons lemon juice

Shred potatoes; cover with lemon juice. Place in a shallow pan. Add butter, sugar, orange juice, and syrup. More liquid may be added, if desired, but remember the potatoes will give some moisture. Bake at 350 degrees until done.
Mrs. Robert Lee (Mildred)

GRAM'S SWEET POTATO PUDDING

4 cups raw, sweet potatoes,
  grated
1 tablespoon cornmeal
1 cup light brown sugar
1 cup sugar

1 small can coconut
1 stick butter
2 cups milk
4 eggs

In a bowl toss together grated sweet potatoes, coconut, cornmeal, sugar, and brown sugar. Heat milk and butter in a saucepan until the butter has melted. Cool. Beat eggs and stir into the milk. Add milk mixture to potato mixture and place in a buttered casserole. Bake at 350 degrees for about 1 hour or until set.
Mrs. E. Clay Lewis, III (Marsha)

CORN STUFFED TOMATOES

6 large tomatoes
4 slices of bacon
1 12-ounce can whole kernel corn,
  drained
2 tablespoons pimiento
¼ cup green onion, sliced

½ cup celery, chopped
½ cup soft bread crumbs
1 cup sharp cheese, grated
1 teaspoon salt
1 teaspoon sugar

Wash tomatoes; cut off tops, hollow out, and save pulp. Leave shell. Place in a shallow baking dish and set aside. Cook bacon crisp; combine with other ingredients including tomato pulp. Put into tomato shells and bake at 350 degrees for 20 minutes.
Mrs. J. C. Harris (Ruby)   *Cove Hotel*

SPINACH AND ARTICHOKE CASSEROLE

2 10-ounce packages frozen,
  chopped spinach
1 package frozen artichokes
½ cup butter, melted

1 8-ounce package cream cheese,
  softened
1 teaspoon lemon juice
Cracker or bread crumbs

Cook spinach and artichokes according to package directions. Drain well. Add butter, cream cheese, and lemon juice to spinach. Place artichokes in bottom of a buttered casserole. Add spinach mixture. Top with cracker crumbs. Dot with butter and bake at 350 degrees for 25 minutes. Serves 6.
Mrs. John Robert Middlemas (Kendall)

SPINACH ELIZABETH

2 packages frozen, chopped spinach
1 tablespoon butter
1½ tablespoons Lipton Onion
   Soup Mix

2 tablespoons cream cheese
1 egg yolk, grated

Cook spinach. Drain excess liquid. Just before serving, add butter, soup mix, and cream cheese. Simmer until hot. Garnish with egg yolk. Serves 6-8.
Mrs. Gordon Hindsman (Helen)

SPINACH MADELEINE

2 packages frozen, chopped
   spinach
4 tablespoon butter
2 tablespoons flour
2 tablespoons onion, chopped
½ cup evaporated milk
½ cup spinach liquor
½ teaspoon black pepper

¾ teaspoon celery salt
¾ teaspoon garlic salt
½ teaspoon salt
1 6-ounce roll of Jalapeños
   cheese
1 teaspoon Worcestershire sauce
Red pepper to taste

Cook spinach according to package directions. Drain and reserve liquor. Melt butter in saucepan; add onion and cook until tender. Add flour and stir until smooth. Stir in vegetable liquor and milk slowly, stirring constantly, and cook until thick. Continue stirring while adding seasonings and cheese which has been cut into small pieces. Stir until melted. Combine with cooked spinach. Place in a buttered 1½-quart casserole. Flavor is improved if kept in refrigerator overnight before cooking. Bake at 350 degrees for 30 minutes or until heated throughout. Serves 4-5.
Mrs. John Fishel (Louise)

RICE O'BRIEN

1 cup white rice
2½ cups rich chicken broth
1 teaspoon seasoned salt
¼ cup butter

½ cup green pepper, slivered
½ cup green onions (including tops),
   chopped
3 tablespoons pimiento, diced

Cook rice in broth with seasoned salt. Melt butter and saute' onions and pepper until tender. Add rice. Add pimiento and serve.
Mrs. John Christo, Jr. (Mary Lee)

BUTTER BAKED RICE

2 teaspoons salt
2 cups water
1 cup long grain rice
⅓ cup butter
1¾ cups chicken broth

¼ cup toasted slivered almonds
Dash of garlic salt
Dash of monosodium glutamate
Parsley, finely snipped

Add salt to water and bring to boil. Pour over rice. Let stand for 30 minutes. Rinse rice with cold water; drain well. Melt butter in skillet. Add rice and cook over medium heat, stirring frequently, until butter is almost absorbed, about 5 minutes. Turn rice into a 1-quart casserole. Sprinkle with garlic salt and monosodium glutamate. Pour chicken broth over rice. Bake covered at 325 degrees for 45 minutes. Add parsley and fluff with fork. Sprinkle with almonds. Bake uncovered 10 minutes longer. Serves 6-7.
Mrs. James A. Poyner (Nell)

DIRTY RICE

1 medium onion, chopped
1 rib of celery, chopped
4 sprigs of parsley, minced
2 tablespoons oil

1 link sausage (approximately
  ½ pound)
4 cups cooked rice

Saute onion, celery, and parsley in oil until tender. Add skinned, mashed sausage and simmer until cooked. Add rice and mix thoroughly. Let stand. Reheat when served. Serves 6-8.
Mrs. Warren Middlemas, Sr. (Emaline)

GREEN RICE

2 cups rice
1 package frozen, chopped
  broccoli
2 eggs, beaten
½ cup vegetable oil
1 onion, chopped

Parsley flakes
1 clove garlic, minced
1 cup milk
1 pound Cheddar cheese, grated
Salt
Pepper

Cook rice as usual. Cook and drain broccoli. Combine rice and broccoli; add remaining ingredients. Bake in a buttered casserole for one hour at 350 degrees. Serves 10-12.
Mrs. Stanley Worsham (Mildred)

STUFFED YELLOW SQUASH

Squash
Green onions
Salt
Pepper
Dash of oregano
Sausage patties

Pepperidge Farm Herb Seasoned
   Crumbs
Butter
Cheese
Paprika
Parsley

Select medium, tender, yellow squash. Wash. Boil whole in salted water about 10 minutes. Halve. Scoop centers into a bowl and save. Dice extra squash to add to squash centers. Sauté a few green onions in butter. Add squash pieces and cook about 15 minutes. Season with salt, pepper, and oregano. Fry several patties of pork sausage. Drain. Crumble into squash pulp. Add only enough crumbs and melted butter to make firm consistency. Stuff squash halves. Top with grated cheese. Bake at 350 degrees for 30 minutes. Sprinkle with paprika and garnish with parsley.
Mrs. H. Mack Lewis (Eleanor)

CAROL'S SQUASH CASSEROLE

1½ pounds squash, sliced
1 onion, sliced
¾ teaspoon sugar
½ cup sharp cheese, grated

Buttered bread cubes
Salt
Coarsely ground pepper

Cook squash and onion until tender. Drain. Place in casserole and sprinkle with sugar, salt, pepper, and cheese.
Cheese Sauce:
3 tablespoons butter, melted
2½ tablespoons flour
1¼ cups milk

½ teaspoon salt
½ teaspoon cayenne pepper
¾ cup sharp cheese, grated

Combine all ingredients for cheese sauce. Pour over squash, top with buttered bread cubes, and bake at 350 degrees for 30 minutes. Serves 8.
Mrs. Herbert Mizell, III (Carol)

STUFFED SQUASH

5 medium yellow squash
1 pound ground round steak
½ cup onion, finely chopped
1 rib of celery, finely chopped
¼ cup bread crumbs

2-3 tablespoons Parmesan cheese
1 8-ounce can tomato sauce
  with mushrooms
Salt
Pepper

Boil squash in salted water until tender. Cool, split lengthwise, scoop out pulp and reserve. Sauté meat, onion, and celery. Add squash pulp, bread crumbs, cheese, salt, and pepper. Stuff shells. Place in a casserole dish. Pour tomato sauce over squash. Sprinkle with cheese. Bake at 350 degrees about 35 minutes.
Mrs. John Christo, Jr. (Mary Lee)

SQUASH-SHRIMP CASSEROLE

5 or 6 medium squash
1 small onion, chopped
3 slices toasted bread
2 eggs
1 cup milk
½ stick butter or oleo

2 cups cooked shrimp
Salt
Pepper
½ cup buttered cracker crumbs
½ cup cheese, grated

Cook squash in salted water until tender. Beat eggs and add toasted bread, milk, and onion. Combine drained squash with bread and egg mixture. Add shrimp. Pour into a buttered 10-inch shallow baking dish. Sprinkle cheese and cracker crumbs on top. Bake covered for 30 minutes at 350 degrees.
Mrs. Ralph Segrest, Jr. (Jane)

ZUCCHINI SQUASH CASSEROLE

8 zucchini squash, sliced
6 tomatoes, sliced
5 yellow onions, sliced

1 stick margarine
1 cup sharp cheese, grated

Melt margarine and sauté zucchini a little at a time. Sauté onions. In a casserole, alternate layers of cooked zucchini, fresh sliced tomatoes, cooked onions, and grated cheese. Sprinkle bread crumbs on top and dot with butter. Bake 25-30 minutes at 350 degrees.
Mrs. Oliver Oxford   *Americus, Georgia*

SQUASH CASSEROLE

2 pounds summer squash, sliced	1 carton sour cream
1 small jar pimiento, chopped	1 package herb seasoned dressing mix
2 carrots, grated	Salt
1 can cream of chicken soup	Pepper
1 onion, chopped	1 stick margarine

Cook squash until tender. Drain. Season with salt, pepper, and 4 tablespoons margarine. Mix soup, sour cream, onion, carrots, and pimiento together. Melt remaining margarine and toss with dressing mix. Fold squash into soup mixture. Place half of dressing mix in bottom of casserole. Put squash mixture in the middle. Use other half of dressing mix on top. Bake at 350 degrees for 30 minutes.
Mrs. D. B. James (Gertie)

ZUCCHINI CASSEROLE

3 medium zucchini squash, cubed	Dash of paprika
½ cup sour cream	1 egg yolk, beaten
1 tablespoon butter	1 tablespoon onion, chopped
2 tablespoons cheese, grated	Cornflakes
Salt	

Simmer zucchini in a small amount of water until tender, about 8-10 minutes. Drain well. Mix sour cream, butter, cheese, and salt. Stir over low heat until butter and cheese have melted. Stir in beaten egg yolk, onion, and paprika. Place zucchini in a well-buttered baking dish and add cream mixture. Top with slightly crushed cornflakes and additional grated cheese. Bake at 375 degrees until top is golden brown. Serves 6.
Mrs. Sam Fleming (Irene)

Breads

FRENCH BREAD

1½ cups warm water
1 tablespoon sugar
4 cups flour

1 package dry yeast
1 tablespoon shortening
1½ teaspoons salt

Dissolve yeast in water; add sugar, salt, shortening, and flour. Mix and let rest 10 minutes. Roll out into a rectangle then roll into a loaf. Let rise 1½ hours. Brush with melted shortening. Bake at 350 degrees for 30 minutes or until done.

Mrs. James C. Feltman (Shirley)

HERBED FRENCH BREAD

1 long loaf French bread
1 stick butter

Fines herbs
1 package onion soup mix

Split loaf of bread in half lengthwise. Soften butter, adding herbs and soup mix. Cream mixture well and spread on bottom half. Replace top. Wrap loaf in aluminum foil and bake in oven at 350 degrees for 20 minutes. Leave foil partially open to keep loaf crisp.

Mrs. Charles Ireland (Caroline)

PATTY'S CHEESE BREAD

1 loaf barbecue bread
1½ cups sharp Cheddar cheese, grated
½ cup mayonnaise
½ teaspoon salt

½ cup scallions (including some green tops), thinly sliced
1 tablespoon parsley, snipped
Dash or two of Tabasco

Combine cheese, mayonnaise, salt, scallions, parsley, and Tabasco. Pull bread apart and place on baking sheet. Spread cheese mixture over bread and broil until cheese begins to melt and edges of bread brown.

Mrs. David J. Turner (Patty)

ONION-CHEESE BREAD

3¾ cups Bisquick
1¼ cups sharp cheese, shredded
1 egg, beaten
2¼ cups milk

½ teaspoon dry mustard
2 tablespoons dehydrated onions
Sesame seeds

Combine all ingredients except sesame seeds. Beat one minute. Pour into a greased 2-quart baking dish. Sprinkle top with sesame seeds. Bake in a pre-heated oven at 325 degrees for 55 to 60 minutes. Cool slightly before slicing.
Mrs. Gary Harrington (Ruthie)

CARAWAY BREAD STICKS

1 package hot dog buns
Butter

Caraway seeds
Paprika (optional)

Cut each hot dog bun in half, then cut lengthwise and crosswise into four equal pieces. Butter each piece of bread generously and sprinkle with caraway seeds and paprika. Toast in oven until golden.
Mrs. Ran Humphreys (Ann Cook)
First President of the Junior Service League of Panama City, Florida

DILLY CASSEROLE BREAD

. . .no kneading—just mix the savory batter, let it rise,
then turn into a casserole. . .

1 package yeast
¼ cup warm water
1 tablespoon instant minced onion
1 tablespoon butter
2 teaspoons dillseed
1 teaspoon salt

1 cup creamed cottage cheese
2 tablespoons sugar
¼ teaspoon soda
2¼-2½ cups flour
1 egg

Soften yeast in water. Combine in mixing bowl cottage cheese, sugar, onion, butter, dillseed, salt, soda, egg, and softened yeast. Add flour to form a stiff dough, beating well after each addition. Cover. Let rise in a warm place (85-90 degrees) until light and doubled in size (50-60 minutes). Stir down dough. Turn into a well-greased 8-inch casserole (1½ to 2 quart). Let rise in a warm place until light (30-40 minutes). Bake at 350 degrees for 40-50 minutes until golden brown. Brush with butter and sprinkle with salt. Remove from casserole. Makes one round loaf.
Mrs. William E. Lark (Ruthie)
Mrs. Harold E. Wager (Margaret)

WHOLE WHEAT BREAD

1 package yeast	1 cup hot water
¼ cup warm water	¾ cup warm water
½ cup brown sugar, firmly packed	4 cups whole wheat flour
3 tablespoons shortening	1½-2 cups white flour
1 tablespoon salt	

Soften yeast in ¼ cup warm water. Combine sugar, salt, and hot water in a large bowl. Add remaining warm water and stir in yeast mixture. Add shortening, whole wheat flour, and white flour to form stiff dough. Knead on lightly floured surface 7 to 10 minutes. Place in a greased bowl; cover. Let rise in a warm place about 2 hours. Punch down; let rise 30-35 minutes. Divide dough in half; shape into two loaves. Place in greased loaf pans. Cover. Let rise 1 hour. Bake 50-60 minutes at 350 degrees.
Mrs. Henry A. Dusseault (Lillian)

POTATO BREAD

2 packages yeast	2 tablespoons butter
5½-6 cups all-purpose flour, sifted	2 teaspoons salt
1½ cups milk	1 can cream of potato soup
2 tablespoons sugar	

Combine yeast and 2½ cups flour. Heat milk, butter, sugar, and salt just until warm. Add to dry ingredients in mixing bowl. Add potato soup. Beat at low speed for ½ minute, scraping sides of bowl. Beat 3 minutes at high speed. Stir in by hand enough of remaining flour to make a moderately stiff dough. Turn out onto lightly floured board. Knead until smooth, 5-8 minutes. Place in a greased bowl, turning once. Cover; let rise until double in size, 50-60 minutes. Punch down. Cover; let sit 10 minutes. Divide dough in half; shape into two loaves. Place in 2 greased 8½x4½x2½-inch loaf pans. Let rise until double in size, about 25 minutes. Bake at 400 degrees for 25-30 minutes.
Mrs. James E. Preston (Sandra)

PERFECT BISCUITS

2 cups self-rising flour	4 tablespoons mayonnaise
1 cup milk	

Combine all ingredients. Drop into greased muffin tins. Bake at 450 degrees until done.
Mrs. B. E. Davis
Mrs. Curtis Bane (Ann)

ANGEL BISCUITS

5 cups all-purpose flour	1 tablespoon baking powder
¾ cup Crisco	2 cups buttermilk
1 teaspoon soda	1 package yeast
1 teaspoon salt	½ cup warm water
3 tablespoons sugar	

Dissolve yeast in warm water. Sift dry ingredients and cut in shortening until mixed thoroughly. Add buttermilk and dissolved yeast. Mix well. Roll on floured board and cut as for biscuits. Bake at 400 degrees for about 12 minutes. Makes 6 dozen. You may cook small amount and store unused dough in refrigerator in a covered bowl. Will keep two weeks or more.
Mrs. Thomas Harding (Jewel)

SOUR CREAM BISCUITS
. . .very light and tasty. . .

2 cups enriched self-rising flour   1 cup sour cream

Blend together, knead slightly, roll, cut, and bake at 400 degrees for 12-15 minutes or until done and golden. Makes about 24 2-inch biscuits.
Mrs. Harold L. Ross (Sarah)

PEGGY HUGHES' BISCUITS

1 cup flour	¼ teaspoon sugar
½ cup Crisco	⅓ cup milk
1 teaspoon baking powder	⅓ cup additional flour
½ teaspoon salt	

Sift dry ingredients with one cup flour. Cut Crisco into flour mixture until fine balls form. Add milk gradually. (Mixture will be soupy.) Then add more flour until you can form a ball. (Add as little flour as possible—between ¼ and ⅓ cup usually.) Roll dough; fold in half and roll again. Cut into biscuits with a small juice glass. Bake at 450 degrees until brown.
Mrs. W. Gerald Harrison (June)

BEER BREAD

4 cups Bisquick
3 tablespoons sugar

1 can *light* beer
(room temperature)

Mix all ingredients together. Mixture will be a little lumpy. Pour into a greased loaf pan and bake at 375 degrees for 45 minutes or until done.
Mrs. Tommy Cooley (Olivia)

CORN GEMS
...good with seafoods...

½ cup cornmeal
3 teaspoons sugar
¼ cup flour
2 teaspoons baking powder
Onion, chopped

¼ teaspoon salt
1 egg
½ cup milk
1 tablespoon butter, melted

Combine above ingredients except butter and beat for two minutes. Melt butter and grease muffin tins. Fill each cup half full with batter. Bake at 350 degrees for approximately 20 minutes. May also be fried in hot grease. Drain well.
Elizabeth Wing Byrd

HUSHPUPPIES

1 cup cornmeal
⅓ cup flour
1 teaspoon salt
2 teaspoons baking powder

1 medium onion, chopped
Cold water—enough to mix well
(about ¾ cup)

Mix together and let stand 30 minutes to 1 hour. Add more water if necessary. Drop by teaspoonfuls into hot, deep grease, dipping spoon in grease each time.
Variation I: To make beer hushpuppies, follow above instructions using beer instead of water (about ¾ bottle of beer). If more liquid is needed, use water. *Be sure beer is room temperature.*
Mrs. H. Patrick Mathis (Bernie)
Variation II: Add 1 small can shoe peg corn, drained, to hushpuppy batter.
Mrs. W. F. Harrison, Jr. (Ruth)

GRANNY RUSS' CORN BREAD

1½ cups cornmeal
1 cup flour
2 teaspoons baking powder
1 teaspoon soda

1 teaspoon salt
2 eggs
5 tablespoons Mazola Oil
2 cups buttermilk

Heat 2 tablespoons of the oil in a skillet. Mix remaining ingredients until almost smooth. Pour into a hot skillet. Bake at 375 degrees for 30 minutes.
Variation: Cracklin' Bread
Add 1 cup cracklins to above mixture and omit 3 tablespoons oil.
Mrs. Benjamin W. Redding (Dee)

SKILLET CUSTARD CORN BREAD
...delicious with broiled ham slices or any country dinner....

1½ cups cornmeal
½ cup flour
1 teaspoon baking powder
1 teaspoon salt
1 teaspoon soda

1 tablespoon brown sugar
2 eggs, beaten
1 cup buttermilk
2 cups milk, divided
3 tablespoons butter

Mix dry ingredients together. Beat eggs until light. Mix with buttermilk and 1 cup of milk. Combine with dry ingredients. Melt the butter in a 10-inch iron skillet, coating bottom and sides. Put batter in skillet and pour the second cup of milk in the center. *Do not stir!* Bake at 350 degrees for 30 minutes. Serve in wedges with butter.
Mrs. Warren Middlemas, Jr. (Martha)

CORN BREAD FOR TWO

4 heaping tablespoons cornmeal
4 heaping tablespoons flour
⅓ teaspoon salt
½ teaspoon sugar

1 teaspoon baking powder
1 egg
Milk

Sift dry ingredients together. Add egg and enough milk to moisten. Do not overmix; batter should be lumpy. Pour into greased muffin tins. Bake at 425 degrees for 30 minutes.
Mrs. Frank Parker (Dorothy Sue)

ROSIE'S FRIED HOT WATER CORN BREAD

1½ cups white cornmeal
1 tablespoon flour
1 teaspoon salt

1 tablespoon melted shortening
1½-2 cups boiling water

Mix dry ingredients together and add boiling water, making a thick batter. Shape into pones with hands or drop by teaspoonfuls into shallow hot grease.
Miss Eloise Wall   El Dorado, Arkansas

MEXICAN CORN BREAD

1 cup cornmeal
1 cup buttermilk
½ teaspoon salt
¾ teaspoon soda
1 8-ounce can cream-style corn
2 eggs
Small onion, chopped

¼ cup oil
2 Jalapeño peppers, chopped
¼ pound mild Cheddar cheese, grated
¼ pound sharp Cheddar cheese, grated

Combine above ingredients, except cheese. Heat oil in heavy skillet. Pour in half of batter. Sprinkle half of cheese over batter. Pour in remaining batter and top with remaining cheese. Bake at 400 degrees for 30 minutes.
Mrs. Joe Cornett (Marianne)
Mrs. Frank Coleman (Camille)

CHARLES' SPOON BREAD

1 cup cornmeal
1 tablespoon baking powder
1½ teaspoons salt
½ cup corn oil

1 cup sour cream
2 eggs
1 cup cream-style corn

Combine all ingredients. Pour into a greased casserole dish. Bake at 400 degrees until golden brown, about 30 minutes. Serve at once.
Mrs. John Bell (Ethel)

CORN SPOON BREAD

2 eggs, slightly beaten
1 8½-ounce package
  corn muffin mix
1 8-ounce can cream-style corn
1 8-ounce can whole kernel corn,
  drained

1 cup dairy sour cream
½ cup butter or margarine, melted
1 cup (4 ounces) Swiss or Cheddar
  cheese, shredded

Combine eggs, muffin mix, both corns, sour cream, and butter. Spread in a
11x7x1¾-inch baking dish. Bake at 350 degrees for 35 minutes. Sprinkle
cheese on top; bake 10-15 minutes more or until knife comes out clean.
Mrs. Rex Rowell, Jr. (Nancy)

CORN FRITTERS

6 ears fresh corn, or 1 8-ounce
  can cream-style corn
3 eggs, separated
1 scant cup flour

1 teaspoon paprika
1 tablespoon sugar
2 teaspoons baking powder
1 teaspoon salt

Beat egg yolks. Add corn, flour, and seasonings. Fold in stiffly beaten egg
whites; add baking powder. Drop by tablespoonfuls into hot grease. Serves 6.
Mrs. Benjamin W. Redding (Dee)

CILLE'S CREOLE BREAD DRESSING

1 stick margarine
1 pound Swift or Owens
  Hot Sausage
1 cup celery, diced

1 box herb seasoned croutons
4 large onions, diced
1¾ cups hot milk
Pecan halves

Peel skin from sausage. Combine with onions and celery. Fry in margarine
until vegetables become limp. Gently add croutons. Do not mash or drain
mixture. Dampen with hot milk (you may add more or less depending on
desired consistency). Top with pecans. Bake at 350 degrees for 30 minutes.
Mrs. Sterrett Procter   *Lafayette, Louisiana*

222

CRANBERRY BREAD

1 cup raw cranberries
1 cup nuts, chopped
1 orange, juice and rind
1 egg, beaten
2 tablespoons Wesson Oil

1 cup sugar
2 cups flour
½ teaspoon salt
1½ teaspoons baking powder
½ teaspoon soda

Combine dry ingredients. Slice cranberries in 3 or 4 slices with sharp knife. Grate rind of orange and squeeze out juice. Put juice in cup with Wesson Oil and add enough boiling water to make ¾ cup liquid. Combine liquid with dry ingredients and beaten egg. Add sliced cranberries and nuts. Bake at 325 degrees for 50-60 minutes. When cool, wrap in foil and refrigerate until ready to slice.
Mrs. A. L. Fulton (Evelyn)

RAISIN-PRUNE BREAD

1½ cups water
½ cup prune juice
2 tablespoons butter
2 teaspoons soda
1 box raisins

2 eggs, slightly beaten
1½ cups sugar
4 cups plain flour, sifted
1 teaspoon salt
1 teaspoon cinnamon

Bring water and prune juice to a boil. Add butter, soda, and raisins. Let stand for 1 hour. Combine eggs and sugar. Stir in dry ingredients which have been sifted together. Stir in raisin mixture. Grease six No. 2 cans well and fill a little over half full. Bake for 1 hour at 325 degrees. Put a pan of hot water on lower rack of oven while baking. When done, invert on waxed paper and cover with wet tea towels. Let stand for 1 hour and remove from cans. When cool, wrap in aluminum foil. Slice in rounds when serving. Keeps well and may be frozen. Makes nice canapés with cream cheese filling.
Mrs. Lester Brock (Martha)

BANANA BREAD

1 cup sugar
¼ cup oil
2 eggs
1 cup mashed bananas

2 cups biscuit mix
1 small can crushed pineapple, drained
½ cup nuts

Beat eggs, sugar, and oil until fluffy; add bananas. Then blend in biscuit mix, pineapple, and nuts. Bake in a loaf pan at 350 degrees for one hour.
Mrs. B. H. DeSear (Ruth)

BANANA NUT BREAD

1 cup butter
1 cup sugar
2 eggs, beaten
3 bananas

2 cups flour, sifted
1 teaspoon soda
1 cup nuts, chopped

Cream butter and sugar together. Add eggs. Cream bananas until light and fluffy. Add to the sugar mixture alternately with the dry ingredients. Add nuts. Pour mixture into a greased loaf pan and bake for 1 hour at 350 degrees.
Mrs. Deck Hull (Nancy)

FRENCH MARKET DOUGHNUTS

1 cup boiling water
¼ cup Crisco
½ cup sugar
1 teaspoon salt
1 cup evaporated milk
1 package yeast

½ cup lukewarm water
2 eggs, well beaten
Flour, approximately 7½
   cups, sifted
Confectioners' sugar

Pour boiling water over shortening, sugar, and salt. Add milk; let cool until lukewarm. Dissolve yeast in lukewarm water and stir into cooled mixture. Add beaten eggs. Stir in 4 cups flour. Beat. Add enough flour to make soft dough. Place in a greased bowl. Brush with melted butter and cover with damp cloth. Chill until ready to use. Roll dough into ⅛-inch thickness. Cut into small squares, and fry in deep hot fat (360 degrees). Turn to brown. *Do not* let dough rise before frying. Drain on absorbent paper. Sprinkle with confectioners' sugar. Makes about 60 doughnuts.
Mrs. Hertha Carter

POPOVERS

1 cup milk
1 cup sifted flour
½ teaspoon salt

1 tablespoon melted butter
2 eggs

Pour milk into small mixing bowl. Sift in flour and salt. Beat until batter is smooth. Add butter and eggs. Beat about 1 minute. Fill 7 well-greased custard cups half full. Bake at 375 degrees for 50 minutes. *Do Not Open* oven door for first 30 minutes or popovers may collapse. Serve immediately.
Mrs. James E. Lewis, Jr. (Lida)

COOL RISE ROLLS

5-6 cups flour	½ cup margarine
2 packages yeast	1½ cups hot, tap water
½ cup sugar	2 eggs
1½ teaspoons salt	

Combine two cups of flour, undissolved yeast, sugar, and salt in large bowl. Stir well to blend. Add softened margarine and hot water. Beat with an electric mixer at medium speed for 2 minutes. Add eggs, which should be room temperature; add one more cup of flour. Beat with mixer at high speed for 1 minute. Stir in remaining flour with a wooden spoon. Use just enough flour to make a soft dough that leaves the sides of bowl. Turn dough onto a floured board. Round dough into a ball and knead for 5 minutes. Cover with plastic wrap and a towel. Let the dough sit for 20 minutes. Punch dough down and shape into rolls. Place on greased baking sheets. Brush top of rolls with oil. Cover pans loosely with plastic wrap. Refrigerate 2 to 24 hours. When ready to bake, remove from refrigerator, uncover and let stand for 10 minutes. Bake at 375 degrees for 20 to 25 minutes on lower oven rack. Rolls may be frozen.

Mrs. Robert Gary Lee (Jean)

BUTTERHORNS

1 cup milk	½ cup sugar
¼ pound butter	½ teaspoon salt
1 package yeast	4 cups sifted flour
3 eggs	

Scald milk. Add butter and cool to lukewarm. Crumble yeast in lukewarm milk and stir until dissolved. In a separate bowl, beat eggs. Add sugar and salt. Combine above mixtures and add flour gradually. Knead and add a little flour until you can handle it. Place in a bowl and let rise 3 hours. Pat down and let rise again (about 1 or 2 hours) or until doubled in size. Put in refrigerator. When ready to use, divide into thirds and roll as for pie crust (about ⅛-inch thick). Cut into sixteen pie-shaped wedges. Start at wide edge of each piece and roll. Bake at 350 degrees for 20 minutes. Makes 48 rolls.

Mrs. Maurice F. Smith (Olive)

CRESCENT NUT ROLLS

Pastry:

4½ cups flour
1 pound margarine
¼ teaspoon salt
4 egg yolks, beaten

2 packages yeast
1 cup sour cream
3 tablespoons lemon juice

Blend flour, margarine, and salt together with **pastry** blender. Add egg yolks and lemon juice. Dissolve yeast in ¼ cup warm water. Add dissolved yeast to sour cream and combine with mixture. Chill dough overnight. Break off small piece of dough, keeping remainder in refrigerator. Sprinkle pastry board lightly with sugar. Place rolling pin stocking on rolling pin and roll dough thin. Fold over, roll again. Repeat, working quickly. Cut dough into 2-inch squares. Place a small spoonful of filling in the center of each square. Roll from corner to corner. Form in crescent shapes. Bake at 375 degrees for 15 minutes or until brown.

Filling:

½ cup butter, melted
¾ cup sugar
Dash of salt

1 teaspoon vanilla
1½ cups nuts, chopped

Blend ingredients together to make a paste and fill crescents.
Mrs. Bill S. Janos (Cathie)

BUTTERY BREAD STICKS

⅓ cup butter
2¼ cups flour, sifted
1 tablespoon sugar
1 cup milk

1½ teaspoons salt
3½ teaspoons baking powder
Sesame seeds

Melt butter in an oblong pan in 450 degree oven. Sift dry ingredients into bowl. Add milk, stirring slowly until dough clings together. Knead about 10 times on well-floured board. Roll in a rectangle to ½-inch thickness. Cut lengthwise, then crosswise, into 16 strips. Dip each piece in melted butter and place in 2 rows in pan. Sprinkle sesame seeds over pieces. Bake in hot oven 15 to 20 minutes.
Mrs. W. A. Heim (Ann)

CARAWAY ROLLS

2 packages yeast
½ cup warm water
2 tablespoons caraway seeds
2 cups creamed cottage cheese
¼ cup sugar

2 teaspoons salt
½ teaspoon soda
2 eggs, slightly beaten
4⅔ cups flour

Dissolve yeast in warm water. Add caraway seeds. Heat cottage cheese until just lukewarm. Mix cottage cheese, sugar, salt, soda, and eggs into yeast mixture. Slowly add flour, mixing until dough cleans bowl. Let rise about 1 hour. Stir down dough. Divide among 24 well-greased muffin cups. Cover and let rise again until doubled, about 45 minutes. Bake at 350 degrees about 20 minutes. Brush with butter. These rolls freeze nicely. Makes 2 dozen.
Mrs. James E. Lewis, Jr. (Lida)

REFRIGERATOR ROLLS

2 packages yeast
1½ cups warm water
1½ cups milk
1 tablespoon salt

½ cup sugar
7 cups sifted flour
⅓ cup shortening
2 eggs

Melt shortening and allow to cool. Dissolve yeast in warm water. Let stand. Scald milk. Add salt and sugar, stirring until dissolved. Cool. Stir yeast solution and add to milk mixture. Add half of the flour and mix well. Stir in shortening and unbeaten eggs. Beat well after each addition. Add remaining flour and mix well. Brush top of dough lightly with shortening. Cover with damp towel and waxed paper. Chill in refrigerator. About two hours before baking, remove desired amount. Shape into rolls. Let rise. Bake at 375 degrees until golden brown. Makes 30 rolls.
Mrs. Ted McLane (Mary Ann)

PERFECT WAFFLES

1¼ cups sifted flour
½ teaspoon salt
2 teaspoons baking powder
1 tablespoon sugar

1 egg, beaten
1½ cups milk
½ cup soft shortening

Combine ingredients and blend. Beat until smooth. Batter will be thin. Makes about 4 waffles.
Mrs. Curtis Bane (Ann)

SOUR CREAM PANCAKES

1 cup pre-sifted flour
1 tablespoon baking powder
¼ teaspoon salt
1 tablespoon sugar

1 egg
1 cup milk
¼ cup sour cream
2 tablespoons butter, melted

Sift together flour, baking powder, salt, and sugar. Add remaining ingredients and beat until smooth. Fry on hot griddle until nicely browned.
Mrs. James E. Lewis, Jr. (Lida)

DUTCH BABIES

3 eggs
½ cup pre-sifted flour
½ teaspoon salt

½ cup milk
3 tablespoons butter
Confectioners' sugar and/or syrup

Beat eggs at low speed with mixer. Gradually add flour and salt. Add milk and blend. Spread bottom and sides of a cold No. 8 iron skillet with butter. Pour in the batter and put in very hot oven (450 degrees). Bake until crust is brown. The sides and sometimes the center will puff up unevenly. Cut the pancake into two halves. Pour a little melted butter over them to taste. Sprinkle with confectioners' sugar and/or syrup. Serve with bacon and coffee.
Mrs. Lauren Merriam, Jr. (Margaret)

PUMPKIN BREAD

1½ cups sugar
½ cup oil
2 eggs, beaten
1 cup pumpkin
½ teaspoon salt

1 teaspoon cinnamon
1⅔ cups flour
1 teaspoon soda
1 teaspoon baking powder
⅓ cup water

Combine all ingredients and place in a greased loaf pan. Bake at 350 degrees for 1 hour and 30 minutes. Place foil over top for the last 30 minutes.
Mrs. Hertha Carter

PRESBYTERIAN MUFFINS

⅔ cup butter
1½ cups brown sugar
2 eggs
1 teaspoon vanilla
1¾ cups flour

¼ teaspoon salt
1 teaspoon soda
¾ cup buttermilk
1 cup nuts, chopped

Cream butter and sugar. Add eggs and beat well; add vanilla. Sift flour, soda, and salt together. Add alternately with buttermilk. Fold in nuts. Bake at 350 degrees in well-greased, small muffin cups for 18-20 minutes.
Mrs. Lauren Merriam, Jr. (Margaret)
Mrs. Hugh Nelson (Lila)

BRAN MUFFINS

2 cups All Bran
2 cups hot water
3 cups sugar
1 cup oleo
4 eggs, beaten
1 quart buttermilk

5 cups flour
3 tablespoons soda
1 tablespoon salt
4 cups bran flakes
1 cup raisins

Pour hot water over All Bran and let stand. Cream oleo and sugar. Add beaten eggs, buttermilk, and bran mixture. Sift flour, soda, and salt; add to the above mixture. Fold in bran flakes and raisins. Refrigerate for 24 hours before cooking. Fill greased muffin tins ¾ full. Bake at 400 degrees for 15 minutes. Makes 48. Batter will keep in refrigerator for six weeks to be used as desired.
Mrs. C. Edward Miller (Mary Ola)

FRESH STRAWBERRY MUFFINS

1 cup fresh strawberries
1¼ cups flour
4 teaspoons baking powder
½ cup sugar
Pinch of salt

2 eggs
¾ cup milk
5 tablespoons butter, melted
Confectioners' sugar

Sift dry ingredients together. Add eggs, milk, and butter. Fold in flour-sprinkled strawberries. Bake at 375 degrees for 20-25 minutes. Sprinkle with confectioners' sugar. Butter and serve piping hot.
Mrs. John Robert Middlemas (Kendall)
Mrs. Florence Hood   Moultrie, Georgia

BLUEBERRY MUFFINS

⅓ cup shortening
¾ cup sugar
1 egg
2 cups flour

2 teaspoons baking powder
¼ teaspoon salt
¾ cup milk
1 cup blueberries

Cream shortening and sugar. Add well-beaten egg. Combine flour, baking powder, and salt; add alternately with milk. Gently fold in blueberries. Bake at 350 degrees for 25 minutes in well-greased muffin tins. Makes 12 large muffins.

Mrs. J. C. Watson (Edna)

CHERRY-GO-ROUND

1 cup milk
½ cup sugar
1 teaspoon salt
1 stick oleo

1 package yeast
1 egg
¼ cup warm water
4 cups flour, unsifted

Scald milk and add sugar, salt, and oleo. Cool mixture to lukewarm. Dissolve yeast in warm water and add to milk mixture. Add egg and two cups of flour. Beat mixture until smooth and stir in remaining flour. Batter will be stiff. Cover tightly and refrigerate for two hours or up to two days.

Filling:

1 pound can red, tart,
    pitted cherries
½ cup brown sugar

½ cup sugar
½ cup flour
½ cup nuts, chopped

Divide dough and roll into two 14x7-inch pieces. Spread with well-drained cherries and a mixture of brown sugar, white sugar, flour, and nuts. Roll dough and mixture lengthwise. Seal ends and edges by folding over. Form two half circles, sealed edges down on greased pan. Cut two-thirds through rolled dough at one-inch intervals, twisting each one-inch section sideways. Cover and let rise in a warm place until doubled in size, about one to two hours. Bake at 375 degrees for 25 minutes. Pineapple may be substituted for cherries.

Icing:

3 tablespoons cherry juice
Vanilla

1-2 cups confectioners' sugar

Combine above ingredients adding a few drops of vanilla. Mixture should have consistency of molasses. Frost Cherry-Go-Round while still warm.

Mrs. Victor P. Frohlich (Dorothy)

LYNCHBURG MUFFINS

3 eggs
1⅓ cups sugar
1½ cups flour
½ teaspoon salt

1½ teaspoons baking powder
½ cup water
1 teaspoon vanilla

Beat eggs with sugar. Sift flour, salt, and baking powder together. Add to egg mixture with water and vanilla. Fill greased muffin pans ¾ full. Bake at 350 degrees for about 20 minutes. Drop muffins in glaze; then drain on wire rack.
Glaze:
Juice and grated rind of 1 lemon
Juice and grated rind of 1 orange

Pinch of salt
2 cups sifted confectioners' sugar

Combine all ingredients.
Mrs. J. C. Harris (Ruby)   *Cove Hotel*

STREUSEL FILLED COFFEE CAKE

Streusel Filling and Topping:
½ cup brown sugar
2 teaspoons cinnamon

2 tablespoons Gold Medal flour
2 tablespoons melted butter

Mix above ingredients together with a fork before mixing coffee cake.
Coffee Cake:
1½ cups sifted Gold Medal flour
3 teaspoons baking powder
¼ teaspoon salt
¾ cup sugar

¼ cup shortening
1 egg
½ cup milk

Sift dry ingredients together and cut in shortening. Blend in well-beaten egg which has been mixed with milk. Spread half of batter in a buttered and floured 6x10-inch pan. Sprinkle with half the streusel mixture. Add other half of cake mixture. Sprinkle remaining streusel over top. Bake at 375 degrees for 25-30 minutes.
Mrs. James E. Carter (Jeri)

SOUR CREAM COFFEE CAKE

2 cups flour, sifted
1 teaspoon baking powder
1 teaspoon baking soda
½ teaspoon salt
1 cup sugar

1 stick margarine, softened
2 eggs
1 teaspoon vanilla
1 cup sour cream

Sift flour, baking powder, soda, and salt together. Cream margarine and sugar together. Add eggs one at a time. Gradually add flour mixture alternately with sour cream. Add vanilla and beat until batter is smooth.
Topping:
1 cup pecans, finely chopped
¼ cup butter, melted
¼ cup sugar

⅓ cup brown sugar
1 teaspoon cinnamon

Combine nuts, sugars, and cinnamon. Toss mixture with melted butter. Pour half of cake batter into a greased 9-inch spring form pan. Add half of topping. Repeat with remaining batter and topping. Bake at 350 degrees for 45-55 minutes.
Mrs. Steve Wilson (Sandra)

HUNGARIAN COFFEE CAKE

1 stick butter
1 cup sugar
2 eggs
2 cups flour
1 8-ounce carton sour cream
1 teaspoon baking soda

1½ teaspoons baking powder
½ teaspoon salt
1 teaspoon vanilla
½ cup sugar
2 teaspoons cinnamon
¾ cup nuts

Cream butter and 1 cup sugar; add eggs. Sift together flour, baking soda, baking powder, and salt. Add to creamed mixture alternating with sour cream. Add vanilla. Pour into a greased and floured tube pan. Cut mixture of ½ cup sugar, nuts, and cinnamon into cake batter. Bake at 350 degrees for 1 hour. Cool at least 1 hour before removing from pan. Serve warm. Serves 15-20.
Mrs. John Colmery (Maxine)

APPLE STRUDEL

Dough:

3 3-ounce packages cream cheese
½ cup unsalted butter

1½ cups plain flour, sifted

Filling:

4 medium yellow apples
Sugar and cinnamon to taste
   (approximately ¼ cup)

1 cup raisins
4 ounces unsalted butter, melted
Confectioners' sugar

Mix softened cream cheese with butter and flour. Refrigerate for approximately one hour. Peel apples and slice very thin. Cover with sugar-cinnamon mixture and set aside. This makes two small strudels or one large one. Roll out dough on floured surface to ⅛-inch thickness. Make a rectangle with the long side facing you. Sprinkle with more cinnamon sugar, raisins, and apples. Fold short sides of the dough ends approximately 2 inches over the apples. Roll the long side of dough toward you. Brush roll with melted butter. As this tears easily, carefully roll dough off edge of counter onto a floured baking sheet seam side down. Bake at 350 degrees for approximately 25 minutes. Brush roll twice with butter during baking process and after removing from oven. Cool and dust generously with confectioners' sugar.

Mrs. William E. Holland, III (Hannelore)

Cakes & Icings

MRS. CAMPBELL'S BAVARIAN CAKE

4 eggs, separated
1 cup sugar
1 tablespoon flour
Dash of salt
2 cups milk, scalded
1 envelope unflavored gelatin

½ cup cold water
1 teaspoon almond extract
1 angel food cake
2 cups whipping cream, divided
1 7-ounce package frozen coconut, thawed

In a double boiler, beat egg yolks well. Add flour, sugar, and salt. Slowly add milk and cook over medium heat, stirring constantly until custard coats spoon. Dissolve gelatin in cold water and add to hot custard. Cool. Add flavoring. Beat egg whites until stiff. Fold into custard. Whip 1 cup of the cream and fold into custard. Slice cake thinly and tear into pieces. Line the bottom of a 9x14-inch pan with cake. Pour in half of the custard. Sprinkle with half of the coconut. Make another layer of cake, then custard. Before serving, top with the other cup of whipped cream and sprinkle with remaining coconut. Serves 15.
Mrs. W. Gerald Harrison (June)

MRS. GREEN'S SHERRY CAKE

6 eggs, separated
¾ cup sugar
¾ cup sherry
1½ envelopes gelatin
½ cup milk

1½ cups whipping cream
¾ cup Confectioners' sugar
1 round angel food cake
Maraschino cherries

Beat egg yolks well. Add sugar and sherry. Mix well. Cook in double boiler until thick. Dissolve gelatin in milk. Add to hot mixture. Beat egg whites until stiff. Set aside. Beat whipping cream until stiff. Fold whipping cream and egg whites together. Fold in confectioners' sugar. *Lightly* fold this into the cooled, cooked mixture. Tear or cut angel food cake into small pieces. Use a 9x13x2-inch pan and alternate a layer of cake with custard mixture until pan is filled, beginning with cake and ending with custard on top. Refrigerate overnight until set. When ready to serve, cut in squares, top with whipped cream and a cherry.
Mrs. A. Horten Lisenby (Elizabeth)

CHOCOLATE ANGEL DELIGHT

1 angel food cake
1 package chocolate fudge frosting
  mix

2 cups whipping cream
1 medium banana, mashed
½ cup nuts, chopped

Combine frosting mix and whipping cream. Cover and chill 1 hour. Slice one inch off top of cake. Make a small cavity completely around the inside of the remaining piece by removing a small amount of the cake. Beat frosting mixture until soft peaks form. Fold mashed banana into 1 cup of the frosting mixture. Fill cavity in cake. Replace top. Frost entire cake with remaining frosting mixture. Sprinkle nuts on top. Keep refrigerated.
Mrs. Robert Gary Lee (Jean)

CHEW CAKE

This cake won "Best in Show" at the 1973 Bay County Fair.

4 eggs
1 box brown sugar
2 cups self-rising flour

2 cups pecans, chopped
1 teaspoon vanilla
Confectioners' sugar

Beat eggs well. Add brown sugar and mix well. Cook together only until sugar melts. Cool. Add flour and pecans that have been dredged in some of the flour. Add vanilla. Pour into a greased 9x13-inch pan. Bake at 300 degrees for 35-40 minutes. Sprinkle with confectioners' sugar when cool, if desired.
Deborah Sue Talley

RUM CAKE

1 package Duncan Hines Golden
  Cake Mix
1 small package Jello Instant
  Vanilla Pudding

½ cup light rum
½ cup milk
½ cup Crisco Oil or Shortening
4 eggs

Mix all ingredients and pour into a greased and floured tube pan. Bake at 325 degrees for 1 hour. Cool 10 minutes.
Topping:
1 cup sugar
1 stick butter

½ cup rum
½ cup water

Combine ingredients and boil 3 minutes. Pour slowly over cake until all is absorbed.
Mrs. James W. Marshall, Jr. (Margie)

FRESH APPLE CAKE I

1¼ cups oil
2 cups sugar
3 eggs, well beaten
3 cups fresh apples
1 cup pecans, chopped

3 cups plain flour
1 teaspoon salt
1 teaspoon baking soda
2 teaspoons vanilla

Combine the following ingredients in a large bowl in the following order: oil, sugar, and eggs. Peel, core, and chop fresh apples and add to the first mixture. Add nuts. In a separate bowl, sift flour, salt, and baking soda together three or four times. Add to apple mixture. Add vanilla and mix well. Pour batter into a greased long sheet pan or two 9-inch cake pans. Put cake in *cold* oven and bake at 325 degrees for about 45 minutes.

Icing:

1 stick oleo
1 cup light brown sugar

¼ cup evaporated milk
1 teaspoon vanilla

Heat oleo and sugar together over low heat. Add milk and let come to a full boil. Remove from heat and cool. Add vanilla. Frost cake.

Mrs. James W. Marshall, Jr. (Margie)
Mrs. Foster H. Kruse (Helen)

FRESH APPLE CAKE II

2 cups cake flour
1¾ cups sugar
2 teaspoons baking powder
2 teaspoons baking soda
4 eggs

1 cup corn oil
2 teaspoons cinnamon
Pinch of salt
2 cups grated apple
2 cups nuts, chopped

Put dry ingredients in mixer and blend. Add eggs, oil, apples, and nuts. Pour into a sheet cake pan. Bake at 350 degrees for 30-35 minutes. Frost.

Icing:

1 box confectioners' sugar,
   sifted

8 ounces cream cheese
1 stick oleo

Cream oleo and cream cheese together. Add confectioners' sugar mixing well.

Mrs. Curtis Bane (Ann)

APPLE POUND CAKE

2 cups sugar
1½ cups vegetable oil
3 large eggs
3 cups plain flour
1 teaspoon baking soda

1 teaspoon salt
1½ teaspoons vanilla extract
¾ cup flaked coconut
3 cups firm apples, diced
1 cup pecans or walnuts, chopped

Mix together sugar and oil. Add eggs and beat well. Combine flour, baking soda, and salt. Add to oil mixture. Stir in vanilla, apples, coconut, nuts, and mix well. Pour batter into a greased 9-inch tube pan. Bake at 325 degrees for 1 hour and 20 minutes or until cake is done.
Mrs. J. R. Arnold (Helen)

APPLESAUCE CAKE

1 stick butter
1 cup sugar
1 teaspoon cinnamon
⅛ teaspoon cloves
½ teaspoon allspice
½ teaspoon nutmeg
½ teaspoon salt

2 cups flour
1 cup raisins
1 cup pecans, chopped
½ cup pineapple, crushed
1 cup applesauce
1 teaspoon baking soda

Sift flour, salt, and spices together. Dredge nuts and raisins in 3-4 tablespoons of this mixture; set aside. Cream butter and sugar. Add baking soda to the applesauce. Add flour and applesauce mixture alternately to butter. Add pineapple and nuts. Blend well. Pour into a greased and waxed paper-lined tube pan. Bake at 350 degrees for 1 hour or until done.
Mrs. Theodore G. Elchos (Jimmie)

VANILLA WAFER CAKE

1 14-ounce box vanilla wafers, crushed
2 sticks oleo
2 cups sugar

6 eggs
½ cup milk
1 7-ounce can Angel Flake coconut
1 cup pecans, chopped

Cream oleo and sugar. Add eggs one at a time. Add milk alternately with wafer crumbs. Add nuts and coconut. Blend well. Pour into a greased and floured tube pan. Bake at 275 degrees to 300 degrees for 1½ to 2 hours.
Mrs. Joe L. Johnson (Anne)
Mrs. Deck Hull (Nancy)

SOUR CREAM BANANA PECAN CAKE

½ stick butter or oleo
1 ⅓ cups sugar
2 eggs
1 teaspoon vanilla
2 cups sifted plain flour
1 teaspoon baking powder
1 teaspoon baking soda
¾ teaspoon salt
1 cup sour cream
1 cup ripe bananas, mashed
  (2 medium)
½ cup pecans, chopped

Cream butter and sugar. Add eggs, one at a time. Add vanilla. Sift dry ingredients together and add to creamed mixture alternately with sour cream. Add bananas and pecans and mix well. Pour into a greased and floured 13x9x2-inch baking pan. Bake at 350 degrees for 40 minutes. Frost with Quick Caramel Icing.

Variation:

This recipe also makes a delicious banana bread if baked in a loaf pan.

Quick Caramel Icing:

1½ sticks butter or oleo
¾ cup brown sugar, firmly packed
6 tablespoons evaporated milk
3½ cups confectioners' sugar
1½ teaspoons vanilla

Heat butter and brown sugar over low heat, stirring constantly until sugar melts. Blend in milk. Cool. Gradually beat in confectioners' sugar until spreading consistency is reached. Add vanilla.

Mrs. Owen Reese, Jr. (Anne)

CHOCOLATE ICE-BOX CAKE

4 4-ounce packages German's
  sweet chocolate
2 tablespoons confectioners' sugar
3 tablespoons hot water
6 eggs
1 teaspoon vanilla
Vanilla wafers

Melt chocolate, water, and confectioners' sugar in double boiler, stirring constantly. When melted, remove from heat and cool. Add beaten egg yolks and vanilla. Fold in beaten egg whites. Line a loaf pan with waxed paper. Alternate a layer of vanilla wafers with a layer of chocolate mixture, ending with a layer of wafers. The cake makes about three layers. Cover tightly and let stand in refrigerator overnight. Slice and top with whipped cream, if desired. May substitute lady fingers in place of vanilla wafers. Serves 12.

Mrs. D. E. McCloy   *Monticello, Arkansas*

BANANA SPICE LAYER CAKE

2½ cups sifted cake flour
2½ teaspoons baking powder
½ teaspoon baking soda
¾ teaspoon salt
⅛ teaspoon cloves
1¼ teaspoons cinnamon
½ teaspoon nutmeg
½ cup shortening
1¼ cups sugar
2 eggs
1 teaspoon vanilla
1½ cups ripe bananas (4-5), mashed

Sift together flour, baking powder, baking soda, salt, and spices. Cream shortening and sugar. Add eggs one at a time. Add vanilla. Add flour mixture alternately with bananas. Pour into two layer pans that have been greased and floured. Bake at 325-350 degrees for about 25 minutes or until done. Frost with Banana Butter Icing.

Banana Butter Icing:
½ cup ripe banana (1 large), mashed
½ teaspoon lemon juice
¼ cup butter
3½ cups sifted Confectioners' sugar

Beat butter until creamy. Combine banana and lemon juice and add to butter alternately with sugar.
Mrs. Theodore G. Elchos (Jimmie)

BUTTERMILK CAKE

2 sticks butter
2 cups sugar
4 eggs, separated
1 cup buttermilk
1 teaspoon baking soda
1 teaspoon cream of tartar
3 cups sifted cake flour
½ teaspoon vanilla

Cream butter and sugar. Add egg yolks, one at a time. Add sifted dry ingredients alternately with buttermilk. Beat egg whites until stiff but not dry. Fold into batter and add vanilla. Pour into a greased and floured 9x13x3-inch pan. Bake at 350 degrees for 40-50 minutes. Spread frosting on cake and broil. Watch until it crusts over. Do not burn.

Broiled Icing:
1 tablespoon butter (melt before
   measuring)
1 cup brown sugar
6 tablespoons evaporated milk

Stir sugar into melted butter until all lumps are dissolved and add milk. Broil 3 minutes.
Mrs. Foster H. Kruse (Helen)

YELLOW BUTTERMILK CAKE

2 sticks butter
2 cups sugar
3 eggs
3 cups flour

½ teaspoon salt
½ teaspoon baking soda
1 cup buttermilk
1 teaspoon vanilla

Cream butter and sugar. Add eggs one at a time. Sift flour, salt, and baking soda and add alternately with buttermilk. Add vanilla. Pour into a greased and floured 13x9-inch pan or layers if desired. Bake at 350 degrees for 25-30 minutes. Frost with Minute Fudge Icing.

Minute Fudge Icing:

2 cups sugar
¼ cup light corn syrup
½ cup milk
½ cup shortening

2 squares unsweetened chocolate
(cut up)
¼ teaspoon salt
1 teaspoon vanilla

Combine all ingredients in a saucepan except vanilla. Stir over low heat until chocolate and shortening melt. Bring to a full rolling boil, stirring constantly. Boil *1* minute. Remove from heat and beat until lukewarm. Add vanilla. Continue beating until smooth.

Note: For layer cake, increase recipe by one-half.

Mrs. J. R. Moody, Sr. (Corine)

BUTTERMILK CHOCOLATE CAKE

4 ounces semi-sweet chocolate
1 stick oleo
1 cup water
2 cups sugar
½ cup buttermilk

2 eggs
2 cups unsifted plain flour
1½ teaspoons baking soda
½ teaspoon salt
1½ teaspoons vanilla

Melt chocolate, oleo, and water together in a saucepan. Set aside. In a mixing bowl, combine and beat sugar, eggs, and buttermilk. Add flour, salt, soda, and vanilla alternately with liquid chocolate mixture. Mix well. Pour into three greased and floured cake pans. Bake at 350 degrees for 30 minutes or until done. Cake should almost cool before removing from pans. Frost as desired.

Mrs. R. William Lawrence (Linda)

BUTTERNUT CAKE

2 sticks butter or oleo
2 cups sugar
4 eggs
3 cups flour

2 teaspoons baking powder
1 cup sweet milk
1 tablespoon butternut flavoring

Cream butter and sugar. Add eggs one at a time. Sift flour and baking powder together and add alternately with milk. Add flavoring. Pour into four greased and floured layer pans. Bake at 350 degrees for 15 minutes or until done. Frost when cool.

Butternut Icing:
1 box confectioners' sugar
1 stick butter or oleo
8 ounces cream cheese

1 cup nuts, chopped
1 tablespoon butternut flavoring
Pinch of salt

Cream butter and cream cheese. Gradually add sugar. Add flavoring, salt, and nuts. Frost.
Mrs. Donald G. Craft (Loyce)

CARROT CAKE WITH PINEAPPLE

3 cups plain flour
½ teaspoon salt
2 teaspoons baking soda
3 teaspoons cinnamon
3 eggs
2 cups sugar

1½ cups cooking oil
1 8¼-ounce can crushed pineapple
2 cups carrots, grated
½ cup nuts, chopped
2 teaspoons vanilla

Sift dry ingredients together. Beat eggs slightly; add sugar and beat until fluffy. Add oil gradually. Add dry ingredients. Add pineapple and carrots. Add nuts and vanilla, and blend well. Pour into two 9-inch greased and floured cake pans. Bake at 350 degrees for 30 minutes or until done.

Cream Cheese Icing:
1 8-ounce package cream cheese
1 16-ounce box confectioners' sugar, sifted
1 teaspoon vanilla

½ stick butter, melted
½ teaspoon lemon extract
1 cup nuts, chopped (optional)

Cream cheese until fluffy. Gradually add sugar, alternating with *cool* melted butter. Add extracts. Frost.
Mary Lee Davenport (Mimi)

CARROT CAKE

2 cups plain flour
2 teaspoons baking soda
½ teaspoon salt
2 teaspoons cinnamon

4 eggs
2 cups sugar
1½ cups cooking oil
2 cups carrots, grated

Sift dry ingredients together. Beat eggs slightly. Add sugar and beat until fluffy. Add oil gradually. Add dry ingredients. Add carrots and blend well. If desired, some chopped nuts may be added to the batter. Pour into two 9-inch greased and floured cake pans. Bake at 350 degrees for 30-40 minutes or until done. Frost with Cream Cheese Icing.
Mrs. Jimmy T. Patronis (Helen)
Mrs. H. Lamar Sikes (Patty)

CARAMEL CAKE

1 cup butter
2 cups sugar
4 eggs
1 cup milk

3 cups flour
2 teaspoons baking powder
1 teaspoon vanilla

Cream butter and sugar. Add eggs one at a time. Sift together flour and baking powder. Add to creamed mixture alternately with the milk, beginning and ending with the dry ingredients. Add vanilla. Pour into three greased and floured cake pans. Bake for approximately 20 minutes at 375 degrees.
Icing:
3½ cups sugar, divided
1 5⅓-ounce can evaporated milk
1 cup milk

1 stick butter
1 teaspoon vanilla
Pinch of baking soda

Place ½ cup sugar in a small iron skillet. Melt over low heat until brown. While sugar is browning, combine evaporated milk, milk, butter, and remaining sugar in a large saucepan. Cook over low heat, stirring until sugar melts. Just before it comes to a boil, add soda and melted sugar from skillet. Cook until it forms a firm ball or 236 degrees on a candy thermometer. Add vanilla. Cool to 110 degrees. Beat until it loses its gloss. Spread on cake. Do not make on a rainy day.
Mrs. W. H. Byers (Jeanette)

CHEESE CAKE I

...pretty and delicious with fresh strawberries served on top...

Crust:

20-22 (2½x2½-inch size)
  graham crackers, crushed

½ cup melted shortening
2 tablespoons sugar

Crush graham crackers. Add sugar and melted shortening. Mix well and press into a 3-quart container (does not have to be a spring-form pan).

Filling:

5 eggs, separated
1 pound cream cheese
1 pint sour cream

1 cup sugar
1 teaspoon vanilla
1 teaspoon lemon juice

Follow instructions exactly. Have ingredients at room temperature. Preheat oven to 300-325 degrees. Beat egg whites stiff. Set aside. Cream cheese; add sour cream. Add sugar gradually; mix well. Add beaten egg yolks. Add flavorings. Fold in egg whites. Pour into a pan lined with cracker crumb crust. Bake 1 hour. Turn off oven heat and let stand in closed oven for 1 hour. (Do not peek.) Open door and let stand for 30 minutes. Remove from oven. Turn out after 5-10 minutes if spring-form pan is not used.

This is an original Turkish recipe that I have baked for 20 years.
Mrs. Lauren E. Merriam, Jr. (Margaret)

CHEESE CAKE II

¼ cup graham cracker crumbs
½ teaspoon cinnamon
1¼ cups sugar
3 tablespoons flour
18 ounces cream cheese

6 eggs, separated
1 cup sour cream
1½ teaspoons vanilla
⅛ teaspoon salt
½ teaspoon cream of tartar

Have everything at room temperature. Butter a 9-inch spring-form pan and sprinkle with graham cracker crumbs mixed with cinnamon. Add salt to egg whites and beat until foamy. Add cream of tartar and beat until mixture stands in soft, stiff peaks. Gradually beat in ½ cup sugar. Set aside. Cream cheese until fluffy and add beaten egg yolks. Add sour cream and vanilla. Combine ¾ cup sugar with flour and gradually add to cheese mixture. Beat until very smooth. *Fold* beaten egg whites into cheese mixture. Pour into the spring-form pan. Place on rack in a large pan. Pour in hot water, having it come to the top of the rack, but not touching the cheese cake pan. Bake at 325 degrees for 1 hour and 45 minutes. Let cool and refrigerate.

Mrs. James E. Lewis, Jr. (Lida)

CHOCOLATE MAYONNAISE CAKE

2 cups flour
1 cup sugar
4 tablespoons cocoa
1 teaspoon baking powder

1 teaspoon baking soda
1 cup mayonnaise
1 cup cold water
1 teaspoon vanilla

Sift together flour, sugar, cocoa, baking powder, and baking soda. Add mayonnaise, cold water, and vanilla. Beat two minutes. Pour into a greased and floured 11x7-inch pan or two 9-inch layer pans. Bake at 350 degrees for 30 minutes or until done. Frost with chocolate icing, if desired.
Mrs. Gordon S. Hill (Mary)

PRIZEWINNING CHOCOLATE SHEET CAKE

2 cups sifted cake flour
2 cups sugar
1 stick oleo
½ cup oil
1 cup water
3 tablespoons cocoa

½ cup buttermilk
1 teaspoon baking soda
2 eggs, beaten
⅛ teaspoon salt
1 teaspoon vanilla

Mix the flour and sugar together. Combine oleo, oil, water, and cocoa in saucepan and bring to a boil. Pour over the flour and sugar mixture. Mix well. Dissolve baking soda in buttermilk. To the chocolate mixture add beaten eggs, salt, vanilla, and buttermilk-baking soda mixture, beating after each addition. Pour into a large greased and floured sheet cake pan. Bake at 350 degrees for 20 minutes.
Icing:
1 box confectioners' sugar, sifted
1 stick oleo
3 tablespoons cocoa

6 tablespoons milk
1 teaspoon vanilla
1 cup pecans, chopped

Combine oleo, cocoa, and milk in a saucepan and bring to a boil. Add confectioners' sugar and vanilla. Mix well. Add chopped pecans. Spread on top of cake while cake is still warm.
Mrs. Frank E. Talley (Shirley)

BLACK RUSSIAN CAKE

1 box deep chocolate Bundt
  cake mix
½ cup salad oil
1 small package instant chocolate
  pudding

4 eggs
¾ cup strong coffee
¾ cup combined Kahlua and crème
  de cacao

Reserve glaze for topping. Combine all ingredients and beat for four minutes at medium speed until smooth. Pour into a well-greased Bundt pan and bake at 350 degrees for 45-50 minutes. Remove cake from oven and when cool, punch holes in cake with a fork or pick.

Topping:

2 tablespoons strong coffee
2 tablespoons Kahlua

Reserved chocolate glaze
4 tablespoons crème de cacao

Combine all ingredients and spoon on cake.
Mrs. John B. Morrow (Jodie)

STRAWBERRY JELLO CAKE

1 package white cake mix
1 3-ounce package strawberry
  Jello
3 tablespoons flour
¼ teaspoon salt
1 cup Wesson Oil

½ cup water
4 eggs
1 10-ounce package frozen
  strawberries (5 ounces for cake
  and 5 ounces for icing)

Sift cake mix, flour, Jello, and salt into a large mixing bowl. Add oil and water. Beat well. Add eggs one at a time. Mix in 5 ounces mashed strawberries. Bake at 300-350 degrees for 30 minutes or until done, according to cake desired. Will yield: 1 large cake, 2 or 3 layers; 1 sheet cake; 42 regular size cup cakes; 125 small cup cakes for teas. Freezes well.

Strawberry Icing:

1 stick oleo

1 box sifted confectioners' sugar

Cream oleo. Gradually add sugar and remaining 5 ounces strawberries until consistency desired for spreading.
Mrs. George Gore (Madelyn)
Mrs. Richard L. Scoggins (Sara)
Mrs. A. D. Teal, Sr.   *Mobile, Alabama*

MRS. ORR'S DUMP CAKE

1 No. 2 can crushed pineapple, drained
1 1-pound can cherry pie filling

1 box yellow or white cake mix
1 cup pecans or walnuts, chopped
2 sticks butter or oleo

Grease a tube pan (not the 2-piece kind). Place pineapple in bottom of pan; cover with pie filling, cake mix, then nuts. Cut butter into pieces and place over cake. Do not mix! Bake at 350 degrees for 1 hour or until brown on top. Serve warm or cold by dipping out with a spoon. Garnish with whipped cream, if desired. Serves 10-12.
Mrs. Milton Gray (Helen)

JELLY ROLL

4 eggs, separated
½ cup plus 1 tablespoon granulated sugar
⅓ cup cake flour, unsifted

¼ cup cornstarch
¼ teaspoon baking powder
2 tablespoons confectioners' sugar
1 teaspoon vanilla extract

Beat egg yolks and granulated sugar together until creamy. Sift flour, cornstarch, and baking powder on top of egg yolk mixture. Set aside. Beat egg whites until frothy. Add confectioners' sugar and beat until stiff. Fold carefully into egg yolk mixture. Add vanilla. Spread on an ungreased jelly roll pan that has been lined with waxed paper. Bake at 350 degrees for 12 to 15 minutes. While jelly roll is baking, take another piece of waxed paper and sprinkle with confectioners' sugar. Turn baked jelly roll onto sugared waxed paper and remove paper that was baked with jelly roll. Roll up immediately and let cool. Unroll and fill with jelly, preserves, or fruit filling. Roll back up and slice to serve.

Fruit Filling:

2 tablespoons water
½ package unflavored gelatin
1 cup heavy cream, whipped
Confectioners' sugar

2 cups cut fresh fruit (peaches or strawberries)
Sugar to sweeten

Dissolve gelatin in water. Fold into whipped cream that has been sweetened with confectioners' sugar. Set aside. Mash fruit with a fork and add sugar to taste. Fold into whipped cream mixture and spread on jelly roll.
Mrs. William E. Holland, III (Hannelore)

FRUIT COCKTAIL CAKE
This isn't a pretty cake, but delicious.

1½ cups sugar
2 eggs
2 cups self-rising flour

2 teaspoons baking soda
1 1-pound can fruit cocktail

Beat eggs and add sugar. Sift flour and baking soda together and add alternately with juice from fruit cocktail. Fold in fruit last. Pour into two greased and floured 9-inch cake pans. Bake at 350 degrees for 15-20 minutes.
Icing:

1½ cups sugar
1 cup evaporated milk
1 stick margarine

1 cup coconut
1 cup pecans, chopped
2 teaspoons vanilla

Blend sugar, milk, and margarine in a saucepan and boil for 10 minutes. Let cool. Stir in remaining ingredients. Frost cake.
Mrs. Dimples Duncan
Mrs. Jim Riggan (Karen)

FEUD CAKE

8 eggs
2 cups sugar
1 cup flour
1 teaspoon salt

4 teaspoons baking powder
1 tablespoon vanilla
5¼ cups pecans, finely chopped

Beat eggs at high speed for 5 minutes. Gradually add sugar and vanilla. Sift dry ingredients together and add to egg mixture. Beat another 5 minutes. Add 5 cups pecans at low speed to moisten well and beat for approximately 1 minute. Pour mixture into 3 greased and paper lined 9-inch cake pans. Bake at 350 degrees for 15 to 20 minutes. Remove immediately from pans to wire cake racks and cool. Cake may fall slightly.
Feud Cake Topping:

1½ quarts whipping cream

1 cup confectioners' sugar

Whip cream until stiff and sweeten with sugar. Frost layers and sides of cake. Sprinkle generously with chopped pecans. Dessert topping may be substituted for whipped cream if desired.
Note: The name of the cake is derived from a legend that two families claimed ownership of the recipe. Their argument turned into a feud. The two families are forgotten but not the cake.
SEVEN SEAS RESTAURANT

FRUIT CAKE

2 cups flour
2 cups sugar
1 cup shortening
6 eggs
1 teaspoon vanilla extract

1 tablespoon rum extract
1 pound candied cherries
1 pound candied pineapple
2 cups pecans, chopped

Dredge fruit and nuts in a small amount of the flour. Cream shortening and sugar together. Add eggs and flour alternately. Add flavorings, fruits, and nuts. Mix well. Bake at 350 degrees for approximately 1½ hours or until done.

Mrs. Douglas B. McDaniel   *Chipley, Florida*

ITALIAN CREAM CAKE

2 cups sugar
½ cup shortening
1 stick butter or oleo
5 egg yolks
1 teaspoon vanilla
2 cups sifted flour

1 teaspoon baking soda
½ teaspoon salt
1 cup buttermilk
5 egg whites
1 cup pecans, chopped
1 3½-ounce can Angel Flake Coconut

Cream butter, shortening, and sugar. Add egg yolks, one at a time. Add vanilla. Sift dry ingredients together and add alternately with buttermilk. Add coconut and nuts. Beat egg whites until they are stiff and fold into mixture. Pour into four round cake pans. Bake at 350 degrees for 25-30 minutes.

Icing:

1 8-ounce package cream cheese
½ stick butter or oleo
1 box confectioners' sugar

1 teaspoon vanilla
2 tablespoons milk, if needed
1 cup nuts, chopped

Cream butter and cheese. Gradually add sugar. Add vanilla and beat until creamy. If needed, add milk. Frost cake and sprinkle with nuts on top and sides.

Mrs. Reynolds E. Pitts (Jean)
Mrs. N. Russell Bower (Jerrie)
Mrs. Paul J. Gwinn, Jr.   *Pine Bluff, Arkansas*

CREAM JAM CAKE

1½ cups sugar
1½ sticks butter
3 beaten eggs
3 cups flour
1 teaspoon baking soda
1 teaspoon cinnamon

1 teaspoon cloves
1 teaspoon allspice
1 teaspoon nutmeg
1 cup buttermilk
1 cup jam
1 cup pecans, chopped

Cream butter and sugar together. Add beaten eggs. Sift flour, baking soda, and spices together three times and add alternately with buttermilk. Add jam and nuts. Pour into two 9-inch greased and floured cake pans. Bake at 350 degrees for 35-40 minutes or until done. Frost with Caramel Icing.

Caramel Icing:
2 cups sugar
½ cup brown sugar
½ teaspoon baking soda

1 cup buttermilk
1 stick butter
1 tablespoon vanilla

Mix first five ingredients in a saucepan and cook until mixture forms a soft ball. Cool and add vanilla. Beat until creamy. Spread on cake.
Mrs. John L. Fishel (Louise)

DATE NUT CAKE

4 eggs, separated
1 cup sugar
1 teaspoon vanilla
1 cup flour
2 teaspoons baking powder

Pinch of salt
1 quart pecans, chopped
2 small or 1 large package
dates, chopped

Beat egg yolks and gradually add sugar. Add vanilla. Sift dry ingredients together. Add dates and pecans to flour mixture. Add to egg yolk mixture. Beat egg whites until soft peaks form. Fold into batter. This makes a *very* stiff batter and the last part of the mixing has to be done by hand. Pour into a greased and paper-lined tube pan. Bake at 250-275 degrees for 50 minutes. Cool in pan.
Mrs. A. Norman Segler (Anita)

ORANGE WINE CAKE

1 stick butter
½ cup shortening
1½ cups sugar
4 eggs
1½ cups buttermilk
3½ cups cake flour, sifted

2 teaspoons baking soda
½ teaspoon salt
2 teaspoons orange extract
1 tablespoon orange rind, grated
1 cup raisins, finely chopped
1 cup pecans, finely chopped

Dredge the raisins and pecans in ½ cup of the flour. Cream butter, shortening, and sugar together. Gradually beat in the eggs. Sift dry ingredients together. Add buttermilk alternately with dry ingredients. Add the orange extract and orange rind. Blend until smooth. Add the raisins and pecans to the mixture. Pour into two greased and floured 9-inch cake pans. Bake at 350 degrees for 30 minutes. Remove from oven and cool for 5 minutes in the pans. Turn out on cooling racks and finish cooling. Frost with Sherry Frosting.

Sherry Frosting:

¼ cup butter
2½-3 cups confectioners' sugar,
   sifted
¼ cup orange juice

½ teaspoon orange extract
½ teaspoon orange rind, grated
Dash of salt
1 tablespoon dry sherry

Cream butter and remaining ingredients together, except sherry. Add enough sherry to make frosting spreading consistency. If frosting is too thin, add more sugar and refrigerate.
Mrs. Foster H. Kruse (Helen)

ORANGE SLICE CAKE

2 sticks oleo
2 cups sugar
4 eggs
3½ cups sifted flour
1 teaspoon baking soda
½ cup buttermilk
2 cups nuts, chopped

1 pound dates, chopped
1 10-ounce package flaked coconut
1 pound candy orange slices,
   finely cut
½ teaspoon salt
¾ cup fresh orange juice
2 cups confectioners' sugar

Cream oleo and sugar. Add one egg at a time. Roll nuts, candy, dates, and coconut in some of the flour. Dissolve baking soda in buttermilk and add alternately with flour. Add salt. Add nuts and candy mixture. Mix well. Pour into a greased and floured tube pan. Bake at 250 degrees for 2½ hours. Mix the fresh orange juice and confectioners' sugar together. Stir until sugar is dissolved. Spoon over cake in pan until all is absorbed. Leave overnight.
Mrs. Lester C. Brock (Martha)

PLUM CAKE

2 cups sugar
1 cup Wesson Oil
4 eggs
2 cups self-rising flour
1½ teaspoons cloves

1½ teaspoons cinnamon
⅛ teaspoon salt
2 small jars plum baby food
(strained)
1 cup pecans, chopped

Combine oil and sugar. Add eggs one at a time. Sift dry ingredients together and add alternately with plums. Add nuts. Pour into a greased and floured Bundt pan. Bake at 350 degrees for 55 minutes or until done. Frost with your favorite Caramel Icing or a Sherry Glaze: ½ box confectioners' sugar and ½ cup dry sherry.

Variation: Add 1 teaspoon each cinnamon, cloves, allspice, and vanilla flavoring. Use two small jars strained apricot baby food instead of plum baby food.

Mrs. Charles F. Anderson (Janet)
Mrs. C. L. Jinks, Jr. (Mary Catherine)
Mrs. Pierce Baymiller   Moss Point, Mississippi

WALDORF TORTE

2 eggs, separated
¼ cup sifted plain flour
½ teaspoon double acting baking
powder
½ teaspoon salt
½ teaspoon cinnamon

½ cup light raisins, snipped
½ cup nuts, pecans or walnuts
1 medium apple
½ cup sugar
¼ teaspoon cream of tartar
½ cup whipping cream

Separate eggs, cover, and let stand at room temperature for 1 hour. Preheat oven to 350 degrees. Grease and line with waxed paper one 9-inch square layer pan. Sift flour, baking powder, salt, and cinnamon together. Toss with raisins, nuts, and apple which has been peeled and cut into small pieces. Beat egg yolks with half of the sugar. Beat egg whites with other half of the sugar and add cream of tartar, beating until soft peaks form. Combine beaten yolks with flour-fruit mixture. Gently fold in beaten egg whites. Pour into prepared pan. Bake for 35 minutes. Cool. Carefully turn onto serving plate. Refrigerate. To serve, frost with whipped cream and serve on individual plates. Serve 6.

Mrs. Sam Ridley (Marge)

BROWN SUGAR POUND CAKE

1 cup shortening	½ teaspoon salt
1 stick oleo	½ teaspoon baking powder
1 pound box brown sugar, sifted	1 cup evaporated milk
5 eggs	2 teaspoons maple flavoring
3 cups flour	

Cream shortening, oleo, and sugar. Add eggs, one at a time. Add sifted dry ingredients alternately with milk. Add flavoring. Pour into a greased and floured Bundt or tube pan. Bake at 300 degrees for 1½ hours or until done. Frost with brown sugar icing, if desired.

Icing:

1 stick oleo	¼ cup milk
1 cup brown sugar	3 cups confectioners' sugar
1 teaspoon vanilla	

Melt oleo. Add brown sugar and stir 1 minute. Add milk, powdered sugar, and vanilla. Blend until creamy.

Miss Elizabeth Knight

GERMAN CHOCOLATE POUND CAKE

2 cups sugar	3 cups flour, sifted
1 cup margarine	1 teaspoon soda
4 eggs	1 teaspoon salt
2 teaspoons vanilla extract	1 4-ounce package German's Sweet
2 teaspoons butter extract	Chocolate
1 cup buttermilk	

Cream sugar and margarine together. Add eggs, extracts, and buttermilk. Sift together dry ingredients and add to creamed mixture. Blend well. Soften chocolate in a warm oven or a double boiler and blend into batter. Pour mixture into a 9-inch greased and floured tube pan and bake at 300 degrees for 1 hour or until done. Remove cake from oven and cover until cool.

Note: If butter is used instead of margarine, omit butter flavoring.

Mrs. Steve Wilson (Sandra)

CHOCOLATE POUND CAKE

2 sticks oleo
2 cups sugar
4 eggs
2½ cups flour
¼ teaspoon salt
½ teaspoon baking soda

1 teaspoon vanilla
1 cup buttermilk
2 5½-ounce cans Hershey's Chocolate Syrup
7 1.26-ounce or 1.4-ounce small, plain Hershey Bars

Cream oleo and sugar. Add eggs one at a time. Sift together flour, salt, and baking soda. Add to the creamed mixture alternating with the buttermilk. Add chocolate syrup. Add melted Hershey bars. Add vanilla. Pour into a greased and floured tube pan. Bake at 325 degrees for 1 hour or until done.
Mrs. James T. Earnest   Northport, Alabama

CREAM CHEESE POUND CAKE
. . .a pretty Christmas cake that freezes well. . .

3 sticks butter
8 ounces cream cheese
3 cups sugar
3 cups cake flour, sifted

6 eggs
1 cup nuts, chopped
1 cup candied cherries, chopped
1 cup dates, chopped

Cream butter and sugar together. Add cream cheese that is room temperature. Add eggs one at a time. Gradually add flour, reserving a small amount. Dredge fruit and nuts in remaining flour and add to mixture. (Dates may be sugared.) Pour into a greased and floured tube pan or two loaf pans. Bake at 325 degrees for 1 hour or until done.
Variation: For a delicious pound cake, leave out fruit and nuts.
Mrs. M. R. Pilcher (Elaine)

7-UP POUND CAKE

2 sticks oleo
½ cup vegetable shortening
3 cups sugar
5 eggs

1 teaspoon lemon extract
3 cups flour
1 7-ounce bottle 7-Up

Cream oleo, shortening, and sugar. Add eggs one at a time. Add lemon extract. Add flour alternately with 7-Up. Pour into a greased and floured tube pan. Bake at 300 degrees for 1 hour and 30 minutes or until done. A glaze of confectioners' sugar, 7-Up, and lemon juice may be poured over cake while still warm.
Milton Acton

COCONUT POUND CAKE

1 7-ounce package frozen coconut, thawed
2 sticks butter
½ cup Crisco Shortening
2½ cups sugar
5 eggs, separated

3½ cups cake flour
¼ teaspoon salt
1 teaspoon baking powder
1 cup milk
1 teaspoon coconut extract

Cream butter, shortening, and sugar. Add egg yolks one at a time. Sift dry ingredients together. Add flavoring to milk. Add dry ingredients to creamed mixture alternately with milk mixture. Add coconut. Fold in stiffly beaten egg whites. Pour into a greased and floured tube pan. Bake at 325 degrees for 1 hour and 15 minutes. Cool in pan about 10 minutes. Freezes well.
Mrs. Richard L. Scoggins (Sara)

GRANNY'S POUND CAKE

1 pound butter
3 cups sugar

3 cups flour, sifted
10 eggs

Cream butter and sugar. Add eggs alternately with flour. Pour into a greased and floured tube pan. Bake at 325 degrees for 1 hour and 30 minutes or until done.
Variation: Nuts and cherries, in the amount desired, may be added for a nice Christmas cake.
Mrs. George J. Dudley (Ruth)

EASY COCONUT POUND CAKE

1 box Duncan Hines Butter Recipe Golden Cake Mix
½ cup Crisco Oil
4 eggs
1 cup water

1 3-ounce package coconut instant pudding
1 7-ounce package shredded coconut

Put all ingredients together in mixer. Blend for 5 minutes at medium speed. Pour into a greased and floured Bundt pan. Bake at 350 degrees for 40 minutes. Cool at least 10 minutes before turning out. Cool thoroughly before cutting and use a *very* sharp knife or cake will crumble.
Mrs. George J. Christo (Judy)

MILLION DOLLAR BAND POUND CAKE
...a tradition of the Bay High Band Boosters...

1 pound butter	6 eggs
3 cups sugar	4 cups flour
2 teaspoons vanilla	¾ cup milk
1 teaspoon almond extract	

Cream butter and sugar. Add flavorings. Add eggs, one at a time. Add flour alternately with milk. Pour into a greased and floured tube pan. Bake at 325 degrees for 1 hour and 45 minutes or until done. Makes a large cake.

POUND CAKE

2 sticks butter	3 cups cake flour
3 cups sugar	2 teaspoons vanilla
1 cup milk	4 teaspoons lemon
1 tablespoon vinegar	extract
¼ teaspoon baking soda	5 eggs

Beat eggs enough to mix and add flavorings. Set aside. Add soda and vinegar to milk. Set aside. Cream butter and sugar. Add flour alternately with milk mixture. Add egg mixture and beat well. Pour into a greased and floured tube pan. Bake at 325 degrees for 1 hour and 30 minutes.
Icing: After cake has cooled, mix lemon juice and confectioners' sugar to spreading consistency, and drizzle over top of cake. Makes a nice glaze on cake.
Mrs. Charles G. Hundley (Frances)

WHIPPING CREAM POUND CAKE

2 sticks butter	½ pint whipping cream
3 cups sugar	2 teaspoons vanilla
6 eggs	1 teaspoon lemon extract (optional)
3 cups sifted flour	

Cream butter and sugar. Add eggs one at a time. Add flour alternately with cream. Add flavoring. Pour into a tube pan that has been sprayed well with Pam or greased and floured. Place cake in a cold oven. Set temperature at 325 degrees and bake for 1 hour and 30 minutes or until done. Cool no more than 15 minutes on a rack. Turn out of pan.
Mrs. Nelson Mahone
Mrs. L. B. Childers (Julia)

SOUR CREAM POUND CAKE I

2 sticks butter	5 eggs
½ cup Crisco (scant)	3 cups cake flour
3 cups sugar	1 teaspoon baking powder
1 teaspoon vanilla	½ pint sour cream
1 teaspoon lemon extract	¼ cup sweet milk
½ teaspoon almond extract	

Have everything at room temperature. Cream butter, Crisco, and sugar. Add flavorings. Add eggs, one at a time. Sift flour and baking powder together and set aside. Mix milk and sour cream together. Add flour mixture, alternating with milk mixture to creamed batter. Pour into greased and floured tube pan. Bake at 325 degrees for 1 hour and 30 minutes or until done.

Mrs. J. Matt Brown (Stuart)

SOUR CREAM POUND CAKE II

2 sticks butter	1 teaspoon almond extract (optional)
3 cups sugar	¼ teaspoon baking soda
6 eggs, separated	3 cups flour
½ pint sour cream	¼ teaspoon salt
1 teaspoon vanilla	

Cream butter and sugar. Add egg yolks one at a time. Add sour cream and flavorings; beat well. Sift dry ingredients together and add to creamed mixture. Beat for five minutes. Fold in stiffly beaten egg whites. Pour into a greased and floured tube pan. Bake at 300-325 degrees for 1 hour and 30 minutes or until done. Cool in pan for 5 minutes.

Variation: If desired, 2 teaspoons vanilla and ½ teaspoon almond may be used.

Mrs. Dempsey J. Barron (Louverne)
Mrs. Custer Russ, Sr. (Irma)

CHOCOLATE ICING

¼ cup butter	1 teaspoon vanilla
2 squares unsweetened chocolate	Cream
1 1-pound box confectioners' sugar	

Melt butter and chocolate. Add sugar and vanilla. Add cream to obtain spreading consistency.

Mrs. Reynolds E. Pitts (Jean)

DECORATORS' ICING

½ cup Crisco
1 pound confectioners' sugar,
sifted
4½ tablespoons water

1 teaspoon flavoring of your choice
½ teaspoon salt
Food coloring, (optional)

Cream Crisco and gradually add sifted sugar. Add water, flavoring, and salt. Beat until smooth. Keep icing covered while not using. It will form a thin crust when exposed to air. This will frost one 8 or 9-inch layer cake. If you have a lot of decorations to make, double recipe.
Note: If using a large amount of food coloring, use less water.
Mrs. W. A. Carpenter (Carol)

CARAMEL ICING

¾ cup brown sugar
1 stick butter
¼ cup confectioners' sugar

¼ cup sugar
¼ cup evaporated milk
5 large marshmallows

Combine first five ingredients and cook 5-7 minutes. Add marshmallows and beat well. Cool (about 1½ hours) until spreading consistency.
Mrs. C. T. Clayton, Jr.   *Birmingham, Alabama*

COCOA FUDGE ICING

1 stick butter or oleo
½ cup Hershey's Cocoa
1 1-pound box confectioners' sugar
7 tablespoons milk

1 teaspoon vanilla
1 tablespoon crushed peppermint
(optional)

Melt butter in a saucepan. Add cocoa and heat 1 minute or until smooth, stirring constantly. Pour into a mixing bowl. Add confectioners' sugar alternately with milk. Beat to spreading consistency. Add vanilla and candy, if used. Will frost two 8 or 9-inch layers.
Mrs. Howard Gray (Carol)

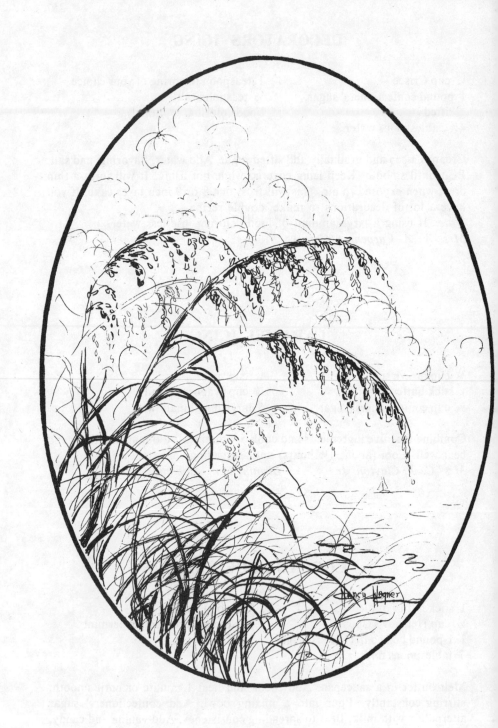

Pies

PÂTE BRISÉE
...a good rich crust for pie, tart, or quiche...

1¼ cups flour
¾ stick butter
2 tablespoons vegetable shortening

¼ teaspoon salt
3 tablespoons ice water

In a large bowl combine flour, butter, shortening, and salt. Blend well. Add water and toss mixture until water is absorbed. Form the dough into a ball. Knead lightly for a few seconds with palm of hand. Shape dough into a ball. Dust with flour, wrap in waxed paper, and chill for 1 hour. Roll dough on floured surface.
Mrs. Warren Middlemas, Jr. (Martha)

TART CRUST

1 cup flour, sifted
½ cup butter
2 tablespoons sugar

1 egg yolk
1 teaspoon grated lemon rind

Sift flour into center of pastry board. Top with butter, sugar, egg yolk, and lemon rind. Mix to a smooth paste. Knead in flour to make a firm dough that cleans the board. Wrap in waxed paper and refrigerate for 1 hour. Good for one 9-inch pie shell or flan crust. Roll dough out on floured surface and press firmly into pan. Prick bottom with a fork. Bake at 400 degrees for 10 minutes; lower heat to 350 degrees for 5 minutes longer.
The Editors

ENGLISH TOFFEE PIE

1 stick butter
2 cups confectioners' sugar
2 eggs, separated
2 tablespoons cocoa
Whipped cream

1 teaspoon vanilla
½ teaspoon salt
1 cup nuts, chopped
1¾ cups vanilla wafer crumbs
Grated chocolate

Cream butter and sugar together. Add beaten egg yolks, cocoa, vanilla, salt, and nuts. Fold in beaten egg whites. Place half of crumbs in a pie plate and add pie mixture. Top with remaining wafer crumbs. Chill overnight and serve with whipped cream. Garnish with grated chocolate.
Mrs. Julian Bennett (Agatha)

BLACK BOTTOM PIE

Crust:

18-20 ginger snap or chocolate   5 tablespoons butter, melted
    cookies

Crush cookies fine. Add melted butter to crumbs and pat into a 9 or 10-inch pie plate. Bake at 425 degrees for 10 minutes. Cool.

Filling:

2 cups milk, scalded	1 teaspoon vanilla
4 eggs	1 tablespoon unflavored gelatin
1 cup sugar	2 tablespoons cold water
1½ tablespoons cornstarch	¼ teaspoon cream of tartar
1½ squares bitter chocolate	2 tablespoons whiskey

Separate eggs and add well-beaten yolks slowly to scalded milk. Combine ½ cup of sugar and the cornstarch and stir into milk mixture. Cook in double boiler for 20 minutes or until mixture coats spoon, stirring occasionally. Remove 1 cup of mixture. Add chocolate to the cup of mixture, and beat as the mixture cools. Add vanilla and pour mixture into pie crust. Chill. Dissolve gelatin in cold water. Add remaining custard to gelatin and chill. Beat egg whites stiff with sugar and cream of tartar and add whiskey. Fold into custard mixture and spread on top of chocolate mixture. Chill.

Mrs. Ray Wagner (Nancy)

DOUBLE CRUST

2¼ cups flour, sifted	¾ cup shortening
1 teaspoon salt	5 tablespoons cold water

Sift flour and salt together in a mixing bowl. Add shortening and cut into flour with a pastry blender. Sprinkle with cold water until well moistened. Form a ball and divide in half. Chill 30-45 minutes. Roll on a lightly floured surface.

Mrs. Philip H. Smith (Ann)

IMPOSSIBLE PIE

...makes its own crust...

4 eggs
1¾ cups sugar
½ cup flour
1 7-ounce can coconut

2 cups milk
1 teaspoon vanilla
½ stick oleo, melted

Butter two 9-inch pie pans. Combine ingredients in order listed. Pour into pie pans and bake at 350 degrees for 30 minutes.
The Editors

GRASSHOPPER PIE

Crust:
24 Oreo cookies

¼ cup oleo, melted

Roll cookies fine and add melted oleo. Line a 10-inch pie plate and pat in place. Refrigerate.
Filling:
40 large marshmallows
1 cup whipping cream
¾ cup milk

2 tablespoons crème de menthe
2 tablespoons white crème de cacao

In double boiler, melt marshmallows and add milk. Cool. Whip cream and add crème de menthe and crème de cacao. Fold whipped cream into marshmallow mixture. Pour into crust and refrigerate. Top with additional whipped cream, if desired. Sprinkle top with Oreo crumbs.
Mrs. Jack Dyer (Jill)

SOUR CREAM PIE

1 cup sour cream
3 egg yolks
½ cup raisins
½ cup nuts
1 cup sugar

¾ teaspoon cinnamon
½ teaspoon ginger
¼ teaspoon nutmeg
1 unbaked pie shell

Mix sour cream and sugar together. Add slightly beaten egg yolks and remaining ingredients. Pour into unbaked pie shell. Bake at 425 degrees for 20 minutes. Reduce heat to 325 degrees and bake 20 minutes longer. Serve with whipped cream, if desired.
Mrs. Paul Eubanks (Maedelle)

EASY EGG CUSTARD PIE

3 eggs, well beaten
2 cups hot water
1 can Eagle Brand milk

1 teaspoon vanilla
2 9-inch pie shells, unbaked

Combine first four ingredients and divide between pie shells. Bake at 450 degrees for 15 minutes. Turn oven down to 350 degrees and bake 25 to 30 minutes longer. Do not overbake. Pie is ready when knife inserted in center comes out clean.
Mrs. B. E. Davis

EGG CUSTARD PIE

⅔ cup sugar
1 tablespoon margarine
4 eggs, separated
1 tablespoon flour

1 teaspoon vanilla
2 cups milk
1 10-inch unbaked pie shell

Combine butter, sugar, flour, and egg yolks together. Gradually stir in milk and add vanilla. Beat egg whites until stiff and fold into mixture. Pour mixture into the pie shell and bake at 350 degrees for 30 or 40 minutes or until knife inserted into pie comes out clean. Mixture will make 6 individual custards instead of pie, if desired. Place custard cups in pan of water to bake.
Mrs. Lowell F. Adams (Lucille)

FRENCH SILK CHOCOLATE PIE

½ cup butter
¾ cup sugar
1 square chocolate
1 teaspoon vanilla
2 eggs

1 baked pie shell or graham cracker
  crust
Whipped Cream
Nuts

Cream butter and sugar together. Blend in melted and cooled chocolate and vanilla. Add eggs one at a time, and beat for 5 minutes with electric mixer at medium speed. Pour mixture into a baked crust or shell. Chill 1-2 hours. Top with whipped cream or nuts, if desired.
Mrs. Henry A. Dusseault (Lillian)

AUNT CLYDE'S BUTTERMILK PIE

1 ⅓ cups sugar
3 tablespoons flour
2 eggs
½ cup margarine
1 cup buttermilk

2 teaspoons vanilla
Juice and pulp of one lemon
(optional)
1 9-inch unbaked pastry shell

Combine sugar and flour. Beat eggs and add to mixture. Add melted margarine and buttermilk. Mix well. Fold in vanilla, lemon pulp, and juice. Pour mixture into chilled pastry shell and bake at 425 degrees for 10 minutes. Reduce heat and bake at 350 degrees for 35 minutes longer without opening door. Meringue may be added, if desired.
Mrs. James W. Marshall, Jr. (Margie)

COCONUT PIE

4 egg yolks
1½ cups sugar
1½ teaspoons vanilla
2½ cups milk
4 tablespoons cornstarch
Meringue:
½ cup sugar
4 egg whites

2 tablespoons light Karo syrup
Dash of salt
1 can shredded coconut
½ stick butter

¼ teaspoon cream of tartar
¼ teaspoon salt

Combine dry ingredients. Add egg yolks, vanilla, milk, syrup, coconut (reserving some to garnish pie), and butter. Cook in a heavy saucepan until mixture thickens. Pour mixture into baked pie crust. To make meringue, beat egg whites with sugar, cream of tartar, and salt until soft peaks form. Top pie with meringue. Garnish with reserved coconut. Place pie in oven to brown meringue. Chill.
Mrs. Judy Waldorff

FRESH STRAWBERRY TART

3 egg whites
½ teaspoon vinegar
¼ teaspoon salt
½ cup sugar
¾ teaspoon vanilla
2 cups fresh strawberries
⅓ cup sugar

2 tablespoons cornstarch
½ cup juice of strawberries
Red food coloring
1 cup whipping cream
1 9-inch baked tart shell
(see index)

Beat egg whites with vinegar and salt until soft peaks form. Gradually add ½ cup of sugar and the vanilla, beating until stiff peaks form. Spread on the bottom and sides of a baked shell. Bake at 325 degrees for 12 minutes. Cool. Mash and sieve strawberries, reserving a few to garnish pie. In a saucepan, blend together the remaining sugar and cornstarch. Add the juice from the strawberries and the mashed berries. Cook and stir until mixture thickens and boils. Cook for 2 minutes. Tint mixture with food coloring. Cool slightly. Spread over meringue and chill until set. Whip cream and cover pie. Garnish with sliced strawberries.
Mrs. Jimmy Christo (Mary Anne)

FRESH STRAWBERRY PIE

1 cup fresh strawberries,
  sliced
1 cup sugar
1 cup water
4 tablespoons strawberry
  gelatin

4 tablespoons cornstarch
1 9-inch baked pie shell
Whipped cream

Combine sugar, water, and cornstarch together. Cook until mixture thickens. Remove from heat and stir in gelatin. Line a cooled, baked 9-inch pie shell with strawberries. Pour gelatin mixture over strawberries and chill. Serve with whipped cream.
Mrs. Ralph Segrest, Jr. (Jane)
Betty Boone Ereckson
Variation: Use 2 cups strawberries. Mash 1 cup strawberries and cook with other ingredients instead of strawberry gelatin. Proceed as above.
Mrs. Charles W. Ireland (Caroline)

CHERRY PIE

2 1-pound cans red, tart cherries, pitted
1 cup sugar
¼ cup brown sugar
4 tablespoons cornstarch
¼ teaspoon cinnamon
½ teaspoon almond extract
2 tablespoons butter
1 double pie crust, unbaked
Few drops red food coloring

Drain cherries and reserve juice. Combine cornstarch with cherry juice. Add sugar, brown sugar, and cinnamon. Cook until clear and mixture thickens. Add cherries, food coloring, and almond extract. Remove from heat and pour into unbaked pie shell. Dot with butter. Cover with other half of pastry. Make about four 1-inch slits in top crust. Bake at 375 degrees for 45 to 55 minutes.
Mrs. Philip H. Smith (Ann)

PECAN PIE

3 eggs
1 cup dark Karo syrup
1 cup sugar
1 teaspoon vanilla
3 tablespoons butter
¾ cup pecans, chopped
1 9-inch unbaked pastry shell

Beat eggs and add to syrup and sugar. Add vanilla and melted butter and mix well. Pour mixture into pie shell and sprinkle pecans over top. Bake at 325 degrees for 35 minutes.
Mrs. Robert Lee (Mildred)

PINEAPPLE PIE

2 sticks oleo
2 cups sugar
4 eggs, beaten
1 teaspoon vanilla
1 small can crushed pineapple, undrained
2 tablespoons cornmeal
2 tablespoons flour

Melt oleo and add remaining ingredients. Pour into 2 unbaked pie shells and bake at 350 degrees for 45 minutes.
Mrs. William E. Lark (Ruthie)

DUTCH APPLE-CRISP PIE

2½ pounds tart apples
1 cup sugar
2 tablespoons flour
½ teaspoon nutmeg
½ teaspoon cinnamon

2 tablespoons lemon juice
½ cup flour
½ cup butter
½ cup nuts, chopped
1 9-inch unbaked pastry shell

Peel apples and slice thin. Mix half of sugar with 2 tablespoons of flour and spices. Toss flour mixture with apples. Pour into pastry shell and sprinkle lemon juice over apples. Mix remaining sugar with ½ cup flour and cut in butter until mixture is crumbly. Sprinkle mixture over apples. Bake at 400 degrees for 45 to 55 minutes. Top pie with chopped nuts 10 minutes before pie is done.
Mrs. James A. Poyner (Nell)

APPLE FLAN

6 tart cooking apples
1 cup sugar
2 tablespoons flour
1 teaspoon cinnamon
1 teaspoon lemon peel, grated
Topping:
½ cup flour
¼ cup sugar
⅛ teaspoon salt

⅛ teaspoon cloves
⅛ teaspoon salt
1 9-inch pie shell
Sour cream

½ cup Cheddar cheese, grated
½ cup butter, melted

Peel and thinly slice apples. Mix together 1 cup sugar, 2 tablespoons flour, cinnamon, lemon peel, cloves, and salt. Toss apple slices with mixture and arrange them in the pie shell, overlapping slices. Combine ingredients for topping and sprinkle over apples. Bake at 400 degrees for 40 minutes. Cover with foil for the last 10 minutes. Cool and serve topped with sour cream.
Mrs. J. R. Moody, Jr. (Jean)

SOUTHERN PECAN PIE

1 cup dark Karo syrup
1½ cups pecan pieces
2 cups sugar
4 eggs, beaten
1 tablespoon butter, melted

1 teaspoon vanilla
1 teaspoon bourbon
Pinch of salt
2 frozen, unbaked pie shells

Put pie shells in a preheated 400 degree oven for 40 seconds. Combine all other ingredients and fill pie shells. Bake at 400 degrees for 10 minutes. Reduce heat to 350 degrees and bake for 45 minutes. These pies freeze well.
Mrs. Abbott Browne (Mary Belle)

APPLESAUCE-APPLE PIE

⅓ cup sugar
⅔ cup brown sugar
½ teaspoon ground cinnamon
¼ teaspoon ground nutmeg
¾ cup flour, sifted

6 tablespoons butter
1 cup applesauce
1 20-ounce can pie sliced
   apples, drained
1 9-inch pie shell

Combine sugar, half of brown sugar, spices, and applesauce. Stir in apple slices. Pour mixture into unbaked 9-inch pie shell. Combine remaining brown sugar and flour. Cut butter into mixture until crumbly. Sprinkle on top of pie. Bake at 400 degrees for 40 minutes.
Mrs. James E. Preston (Sandra)

PUMPKIN PIE

1½ cups pumpkin
1½ cups sugar
3 tablespoons flour, rounded
3 eggs
1 stick oleo, melted

1 small can Pet Milk
1 teaspoon vanilla
1 tablespoon sugar
1 tablespoon nutmeg
2 unbaked pastry shells

Mix all ingredients together except nutmeg and 1 tablespoon of sugar. Add eggs one at a time to the mixture. Pour mixture into pastry shells and bake at 300 degrees for 1 hour and 40 minutes. Remove pies from oven and sprinkle with a mixture of nutmeg and sugar.
Mrs C. C. Price (Gertie)

SWEET POTATO PIE

2 cups sweet potatoes
1 cup sugar
2 eggs
2 tablespoons butter

1 teaspoon vanilla
½ cup milk
Dash of salt
1 unbaked pie shell

Peel and cook sweet potatoes in water until tender. Drain and mash potatoes. Add remaining ingredients to potatoes while still hot. Pour into the pie shell and bake at 350 degrees until pie is firm.
Mrs. Lowell F. Adams (Lucille)

PURPLE PLUM MINCEMEAT PIE

3 cups Purple Plum Mincemeat
   (see index)
2 cups tart apples, sliced
2 tablespoons flour

2 tablespoons sugar
2 tablespoons butter
Pastry for double crust 9-inch pie
Hard Sauce (see index)

In a large bowl combine mincemeat and apples. Combine flour and sugar and add to mincemeat-apple mixture. Pour filling into pie shell and dot with butter. Place top crust over filling. Cut steam vents in crust and flute edges. Bake at 425 degrees about 40 minutes until golden brown and filling is bubbly. If crust gets too brown, cover edges with foil during the last 10 minutes. Serve warm with Hard Sauce or vanilla ice cream.
Mrs. Ray Wagner (Nancy)

SUNNY SILVER PIE

⅓ cup cold water
1½ teaspoons gelatin
4 eggs, separated
1 cup sugar
2-3 tablespoons lemon juice

Grated rind of 1 lemon
⅛ teaspoon salt
1 cup whipped cream
1 baked pie shell

Soften gelatin in cold water. Place egg yolks, rind, lemon juice, salt, and ½ cup sugar in double boiler. Cook until thickened, stirring constantly. Remove from heat and add gelatin. Beat egg whites until stiff and add remaining ½ cup sugar. Beat well. Fold in egg yolk mixture. Pour into pie shell. Top with sweetened whipped cream. Refrigerate 3-4 hours before serving.
Mrs. Harold E. Wager (Margaret)

CHESS PIE

3 eggs
1½ cups sugar
½ cup butter

1 tablespoon vinegar
1 teaspoon vanilla
1 9-inch unbaked pie shell

Cream butter and sugar together and stir in vinegar. Cook over low heat until bubbly. Remove from heat and let cool slightly. Beat eggs and add vanilla. Combine mixtures and pour into the pie shell. Bake at 300 degrees for approximately 30 minutes. Pie is done when knife inserted in center of pie comes out clean.
Note: Substitute 2 tablespoons of lemon juice for vinegar, if desired.
Mrs. Stanley Worsham (Mildred)

SURPRISE PIE

2 cups raisins
1½ cups water
½ cup sugar
2 tablespoons flour

½ cup walnuts, chopped
1 teaspoon lemon peel, grated
3 tablespoons lemon juice
1 unbaked double crust

Cook raisins in water in covered saucepan for 10 minutes or until raisins are plump. Combine sugar and flour and stir into raisins. Cook over low heat, stirring constantly until mixture thickens and bubbles. Cook 1 minute longer and remove from heat. Stir in nuts, lemon peel, and lemon juice. Line a 9-inch pie plate with pastry and add hot raisin mixture. Top with crust and cut slits in top. Bake at 425 degrees for 30 to 40 minutes.
Mrs. W. Roland McArthur (Julie)

LEMON CHESS PIE

2 cups sugar
4 eggs
1 tablespoon flour
1 tablespoon cornmeal
¼ cup milk

¼ cup butter, melted
⅓ cup fresh lemon juice
2 teaspoons grated lemon rind
1 9-inch unbaked pie shell

Combine sugar, eggs, flour, and meal. Add milk, butter, lemon rind, and juice. Pour into the pie shell and bake for 45 minutes at 375 degrees. The cornmeal rises to form crust over pie.
Mrs. Florence Hood   Moultrie, Georgia
Mrs. Charles Anderson (Janet)

LEMON MERINGUE PIE

1½ cups sugar
¼ cup plus 2 tablespoons cornstarch
¼ teaspoon salt
½ cup lemon juice
½ cup cold water

3 egg yolks, well beaten
2 tablespoons butter
1½ cups boiling water
1 teaspoon lemon peel
1 9-inch baked pie shell

Blend sugar, cornstarch, and salt together. Stir in lemon juice, cold water, and egg yolks blending until smooth. Add butter and stir in boiling water. Bring to a boil over medium heat; boil 2-3 minutes. Stir in lemon peel. Cool and put into pie shell.

Meringue:
3 egg whites
¼ teaspoon cream of tartar

6 tablespoons sugar

Beat whites, adding cream of tartar and sugar. Top pie with meringue and bake at 350 degrees for 12-15 minutes or until brown.
Mrs. Richard Erickson (Diane)

LEMON-FILLED MERINGUE SHELL

Shell:
3 egg whites
¾ cup sugar
¼ teaspoon cream of tartar

⅛ teaspoon salt
½ teaspoon vanilla extract

Combine egg whites, cream of tartar, salt, and vanilla. Beat until soft peaks form. Add sugar, 2 tablespoonsful at a time, beating until meringue is glossy. Spread in a buttered 9-inch pie pan. Bake at 250 degrees for one hour. Turn off heat, but leave shell in oven for several hours if not crisp to touch.

Filling:
4 egg yolks
¼ cup sugar
3 or 4 tablespoons lemon juice
1 tablespoon lemon rind

½ pint whipping cream
3 tablespoons sugar
½ teaspoon lemon extract
Strawberries (optional)

In a double boiler, combine yolks and ¼ cup sugar. Add juice and rind and cook together stirring constantly until thick. Cool. Add whipped cream to which 3 tablespoons sugar and lemon extract have been added. Pour into meringue shell and chill 12 to 24 hours. Top with additional whipped cream. Serve with fresh strawberries, if available.
Mrs. H. Mack Lewis (Eleanor)

LIME CHIFFON PIE

½ cup sugar	1 teaspoon grated lime peel
1 tablespoon unflavored gelatin	Few drops green food coloring
¼ teaspoon salt	4 egg whites
4 egg yolks	½ cup sugar
½ cup lime juice	1 cup cream, whipped
¼ cup water	1 9-inch baked pastry shell

In a saucepan combine gelatin, ½ cup sugar, and salt. Beat together egg yolks, lime juice, and water; stir into gelatin mixture. Cook and stir over medium heat just until mixture begins to boil. Remove from heat and stir in grated peel. Add food coloring *carefully* to tint pale green. Chill, stirring occasionally, until the mixture mounds slightly. Beat egg whites to form soft peaks gradually adding ½ cup sugar and beating until stiff. Fold gelatin mixture into egg whites. Fold in whipped cream. Spoon into cooled shell. Chill until firm and decorate with additional whipped cream. Sprinkle with more grated lime peel and decorate with very thin wedges of fresh lime.
Mrs. W. P. Carter, III   *Lumpkin, Georgia*

CHOCOLATE MERINGUE PIE

3 eggs, separated	2 cups milk
½ stick butter or margarine	1½ teaspoons vanilla
1¼ cups sugar	1 9-inch baked pie shell
3 tablespoons flour	6 tablespoons sugar
2 tablespoons cocoa	¼ teaspoon cream of tartar
½ teaspoon salt	

Combine 1¼ cups sugar, flour, cocoa, and salt. Scald milk and add butter. Remove from heat. Stir in sugar mixture and cook until slightly thickened. Remove from heat and add beaten egg yolks. Cook over low heat for 20 minutes, stirring to prevent sticking. Add 1 teaspoon vanilla and pour mixture into baked pie shell. Beat egg whites with 6 tablespoons sugar, cream of tartar, and ½ teaspoon vanilla until stiff peaks form. Spread over pie and bake at 400 degrees until lightly browned. Chill before serving.
Mrs. S. A. Lawhorne   *Pine Bluff, Arkansas*

JIMMY'S CHOCOLATE PIE

1½ cups coconut
2 tablespoons butter, melted
2 tablespoons water

1 teaspoon instant coffee
6 Hershey almond bars
4 cups Cool Whip

Combine coconut and butter and press into an 8-inch pie plate. Bake at 350 degrees for 10 minutes. Cool. Mix coffee with water and add melted Hershey bars. Fold in Cool Whip and pour mixture into pie shell. Freeze.
Mrs. James W. Marshall, Jr. (Margie)

FUDGE PIE

1 cup sugar
½ cup margarine
2 eggs, separated
2 squares unsweetened chocolate
⅓ cup flour, sifted

⅛ teaspoon salt
1 teaspoon vanilla
½ cup pecans, chopped
Whipped cream or vanilla
   ice cream

Cream sugar and margarine together. Add beaten egg yolks. Melt chocolate and add to mixture. Add flour, salt, vanilla, and pecans. Beat egg whites until stiff and fold into mixture. Pour into a greased pie plate and bake at 350 degrees for 30 minutes. Serve with vanilla ice cream or whipped cream. Serves 8.
Mrs. Frank Parker (Dorothy Sue)
Mrs. Rayford Lloyd, Jr. (Genie)

BROWNIE PIE

3 egg whites
Dash of salt
¾ cup sugar
¾ cup fine, chocolate wafer crumbs

½ cup pecans, chopped
½ teaspoon vanilla
Whipped cream

Beat egg whites with salt until soft peaks form. Fold in wafer crumbs, sugar, nuts, and vanilla. Spread in a lightly buttered pie plate. Bake at 325 degrees for 35 minutes. Cool and spread with sweetened whipped cream. Garnish with curls of unsweetened chocolate. Chill for at least 3 or 4 hours.
Mrs. Myron Scales
Mrs. Gordon Hill (Mary)

Desserts

FINNISH STRAWBERRY FOLDOVERS

½ cup butter	Confectioners' sugar
½ cup flour	2 cups milk
½ teaspoon salt	4 cups sliced strawberries
Dash of nutmeg	Whipped Cream
4 eggs	

Sweeten strawberries with a little sugar. Butter two 9-inch cake pans. Line each with buttered, waxed paper. In a large, heavy saucepan, melt butter, and remove from heat. Blend in flour, salt, and nutmeg; stir in milk. Cook over medium heat, stirring constantly until mixture boils for one minute and is very thick. Let cool for 15 minutes. Beat in eggs one at a time until well blended. Pour into prepared pans, dividing evenly. Bake at 400 degrees for 35 minutes until puffy and golden. Sprinkle each cake with confectioners' sugar. Spoon 1 cup of berries over half of each cake. Fold other half of cake over the berries, omelet style. Cover each cake with another cup of berries and sprinkle with additional confectioners' sugar. Cut into wedges and serve warm with whipped cream. Serves 8.
Mrs. James E. Preston (Sandra)

MACAROON TORTE

1 tablespoon unflavored gelatin	½ cup sugar
¼ cup cold water	2 egg whites
½ cup crushed pineapple	1 cup heavy cream, whipped
Hot water	1 8-ounce package macaroon cookies

Soften gelatin in cold water. Drain pineapple and reserve juice. Add enough hot water to pineapple juice to make ½ cup; add to gelatin mixture to dissolve. Chill until partially set. Crush cookies and line bottom of an 8-inch pan, reserving ¼ cup of crumbs. Add pineapple to gelatin. Gradually beat sugar into stiffly beaten egg whites. Fold in whipped cream and pour into pan. Garnish with crumbs. Chill.
Mrs. R. O. Middlemas   *St. Petersburg, Florida*

COVE TORTE

17 soda crackers
1 cup sugar
¾ cup pecans

3 egg whites
¼ teaspoon cream of tartar
1 teaspoon vanilla

Crumble soda crackers and add sugar and nuts. Beat egg whites with cream of tartar until stiff; add vanilla. Fold egg whites into cracker mixture. Pour into a well-buttered square pan and bake for 30 minutes at 350 degrees. Serve with vanilla ice cream topped with fruit or chocolate ice cream and creme de cacao.
Mrs. J. C. Harris (Ruby)   *Cove Hotel*

SPANISH FLAN

1 can condensed milk
1 cup milk
2 eggs

1 teaspoon vanilla
¼ teaspoon salt
1½ cups sugar

Beat eggs and mix with condensed milk. Add milk, vanilla, and salt. Melt sugar over low heat until brown. Pour sugar into casserole dish. Add custard. Place casserole dish in a pan ½ full of water and bake at 300 degrees for 1 to 1½ hours or until knife inserted comes out clean. Cool and serve.
Mrs. William E. Holland III (Hannelore)

CRÈME BRULÉE

2 cups heavy cream
4 egg yolks
2½ tablespoons sugar

½ teaspoon vanilla
Brown sugar

Scald cream in a saucepan. Beat egg yolks until thick and creamy. Beat in 2½ tablespoons sugar. Add hot cream very slowly, stirring constantly. Add vanilla. Pour into a baking dish. Place dish in a roasting pan filled with enough hot water to reach to ⅔ depth of the baking dish. Bake at 350 degrees for 1 hour. To finish, sift ⅓-inch layer of brown sugar on top of cream. Place under broiler 4 to 5 inches from heat until sugar melts and forms a hard crunchy crust. Watch closely. Chill. Serves 4.
Mrs. James E. Lewis, Jr. (Lida)

BOILED CUSTARD

1 quart milk
1 cup sugar
3 or 4 eggs

Pinch of salt
1 teaspoon vanilla

Scald milk. Beat eggs; add sugar and salt. Stir in hot milk and cook in a double boiler, stirring until mixture coats spoon. Cool and add vanilla.
Mrs. Ernest Bennett   *Hartsville, Alabama*

CREAM PUFFS

1 cup water
½ cup butter

1 cup flour
4 eggs

Bring water and butter to a boil. Add flour and beat well. Add eggs one at a time. Drop by a tablespoon onto a cooky sheet. Bake at 425 degrees for 25 minutes. Split and fill with filling. Makes 12-15 puffs.
Filling:

2 cups milk
5 tablespoons flour
⅔ cup sugar

2 eggs, beaten
2 tablespoons butter
1 teaspoon vanilla

Scald milk and add butter. Mix flour and sugar together and gradually add milk. Cook until mixture begins to thicken. Gradually add some of the milk mixture to the eggs. Then pour egg mixture back to milk mixture and cook until thickened; add vanilla.
Mrs. Curtis Bane (Ann)

BREAD PUDDING

2 eggs
½ cup sugar
1 teaspoon vanilla
2 cups milk

6 slices white bread
Pinch of salt
½ small can pineapple chunks
Small box raisins (optional)

Mix eggs, sugar, vanilla, and salt. Add milk. Tear bread into small pieces. Stir into mixture and let stand about 5 minutes. Add pineapple and raisins. Stir until mixed well. Pour into 10-inch pie pan. Bake at 375 degrees for 40 minutes.
Mrs. Michael Wynn (Diane)

CHOCOLATE ICEBOX PUDDING

1 package chocolate morsels
2 tablespoons sugar
1 tablespoon water
1 tablespoon butter

6 eggs, separated
1 package lady fingers
Whipping cream
(optional)

Heat first four ingredients until chocolate melts. Add egg yolks one at a time, beating after each addition. Beat egg whites and fold into first mixture. Arrange lady fingers in a dish and cover with chocolate mixture. Refrigerate for 24 hours. Serve with whipped cream.
Mrs. Maurice Smith (Olive)

PEARS IN WINE

6 ripe, yellow pears
1 cup sugar
1 cup water

1 lemon, thinly sliced
⅓ cup red wine

Peel pears, leaving stems on, and core half-way up from bottom. Boil sugar and water with lemon, and cook pears until tender, for about 15 minutes. Remove pears, cook syrup 5 minutes longer. Remove from stove. Add wine and pears. Chill and serve.
Mrs. Hugh Nelson (Lila)

OZARK PUDDING

2 eggs
1½ cups sugar
5 tablespoons flour
3 teaspoons baking powder
¼ teaspoon salt

2 teaspoons vanilla
2 cups apples, chopped
1 cup pecans, chopped
Whipped cream

Beat eggs well and combine with remaining ingredients. Place mixture in a 2-quart soufflé dish and bake at 350 degrees for 30 minutes. Serve with whipped cream.
Mrs. Troy Barker (Theo)

APPLE CRUMBLE

¾ cup sugar
¾ cup flour
½ cup water (approximately)
4 or 5 apples

Nutmeg (optional)
Cinnamon
¾ stick butter

Cut apples into small pieces and arrange in a greased baking dish. Pour water over apples and sprinkle spices on top. Mix sugar and flour together. Cut in butter and spread on top of apples. Bake at 350 degrees for about 40 minutes or until apples are done.
Mrs. W. G. Cornett (Ola)
Mrs. Robert Lee (Mildred)

FRESH FRUIT COBBLER

3-4 cups fruit, chopped and
   sugared
1 stick margarine
¾ cup milk

2 teaspoons baking powder
¼ teaspoon salt
¾ cup flour
1 cup sugar

Melt margarine in a Pyrex dish. Make a batter of remaining ingredients and pour over melted margarine. *Do not stir.* Pour fruit over mixture. Bake 1 hour at 350 degrees.
Note: Excellent with fresh blueberries, peaches, or blackberries.
Mrs. Murray Crowder (Harriet)
Mrs. John Bell (Ethel)

PINEAPPLE DELIGHT

2 large cans diced pineapple
   (reserve juice)
1 small package miniature
   marshmallows

1 tablespoon cornstarch
Milk
1 pint whipping cream
Maraschino cherries

Heat pineapple juice in double boiler. Mix cornstarch with enough milk and hot pineapple juice to form a paste. Add paste to remaining pineapple juice. Cook until mixture thickens. Pour hot mixture over pineapple and marshmallows which have been sugared. Chill and serve. Garnish with sweetened whipped cream and cherries.
Mrs. Foster H. Kruse (Helen)

CHERRY DELIGHT

1 cup flour
1¼ cups sugar
1 teaspoon baking soda
1 teaspoon cinnamon
½ teaspoon salt
1 tablespoon butter, melted
1 egg, beaten

2 cups sour cherries, drained
  (reserve 1 cup juice)
½ teaspoon almond extract
½ cup English walnuts or pecans,
  chopped
Whipping cream

Sift together dry ingredients. Combine remaining ingredients and add to flour mixture. Bake in a 9-inch square pan at 350 degrees for 45 minutes. Cut into squares and serve with hot Cherry Sauce and whipped cream.
Cherry Sauce:

1 cup cherry juice
1 tablespoon cornstarch
½ cup sugar
¼ teaspoon almond extract

1 tablespoon butter
Dash of salt
1 teaspoon red food coloring

Combine all ingredients and cook for 10 minutes stirring constantly. Reheat to serve.
Mrs. Harvey Brewton (Lillie)

LEMON FLUFF

1 3-ounce package lemon gelatin
1 large can evaporated milk
1 cup sugar

1½ cups hot water
½ cup lemon juice
2½ cups vanilla wafer crumbs

Chill milk for 3 or 4 hours. Dissolve gelatin in hot water and refrigerate until thickened but not firm. Whip until fluffy. Fold in lemon juice and sugar. Beat milk until thick like whipped cream. Fold into gelatin mixture. Line a 9x13-inch pan with crumbs, reserving some crumbs for top. Pour lemon mixture over crust. Sprinkle top with remaining crumbs. Chill until ready to serve.
Mrs. Curtis Bane (Ann)

LEMON SOUFFLÉ

1 cup sugar	4 eggs, separated
4 tablespoons butter	2 cups milk
4 tablespoons flour	Juice of 2 lemons

Cream butter and sugar together and add flour. Add lemon juice to the egg yolks. Mix well. Combine mixtures and add milk. Beat egg whites until stiff and fold into the above mixture. Pour into a soufflé dish and set in a pan of cold water. Bake at 325 degrees for about 40 minutes or until done.
Miss Eloise Wall   *El Dorado, Arkansas*

PECAN SOUFFLÉ

¼ cup butter	½ cup sugar
¼ cup flour	1 cup pecans, finely chopped
½ teaspoon salt	1 teaspoon vanilla
1 cup milk	1 cup whipped cream
3 eggs, separated	½ teaspoon grated lemon rind

Melt butter in double boiler. Stir in flour and salt. Gradually add milk, stirring constantly until a thick paste is formed. Combine beaten yolks, sugar, pecans, and vanilla, mixing well. To this add butter mixture and stir until well blended. Beat egg whites until stiff and carefully fold in. Turn into a buttered soufflé dish or casserole. Place in a pan of hot water and bake at 350 degrees for 45 to 60 minutes or until set. Serve at once with whipped cream to which lemon rind has been added. Serves 6.
The Editors

POT DE CRÈME

1 6-ounce package semi-sweet	1 egg
chocolate	1 teaspoon vanilla
2 tablespoons sugar	¾ cup milk
Dash of salt	Whipped cream

Combine all ingredients except milk in blender. Scald milk and pour into blender. Blend at high speed for one minute. Pour mixture into pot de crème cups or small serving dishes. Chill three hours or until firm. Top with whipped cream. Serves 6.
Mrs. Florence Stewart
Editors' Variation: Flavor the whipped cream with Myers rum and top with toasted slivered almonds.

CHARLOTTE RUSSE

3 eggs, separated
1 cup milk
5 tablespoons rum
½ cup sugar
1 package lady fingers

1 envelope unflavored gelatin
½ pint whipping cream
¼ cup cold water
Cherries (optional)
Chocolate curls (optional)

Scald milk in double boiler. Cool slightly. Pour over egg yolks and sugar. Cook until mixture coats spoon. Combine gelatin and water. Add mixture to gelatin gradually. Cool. Whip cream and add to mixture. Fold beaten egg whites and rum into mixture. Arrange lady fingers in mold and add charlotte. Garnish with cherries. Let set overnight in refrigerator.
Mrs. Charles Lahan (Ann)

ALMOND BISQUE

22 large marshmallows
½ cup milk
Graham cracker crumbs

1 pint whipping cream
2 teaspoons almond extract
Cherries

Pour milk over marshmallows and melt in double boiler. Don't get mixture too hot. When melted, cool pan in ice water. Add almond extract. Whip ½ pint cream and fold into marshmallow mixture. Line an 8-inch square pan with cracker crumbs and spread mixture over. Cover with a light sprinkling of crumbs and freeze. Slice and serve with remaining whipped cream and cherries.
Mrs. J. C. Harris (Ruby)   *Cove Hotel*
Mrs. John Colmery (Maxine)

ICEBOX PINEAPPLE DELIGHT

1 pound vanilla wafers
1½ cups confectioners'
    sugar
1 No. 2 can crushed pineapple

1 cup nuts, chopped
½ cup butter
2 eggs, beaten
½ pint whipping cream

Butter a 13x9x2-inch pan. Roll vanilla wafers and spread half of crumbs on bottom of pan. Cream butter and sugar. Add eggs and beat until smooth and creamy; spread over wafers. Combine drained pineapple, nuts, and whipped cream. Spread on top of egg mixture and sprinkle remainder of crumbs on top. Chill for 24 hours. Cut into squares and garnish with whipped cream and cherries.
Mrs. Lester C. Brock (Martha)

STRAWBERRIES ROMANOFF

2 quarts strawberries,   ½ pint whipping cream
  sugared   Juice of 1 lemon
1 pint vanilla ice cream   4 ounces Cointreau

Whip ice cream slightly and fold in whipped cream. Add lemon juice and liqueur. Pour over whole chilled strawberries.
Mrs. Clark Whitehorn (Ginny)

NORVEGIENNE PENNYE
(Baked Alaska Pennye)

1 loaf pound cake   ½ teaspoon lemon juice
2 pints Neapolitan brick ice cream   1 cup confectioners' sugar
4 egg whites   1 cup brandy
Pinch of salt

Beat egg whites with salt until frothy; add lemon juice and continue to beat until egg whites form soft peaks. Gradually fold in confectioners' sugar and continue to beat until glossy and stiff peaks form. Cut a ¾-inch slice from bottom of cake and place on an oven proof platter or dish. Cover cake with ice cream trying to shape like a loaf pound cake. Slice remaining cake into three thin layers. Place one layer on top of ice cream. Cut second layer to fit sides and third layer to fit ends. Completely enclose ice cream with cake, trimming ends to fit neatly. Spread cake completely with 1-inch layer of meringue. Bake at 425 degrees for 6 to 8 minutes or until golden. Place in freezer until ready to serve. Pour brandy over cake and flame. Serves 8.
Mrs. George Jenkins, Jr.   *Lafayette, Louisiana*

MAPLE PARFAIT

4 egg yolks   1 pint whipping cream
1 cup pure maple syrup

Beat eggs until very light; add syrup. Cook in double boiler until mixture coats a metal spoon. Chill and add one pint of cream, whipped very stiff. Cover with foil and let freeze until firm.
Mrs. John Henry Sherman (Ruth)

BANANAS FOSTER

3 tablespoons brown sugar
3 tablespoons butter
2 tablespoons banana liqueur
⅛ teaspoon cinnamon

1 large ripe banana
2 ounces white rum
1 tablespoon lemon juice
Vanilla ice cream

Peel banana and slice lengthwise. Sauté in sugar and butter until tender. Sprinkle with lemon juice and dust with cinnamon. Heat liqueur and rum. Add to banana mixture and set aflame, basting the banana until the flame dies out. Serve over vanilla ice cream. Serves 2.
Miss Carol Jean Lewis

VANILLA ICE CREAM

½ gallon milk
1 large can evaporated milk
2 cups sugar

6 eggs, well beaten
1 teaspoon salt
3 tablespoons vanilla

Combine all ingredients, except vanilla, in a large, heavy saucepan. Cook over low heat, stirring constantly, until custard forms a coating on a metal spoon. Mashed peaches or strawberries may be added if the milk is decreased. Freeze in ice cream freezer.
Mrs. Earl Preston (Lois)

FRENCH VANILLA ICE CREAM

6 egg yolks
¼ teaspoon salt
2 cups milk

2 cups heavy cream
1 cup sugar
3 teaspoons vanilla

In a double boiler, beat egg yolks and milk with a rotary beater. Add sugar and salt. Cook over simmering water, stirring constantly, until mixture coats a metal spoon. Let cool; then add cream and vanilla. Freeze in an ice cream freezer. Makes about 1½ quarts.
Mrs. H. C. Smith, Jr. (Joyce)

BANANA ICE CREAM

6 bananas
Juice of ½ lemon
3 large cans Pet Milk, chilled

½ pint whipping cream
2½ cups sugar
Milk

In a blender purée bananas adding lemon juice to prevent darkening. Beat whipping cream and set aside. Beat Pet Milk until it becomes foamy and doubles in bulk. Add sugar slowly and continue beating. Combine whipped cream, Pet Milk, and bananas; put in a freezer container. Fill to "fill line" with milk and freeze. Makes 6 quarts.
Variation: Add chopped nuts or strawberries to taste.
Mrs. Joe Keller (Jane)

CHOCOLATE ICE CREAM

1½ squares unsweetened chocolate
    or ¼ cup cocoa
1 cup sugar
⅓ cup hot water

Dash of salt
1 tablespoon vanilla
1 quart half and half cream

In a double boiler, melt chocolate; combine with sugar, water, and cook until smooth. Add salt and vanilla; cool. Add cream and freeze in ice cream freezer.
Mrs. Owen Reese, Jr. (Anne)

MOCHA CHIP ICE CREAM

3 egg yolks
2 cans Eagle Brand milk
½ pint whipping cream
½ gallon milk

1 tablespoon instant coffee
2 teaspoons vanilla
1 German chocolate bar, grated
1 cup nuts, chopped

Make a paste of the instant coffee and a little water. Mix a small amount of milk with egg yolks in blender. Add remaining ingredients, except ½ gallon milk. (German chocolate bar will grate in blender if small pieces are added one at a time.) Pour into ice cream freezer and fill to "fill line" with milk. Freeze as directed. Makes 1 gallon.
Mrs. Joe Keller (Jane)

Tea Time

SPICED PECANS

1 cup sugar
¼ teaspoon cream of tartar
½ teaspoon cinnamon

¼ cup water
2 cups pecans
½ teaspoon vanilla

Combine sugar, cream of tartar, cinnamon, and water. Cook to soft ball stage. Add vanilla and pecans. Stir until pecans are sugary. Pour onto waxed paper and separate pecans.
Mrs. Chester H. Pelt, Jr. (Libbi)

ORANGE BALLS

1 pound vanilla wafer crumbs
1 package confectioners' sugar
1 6-ounce can orange juice

1 stick margarine, melted
1 can coconut
1 cup nuts, finely chopped

Mix together all ingredients except coconut. Form into balls and roll in coconut. Refrigerate.
Variation: Graham cracker crumbs may be substituted for vanilla wafers.
Mrs. Jack Segler (Patty)
Mrs. James R. Patterson (Wanda)
Mrs. John Boling (Martha)

ORANGE SUGARED PECANS

1½ cups sugar
¼ cup water
3 tablespoons frozen orange juice concentrate

½ teaspoon orange rind, grated
Dash or two of cinnamon
3 cups pecan halves

Combine sugar, water, and juice in a saucepan. Bring to a boil over medium heat, stirring constantly. Boil slowly, without stirring, to 240 degrees on candy thermometer or soft boil stage. Remove from heat. Add orange rind, cinnamon, and pecans. Stir until syrup begins to look cloudy. Pour mixture onto a large piece of waxed paper making one layer. Let cool and separate pecans.
Mrs. Owen Reese, Jr. (Anne)

PEANUT BUTTER BALLS

1 12-ounce jar creamy
   peanut butter
2 sticks butter or oleo, melted
1½ boxes confectioners' sugar

Dash of salt
1 6-ounce package chocolate chips
2 ounces paraffin

Combine peanut butter, sugar, butter, and salt. Shape into balls. Melt paraffin and chips in a double boiler. Dip balls in chocolate, using a pick. Place on waxed paper. May be frozen.
Miss Kathleen Pilcher   *Charleston, South Carolina*

CRÈME DE MENTHE BALLS

1 cup vanilla wafer crumbs
¾ cup pecans, finely chopped
1 cup confectioners' sugar

2 tablespoons light
   or dark corn syrup
½ cup white or green crème de menthe

Combine vanilla wafer crumbs, pecans, and sugar. Add corn syrup and crème de menthe, blending with a fork to make a stiff dough. Form into balls and roll in confectioners' sugar. Chill overnight. Store in an air tight container.
Mrs. Richard Laird (Judi)

BOURBON BALLS

1 6-ounce package
   semi-sweet chocolate morsels
½ cup sugar
3 tablespoons light corn syrup

⅓ cup bourbon
2½ cups vanilla wafers,
   finely crushed
1 cup walnuts, finely chopped

Melt chocolate in double boiler. Remove from water and stir in sugar and syrup; blend in bourbon. Combine wafers, walnuts, chocolate mixture, and mix well. Form into one-inch balls and roll in granulated sugar. Allow to ripen in covered container for several days.
Mrs. James E. Carter (Jeri)

BOURBON CANDY

1 pound box confectioners' sugar
2 tablespoons butter
⅓ cup bourbon
Pecans

1 pound Baker's chocolate
2 tablespoons paraffin
1 tablespoon butter

Mix together confectioners' sugar, softened butter, and bourbon. Cover and refrigerate for 3 hours. Shape into small balls placing a pecan in the center of each. If preferred, mix crushed pecans in with the mixture before chilling. After balls are formed, chill again. Make chocolate coating by mixing together the melted chocolate, paraffin, and 1 tablespoon of butter. Using a small skewer, dip balls into coating. Place balls on waxed paper.
Mrs. J. C. Harris (Ruby)   *Cove Hotel*

DATE NUT MERINGUES

3 egg whites
1 cup sugar
1 package dates, chopped

1½ cups pecans, chopped
½ teaspoon vanilla

Beat egg whites until stiff and gradually add sugar. Add dates, pecans, and vanilla. Mix well. Drop on greased cooky sheet and bake at 325 degrees for 12 to 15 minutes.
Mrs. J. C. Harris (Ruby)   *Cove Hotel*

PECAN PUFFS

2 egg whites
2 cups sifted confectioners' sugar
1 teaspoon vinegar

1 teaspoon vanilla extract
2 cups pecans

Beat egg whites until stiff, but not dry, gradually adding sugar. Stir in remaining ingredients. Drop by ½ teaspoonful, two inches apart, onto a greased cooky sheet. Top with pecans which have been broken into quarters. Bake in a preheated 300 degree oven for 12 to 15 minutes.
Mrs. C. H. Beach (Callie)

SHRIMP STACKS

2 cans small shrimp
1 cup celery, finely chopped
Mayonnaise, enough to
  moisten

2 8-ounce packages
  cream cheese, softened
Coffee cream or milk
1 large loaf bread

Stack three pieces of bread; trim crusts and cut in half. Add cream or milk to cream cheese until moist enough to spread. Combine shrimp, celery, and mayonnaise into a spread. Stack layers of bread, shrimp mixture, bread, shrimp mixture, bread in that order. Cover top and sides with cream cheese mixture. Chill on cooky sheet overnight. Slice into bite-sized sandwiches.
Mrs. Jack Dyer (Jill)

MERINGUE PUFFS

2 egg whites
¾ cup sugar
⅛ teaspoon salt

⅛ teaspoon cream of tartar
1 cup chocolate chips
1 cup pecans, chopped

Beat 2 egg whites until soft peaks form. Add sugar, cream of tartar, and salt; beat until stiff. Fold in chocolate chips and pecans. Drop by teaspoonfuls onto a cooky sheet lined with waxed paper. Bake at 300 degrees for 20 minutes.
Mrs. James R. Patterson (Wanda)

PECAN SANDIES

1 stick butter
3 tablespoons confectioners' sugar
1¼ cups flour

½ teaspoon vanilla
½ cup pecans, chopped

Cream butter and sugar. Add remaining ingredients. Shape as desired. Bake on ungreased cooky sheet at 300 degrees for 30 minutes. Roll in confectioners' sugar while still warm. Yields 3 dozen.
Mrs. Jim Dunkerly (June)

SWEDISH TOSCAS

1½ sticks butter	2 cups flour
½ cup sugar	

Cream butter and sugar and blend in flour. Press dough into small, ungreased muffin tins. Bake at 350 degrees for 10 minutes or until pastry is slightly brown on edges.

Filling:

1 cup sugar	1 cup almonds or pecans, chopped
8 tablespoons butter or oleo	1 teaspoon almond or vanilla
6 tablespoons heavy cream or	extract
Pet Milk	8 teaspoons flour

Combine ingredients and stir constantly in saucepan until bubbly and thickened. Spoon into pastry. Bake about 15 minutes. Garnish with whipped cream and crystallized fruit. Makes 60.

Mrs. H. Mack Lewis (Eleanor)

BLACK BOTTOM CUPS

1 8-ounce package cream cheese	1 6-ounce package semi-sweet
1 egg white	chocolate chips
⅓ cup sugar	1 teaspoon vanilla
Pinch of salt	½ teaspoon almond extract

Combine ingredients except for chocolate chips in a small bowl and mix well. Stir in chocolate chips. Set mixture aside.

1 cup sugar	⅓ cup oil
¼ cup cocoa	1 cup water
1 teaspoon baking soda	1 tablespoon vinegar
1½ cups flour, sifted	1 teaspoon vanilla
½ teaspoon salt	Chopped nuts

Sift dry ingredients together. Add remaining ingredients except nuts and mix well. Fill paper muffin cups ⅓ full with chocolate batter. Top each with a heaping teaspoon of cream cheese mixture. Sprinkle with nuts. Bake at 350 degrees for 25-30 minutes. Makes 2 dozen.

Mrs. Lester Brock (Martha)

CHEESE KRISPIES I

1 stick margarine
1 cup sharp cheese, grated
1 cup flour

¼-⅓ teaspoon salt
1 cup Rice Krispies
Dash of cayenne pepper

Cream softened cheese and margarine together with mixer. Turn off mixer. Stir in flour, salt, pepper, and Rice Krispies. Drop by teaspoonfuls onto a greased cooky sheet. Bake 15-20 minutes at 350 degrees. Store in a tight container after cooling. Yields 40.
Miss Carol Jean Lewis

CHEESE KRISPIES II

2 cups flour
¼ teaspoon salt
½ teaspoon paprika
1 teaspoon sugar

2 sticks oleo
½ pound extra sharp
   Cheddar cheese
2 cups Rice Krispies

Cream oleo with grated cheese. Sift flour, salt, paprika, and sugar together. Add to creamed mixture and mix well. Add 2 cups Rice Krispies. Drop by teaspoonfuls onto a baking sheet. Mash flat and bake at 320-350 degrees until golden. Yields 8 dozen.
Mrs. Charley Gramling, III (Jo Ann)

LEMON TARTS

1 3-ounce package
   cream cheese

1 cup flour
1 stick margarine

Cream cheese and margarine. Add flour. Mix well and shape into a ball. Refrigerate for 20 minutes for better handling. Form crust (thick enough to prevent custard from seeping through) to fit into mini-muffin pans. Trim excess crust from top of muffin tin for easy removal. Fill with custard and bake at 350 degrees for approximately 20 minutes. Cool well before removing. Makes 24 tarts.
Custard:
2 egg yolks
1 cup sugar

2 tablespoons butter, melted
3 tablespoons lemon juice

Beat egg yolks. Add sugar and mix well. Add melted butter and lemon juice.
Mrs. S. A. Lawhorne   *Pine Bluff, Arkansas*

TOLL HOUSE CUPCAKES

½ cup butter, softened
6 tablespoons sugar
6 tablespoons brown sugar
½ teaspoon vanilla

1 egg
1 cup plus 2 tablespoons sifted flour
½ teaspoon baking soda
½ teaspoon salt

Combine first four ingredients and beat until creamy. Add the egg. Sift together the dry ingredients and stir into the butter mixture. Spoon by rounded tablespoons into paper-lined muffin tins. Bake at 375 degrees for 10 to 12 minutes. Remove from oven and spoon 1 tablespoon of topping over each cupcake. Return cupcakes to oven and bake for an additional 15 minutes.

Topping:

1 cup brown sugar, firmly packed
1 egg
⅛ teaspoon salt

½ cup nuts, chopped
1 cup semi-sweet chocolate chips
½ teaspoon vanilla

Mix together brown sugar, egg, and salt. Stir in nuts, chips, and vanilla. Makes 18.

Mrs. Kent Hall (Isabel)

DOUBLE DELIGHT

2½ cups sugar
1 cup evaporated milk
½ stick butter
¼ teaspoon salt
1½ cups miniature marshmallows
¾ cup nuts, chopped

1 teaspoon vanilla
1 package semi-sweet chocolate morsels
1 package milk chocolate morsels

In a large saucepan combine sugar, milk, butter, and salt. Bring mixture to a boil and boil for 6 minutes. Remove and stir in marshmallows, nuts, and vanilla. After marshmallows have melted, divide the mixture. To half of it, add semi-sweet chocolate and stir until melted. Pour into an 8-inch square buttered pan. To the remaining mixture add the milk chocolate. When chocolate has melted, pour mixture over first layer. Chill and cut into squares.

Mrs. Richard Green (Vicki)

DIVINITY

1 cup light Karo syrup	4 large egg whites
5 cups sugar	2¼ teaspoons vanilla extract
½ teaspoon salt	2½ cups walnuts, chopped
1 cup water	

Combine first four ingredients in a heavy saucepan. Cook over medium heat stirring until sugar has dissolved. Stop stirring, but continue cooking mixture to a firm-ball stage (248 degrees on a candy thermometer). Before syrup reaches 248 degrees, beat egg whites until stiff. Pour half of syrup over beaten egg whites a little at a time, beating constantly. Cook other half of syrup until soft crack stage (272 degrees on a candy thermometer). Pour slowly over egg whites and first half of mixture; continue to beat constantly until mixture holds its shape. Add vanilla and nuts. Drop from a teaspoon onto waxed paper. Makes about 2½ pounds of candy.
Note: Recipe may *not* be doubled.
Mrs. Philip Smith (Ann)

SHORTBREAD

1 pound oleo or butter	Pinch of salt
1 cup sugar	4½ cups flour

Sift sugar over the flour. Using hands, work softened butter into ingredients. Add salt. Flatten dough to ½ inch thick. Cut with cooky cutter. Bake on cooky sheet at 350 degrees for 20 minutes.
Mrs. Charles Hewitt   Birmingham, Alabama

STRAWBERRY JAM BARS

2 sticks butter	1 cup sugar
2 cups unsifted flour	1 cup nuts, chopped
2 egg yolks	1 cup strawberry jam

Cream butter and sugar together. Add egg yolks. Gradually add flour. Stir in nuts. Divide batter and spread half of it into a buttered 9-inch square pan. Spread the other half on waxed paper and shape into a 9-inch square. Place in refrigerator as this makes handling easier. Spread jam on batter in pan. Place refrigerated batter on top. Bake at 325 degrees for 55 minutes. Cool. Cut into bars.
Mrs. Kent Hall (Isabel)

FUDGE BROWNIES

2 sticks margarine	Pinch of salt
2 tablespoons cocoa	1½ cups flour
4 eggs, beaten	1½ cups pecans, chopped
2 cups sugar	2 teaspoons vanilla extract
1 teaspoon baking powder	4 cups miniature marshmallows

Melt margarine and cocoa in a skillet; set aside. Combine eggs and sugar and beat well. Add flour, baking powder, and salt; mix well. Add chocolate mixture, pecans, and vanilla. Pour into a greased 13x9x2-inch pan and bake at 325 degrees for 30 minutes. Remove brownies from oven and cover top with marshmallows. Brownies may need to go back in oven long enough for marshmallows to melt slightly. After brownies have cooled, spread with frosting.

Frosting:

1 box confectioners' sugar	1 teaspoon vanilla
1 stick margarine	3 tablespoons milk
2 tablespoons cocoa	

Combine sugar and margarine in a mixer; add milk slowly. Add cocoa and vanilla.

Mrs. Buford Ennis (Dot)

LEMON BARS

1 stick butter	¼ teaspoon salt
¼ cup confectioners' sugar	3 tablespoons fresh lemon juice
1 cup flour	2 tablespoons flour
2 eggs	½ teaspoon baking powder
1 cup sugar	

Cream butter, confectioners' sugar, and 1 cup flour together. Spread evenly in an 8-inch square pan. Cook at 350 degrees for 15 minutes. Beat eggs and mix with remaining ingredients. Spread over cooked pastry. Bake at 325 degrees for 30 minutes. Cool. Sprinkle with additional confectioners' sugar. Cut into oblong finger shapes. Store in refrigerator.

Mrs. Foster H. Kruse (Helen)
Mrs. William Carter, III   Lumpkin, Georgia

PINEAPPLE FLAKE SQUARES

3 cups flour
3 tablespoons sugar
3 teaspoons baking powder
Pinch of salt

2 sticks oleo
½ cup sour cream
3 egg yolks
1 egg white

Sift flour, baking powder, and salt together. Work in oleo as for pie dough. Add egg yolks and sour cream. Mix with knife. Roll out ⅔ of dough on floured cooky sheet. Spread with pineapple filling. Roll out remaining ⅓ dough about 13x8 inches. Cut into ½-inch strips. Lay strips criss cross over filling. Beat one egg white slightly and brush over strips; sprinkle with sugar. Bake on cooky sheet at 350 degrees for 30 to 40 minutes, or until golden brown. Cool. Cut into 2-inch squares.

Pineapple Filling:

1 No. 2 can crushed pineapple,
   undrained
1 cup sugar

½ cup orange juice
3½ tablespoons cornstarch

Combine all ingredients and cook until thick. Cool.
Mrs. Victor P. Frohlich (Dorothy)

PEANUT BUTTER BROWNIES

¾ cup cocoa
½ cup plus 2 tablespoons shortening
½ cup plus 2 tablespoons peanut
   butter
1¾ cup plus 2 tablespoons
   sugar

5 eggs
3 teaspoons vanilla
1 cup plus 2 tablespoons flour,
   sifted
2 teaspoons baking powder
½ teaspoon salt

Cream shortening, peanut butter, and sugar together. Add eggs and vanilla, mixing well. Sift dry ingredients together and stir into creamed mixture until well blended. Spread ½-inch thick in a greased 8x8-inch baking dish. Bake at 350 degrees for 25-30 minutes.

Glaze:

2 cups confectioners' sugar
3 tablespoons cocoa

¼ cup warm milk or water

Combine above ingredients and spread on brownies while still warm.
Mrs. Lester C. Brock (Martha)

OLD-FASHIONED TEA CAKES

1 cup sugar
½ cup oleo
1 egg
2½ cups flour

2 teaspoons baking powder
¼ cup milk
1 teaspoon vanilla

Cream sugar and oleo; add egg and beat well. Sift flour with baking powder. Add to sugar mixture alternately with milk and vanilla. Chill well. Roll thin and cut with cooky cutter. Place on greased pan; bake at 350 degrees until light brown. Makes approximately two dozen large cakes.
Mrs. Milton Gray (Helen)

DREAM BARS

1 stick butter
½ cup brown sugar
1 cup flour
2 eggs
1 cup sugar
2 tablespoons flour
¼ teaspoon salt

½ teaspoon baking powder
1 teaspoon vanilla
1 cup coconut
1 cup nuts, chopped
1 tablespoon butter
2 tablespoons lemon juice
1 cup confectioners' sugar

Combine stick of butter, brown sugar, and 1 cup of flour. Press mixture into 9x13-inch Pyrex dish. Bake at 350 degrees for 15 minutes. Combine remaining ingredients except butter, lemon juice, and confectioners' sugar. Spread mixture over crust. Bake for 30 minutes more. Cool slightly and top with mixture of butter, lemon juice, and confectioners' sugar. Cut into squares.
Mrs. W. P. Wilson (Lennie)

HELLO DOLLY SQUARES

1 stick margarine
1 cup graham cracker crumbs
1 cup pecans, chopped

1 small package chocolate chips
1 cup coconut
1 can sweetened condensed milk

Melt margarine. Layer ingredients in a 7x12-inch dish in order listed. Bake at 350 degrees for 45 minutes. Cool and cut into squares.
Mrs. Richard Morley (Ellenor)
Mrs. Thomas H. Gregory   *St. Petersburg, Florida*
Variation: Add one package of butterscotch bits after the chopped pecans.
Mrs. J. C. Harris (Ruby)   *Cove Hotel*
Mrs. Milton Acton (Lois)

ALMOND BARS

1 cup butter
¾ cup sugar
1 egg, separated
½ cup almond paste, softened

2 cups flour, sifted
¼ cup sliced almonds
1 teaspoon almond extract

Cream butter and sugar. Beat egg yolk into the butter-sugar mixture. Beat in almond paste and extract until smooth. Add flour until well blended. Press into a 9x9x2-inch ungreased pan. Beat egg white until frothy; brush over the top of the dough. Cover with almond slices. Bake in preheated oven at 350 degrees for 35 minutes or until golden brown. Cool completely on a wire rack before cutting into bars.
Note: Do not substitute prepared almond filling for the paste.
Mrs. Lester C. Brock (Martha)

CHARLESTON MUD HENS

¾ stick butter
1 cup sugar
2 eggs
1 cup flour, sifted

1 tablespoon baking powder
¼ teaspoon salt
½ teaspoon vanilla

Cream butter and sugar together. Add eggs, then flour, which has been sifted with baking powder and salt. Add vanilla. Spread mixture in a greased 9x13-inch pan.

2 eggs
1½ cups brown sugar
1½ cups pecans, chopped
2 tablespoons flour
2 tablespoons lemon juice

½ teaspoon baking powder
½ teaspoon salt
1 teaspoon vanilla
1½ cups confectioners' sugar
1 tablespoon butter or oleo

Combine above ingredients except confectioners' sugar, softened butter, and lemon juice. Spread over first mixture. Bake at 350 degrees for 25 minutes or until done. Cool. Combine confectioners' sugar and softened butter with just enough lemon juice to obtain spreading consistency. Spread over top and cut into squares.
Mrs. H. Mack Lewis (Eleanor)

BENNE WAFERS

2 cups flour
1 cup sugar
1 stick oleo
1 stick butter

1 egg, separated
2 teaspoons vanilla
½ cup nuts or lightly
   toasted sesame seeds

Combine all ingredients except nuts and egg white. Beat with mixer until light and fluffy. Spread on ungreased cooky sheet. Lightly beat egg white and spread over top. Sprinkle with nuts or sesame seeds. Bake at 250 degrees for 45 minutes to 1 hour. Cool and cut.
Mrs. William Carter, Sr.   *Lumpkin, Georgia*

COCONUT-ORANGE SQUARES

⅔ cup flour, sifted
½ teaspoon baking powder
½ teaspoon salt
¼ cup butter
1 cup sugar
1 egg

1 tablespoon milk
1 teaspoon orange rind, grated
1 cup flaked coconut
4 squares semi-sweet
   chocolate, melted

Sift flour with baking powder and salt. Cream butter. Gradually add sugar; cream until light and fluffy. Add egg, milk, and orange rind; beat well. Add flour mixture and coconut, mixing only enough to blend. Place in an 8-inch square pan which has been lined with paper and then greased. Bake at 350 degrees for 25 minutes. Remove from pan and trim off edges. Spread with melted chocolate. Cool. Cut into squares. Yield: 12 servings.
Variation: Alternate baking pan. This may also be baked in a 9x5-inch loaf pan. Increase baking time to 30 minutes. Cool. Cut into bars. Yield: 12 servings.
Mrs. Foster H. Kruse (Helen)

MARSHMALLOW SQUARES

1 cup sugar
2 eggs, beaten
⅔ cup butter
2¾ cups graham cracker crumbs

1 package miniature marshmallows
½ cup nuts, chopped
1 package chocolate morsels

Combine sugar, eggs, and butter. Cook in double boiler for 30 minutes. Cool and pour over remaining ingredients except chocolate. Mix well and press in an oblong pan. Melt chocolate and spread on top. Refrigerate until chocolate is hard. Cut in squares.
Mrs. James C. Feltman (Shirley)

ICEBOX COOKIES

1½ sticks butter
½ box dark brown sugar
1 egg, slightly beaten

3 cups flour, sifted
2 teaspoons baking powder
1-2 cups nuts, chopped

Cream butter and sugar. Add beaten egg. Add remaining ingredients and mix well. Make rolls of dough and wrap in waxed paper. Refrigerate overnight. Slice and place on greased cooky sheet. Bake at 370 degrees for 10-12 minutes. The tops of cookies do not brown. Remove from cooky sheet while hot. The rolls of dough may be kept in the refrigerator for a week. Cookies may be frozen after baking.
Mrs. Albert M. Lewis, Jr. (Jean)

FROSTED DELIGHTS

1½ cups cake flour, sifted
½ teaspoon salt
1 teaspoon baking powder
½ cup shortening
1 cup sugar

2 eggs, beaten
½ teaspoon vanilla
1 cup brown sugar
1 egg white
1 cup pecans, chopped

Sift together flour, salt, and baking powder. Cream shortening with sugar until fluffy. Add vanilla, eggs, and sifted ingredients; mix well. Spread batter on greased baking sheet. Spread thin. Sift brown sugar and fold into beaten egg white. Spread over batter and sprinkle with nuts. Bake in slow oven at 325 degrees for 30 minutes. Cut into squares and remove from sheet while warm.
Mrs. Buford Ennis (Dot)

CANDY BAR MELT-AWAYS

1 roll Pillsbury Slice and Bake
  Cookies (any variety)
18 to 20 junior size Mars bars

½ cup graham cracker crumbs
½ cup nuts, chopped

Slice cooky dough into ¼-inch slices. Place slices in 13x9-inch pan. Press together to form flat crust. Bake at 375 degrees for 12 to 15 minutes until golden brown. Remove from oven. Arrange candy evenly over crust. Return to oven 2 to 3 minutes until candy softens. With spatula quickly spread candy. Sprinkle with mixture of crumbs and nuts, pressing slightly. Cool and cut into bars.
Mrs. Kent Hall (Isabel)

HAWAIIAN DROP COOKIES

2 cups unsifted flour
2 teaspoons baking powder
¼ teaspoon salt
⅔ cup shortening
1¼ cups sugar
1 cup pecans, finely chopped

½ teaspoon vanilla
½ teaspoon almond extract
1 egg
¾ cup crushed pineapple,
  well drained
½ cup coconut

Cream shortening. Add sugar and flavorings and beat until smooth. Add egg and beat mixture until fluffy. Blend in pineapple, nuts, and the sifted dry ingredients and drop by teaspoonfuls on ungreased cooky sheet about 3 inches apart. Sprinkle with coconut and bake at 325 degrees for about 20 minutes.

Mrs. Gordon Hindsman (Helen)

SNICKERDOODLES

1 cup soft shortening
1½ cups sugar
2 eggs
2¾ cups sifted flour
2 teaspoons cream of tartar

1 teaspoon soda
½ teaspoon salt
2 tablespoons sugar
2 teaspoons cinnamon

Cream shortening and sugar together. Add eggs and mix well. Sift flour, cream of tartar, soda, and salt together and add to first mixture. Chill dough. Shape into balls the size of small walnuts. Roll in a mixture of 2 tablespoons sugar and 2 teaspoons cinnamon. Place about two inches apart on an ungreased cooky sheet. Bake at 400 degrees for 8 to 10 minutes. Makes about 5 dozen.

Mrs. James C. Feltman (Shirley)

CHINESE CHEWS

1 cup dates, chopped
1 cup nuts, chopped
1 cup sugar
1 cup flour
½ teaspoon baking powder

Pinch of salt
¼ cup butter, melted
2 eggs, well beaten
½ teaspoon vanilla
Confectioners' sugar

Mix together all ingredients. Bake in an 8-inch square pan at 350 degrees for 25 to 30 minutes. Cut into small squares and roll in confectioners' sugar.

Mrs. Robert Porter (Betty)

CRISP COOKIES

½ cup butter, melted
½ cup brown sugar
½ cup sugar
1 egg
1 cup flour
1 teaspoon soda

½ teaspoon salt
1 cup quick-cooking rolled oats
1 cup Rice Krispies
1 cup flaked coconut
1 teaspoon vanilla

Combine ingredients. Drop by teaspoonfuls onto an ungreased cooky sheet. Bake at 350 degrees for 8 to 10 minutes.
Mrs. Harold C. Steadman (Elsie)

PEANUT BRITTLE

3 cups sugar
1 cup white Karo syrup
½ cup water
3 cups raw peanuts

3 tablespoons oleo
1 teaspoon salt
2 teaspoons baking soda

Boil sugar, syrup, and water until a thread spins (250 degrees on candy thermometer). Add peanuts and continue cooking, stirring constantly, until it becomes a brownish gold (300 degrees). Remove from heat and add remaining ingredients. Mix well. Quickly pour onto a clean, buttered counter-top as thin as possible. Immediately begin lifting up edges to facilitate cooling and break candy into pieces.
Mrs. Hugh H. Tucker (Betty)

MARTHA WASHINGTON CANDY

1 stick butter
1 can Eagle Brand milk
1 can coconut
1 quart pecans, chopped

1 12-ounce package chocolate chips
¼ pound or 1 stick paraffin
2 boxes confectioners' sugar

Combine first four ingredients and gradually add confectioners' sugar. Roll into balls and chill overnight. Melt chocolate chips and paraffin and dip the balls in the chocolate with a toothpick. Yields 80-90 balls of candy.
Mrs. T. Woodie Smith (Lois)

MELT IN THE MOUTH COOKIES

2 egg whites
⅔ cup sugar

1 cup nuts, chopped
1 cup semi-sweet chocolate morsels

Beat egg whites slightly. Gradually add sugar to egg whites while beating. Beat mixture until peaks form. Fold in nuts and chocolate. Drop by teaspoonfuls onto a greased cooky sheet and place in a preheated oven at 350 degrees. Immediately turn off heat and leave cookies in oven for 3 hours. Makes 70 small cookies.

Mrs. J. D. Donnelly

GINGERBREAD MEN

3¾ cups all-purpose flour
1 teaspoon baking soda
½ teaspoon salt
1 tablespoon cinnamon
2 teaspoons ground ginger
2 tablespoons cocoa
1 teaspoon ground cloves (optional)

1 cup margarine
¾ cup sugar
¼ cup brown sugar
1 egg
½ cup molasses

Sift together flour, baking soda, salt, ginger, cinnamon, cocoa, and cloves. In a separate bowl, beat margarine, adding sugar gradually until fluffy. Beat in egg and molasses. Add flour mixture. Refrigerate. Roll and cut into shapes. Bake at 350 degrees for 8-10 minutes. Decorate.

Mrs. Rayford Lloyd, Jr. (Genie)

FRUIT COOKIES

1½ cups Crisco
2 cups sugar
4 eggs
5½ cups flour
2 teaspoons baking powder
1½ teaspoons soda

½ teaspoon salt
½ teaspoon vanilla
¾ cup raisins
¾ cup dates, chopped
¾ cup nuts, chopped
1 small jar cherries, chopped

Cream shortening and sugar. Add beaten eggs. Sift flour, baking powder, and salt together. Moisten soda in milk or water. Add remaining ingredients. Shape mixture into rolls and wrap in waxed paper. Chill at least two hours. Slice and bake at 375 degrees.

Mrs. W. J. Parish, Jr.   (Nancy)

FRUIT CAKE COOKIES

Step I:

2 pounds candied cherries
2 pounds candied pineapple

2 pounds light raisins
6 cups pecans

Cut up and dredge in flour.

Step II:

3½ cups flour
1 teaspoon soda
½ teaspoon salt

1 teaspoon cinnamon
1 teaspoon nutmeg
1 teaspoon allspice

Sift together.

Step III:

1 stick butter
1½ cups brown sugar
3 teaspoons milk

4 eggs
1 cup bourbon

Cream butter and sugar. Add milk and then eggs, one at a time. Add bourbon. By hand combine flour mixture and butter mixture. Then add fruit mixture. Drop on greased cooky sheet. Bake at 275 degrees for 45 minutes. I usually cut nuts and fruits the day before baking. You may prepare entire recipe the day before, but cover tightly and refrigerate. Makes 400 cookies.
Mrs. Harold E. Wager (Margaret)

BUTTER TEA COOKIES

1 pound unsalted butter
¼ cup confectioners' sugar
1 egg yolk
2 teaspoons vanilla
1 ounce Cognac

5 to 6 cups cake flour
Confectioners' sugar
Nuts (optional)
Cloves (optional)

Soften butter and then whip with mixer until light and fluffy. Add ¼ cup confectioners' sugar, egg yolk, vanilla, and Cognac, beating thoroughly after each addition. Add flour slowly and mix until dough is soft and can be handled easily. Take a teaspoonful of dough and roll into a ball. Place on cooky sheet and press nut or clove in center, if desired. Bake at 350 degrees for 15 minutes. When done, sprinkle with additional confectioners' sugar while still warm.
Mrs. John Cleondis (Caliope)

CANDIED APRICOTS

2 cups sugar
1 pound dried
   apricots (large)

¾ cup water
Pecan halves
Confectioners' sugar

Combine sugar and water and boil apricots for about 10 minutes or until tender. Remove with a fork. Press nut in middle of apricot and roll in confectioners' sugar.
Mrs. John Cluxton (Jay)

DATE FINGERS

1 8-ounce package chopped dates
1 stick butter
1 cup sugar
1 egg, well beaten

½ cup nuts, chopped
2 teaspoons vanilla
2½ cups Rice Krispies
Confectioners' sugar

Melt butter and sugar. Add egg and dates. Bring to a boil and cook on low heat for 10 minutes stirring constantly. Pour over Rice Krispies. Mix and let cool. Form into fingers and roll in confectioners' sugar.
Mrs. James B. Smith

ANNIE MAE'S DATE NUT ROLL

3 cups sugar
1 cup Carnation Milk
½ stick butter
2 teaspoons white Karo syrup

1 package dates, chopped
1 teaspoon vanilla
2 cups nuts, chopped

Cook sugar, syrup, butter, and milk to soft ball stage. Add dates and cook to soft ball stage again. Add nuts and vanilla; beat until creamy. Put on waxed paper and roll. Let harden. Slice, when ready to serve.
Mrs. James Marshall, Jr. (Margie)

DATE SWIRL COOKIES

Filling:

1¼ cups dates
½ cup sugar
½ cup water

1 tablespoon lemon juice
¼ cup nuts, chopped

Combine dates, sugar, and water in a saucepan and cook until thickened, stirring constantly. Remove from heat, add lemon juice and nuts; cool.

¾ cup shortening
1½ teaspoons orange rind, grated
¼ teaspoon lemon rind, grated
1½ teaspoons salt
2 cups brown sugar

2 eggs
3½ cups flour
1½ teaspoons soda
2 tablespoons milk

Combine shortening, fruit rinds, salt, brown sugar, and eggs; beat thoroughly. Sift flour and soda together. Add half of flour to shortening mixture; add milk, then remaining flour, mixing thoroughly. Divide dough in half; roll each half into a rectangle about ¼-inch thick. Spread evenly with date mixture and roll. Wrap in waxed paper and refrigerate until ready to bake. Slice and place on a lightly greased cooky sheet. Bake at 375 degrees for 8-10 minutes.

Mrs. A. L. Aldrich   *Hueytown, Alabama*

Preserves Relishes & Accompaniments

MISS RUTH MARTIN'S KUMQUAT MARMALADE

Miss Martin was a member of one of Northwest Florida's
first pioneer families.

3 pounds kumquats
1 lemon

Sugar
1 can crushed pineapple

Thinly slice and seed kumquats and lemon. Weigh and add the same weight of water. Let kumquats soak in water overnight. Boil until tender. Soak for 24 hours and boil an additional 30 minutes. Weigh mixture again. Add the same weight of sugar and the can of pineapple. Boil for 40 minutes or until syrup begins to jell when placed on a cool saucer. Pour into glass jars and allow to firm before sealing.
Mrs. Warren Middlemas, Jr. (Martha)

EASY ORANGE MARMALADE

4 oranges

4 cups sugar

Prepare oranges by cleaning with a brush. Grind one whole orange omitting seeds. Peel three oranges and grind only the pulp. Combine pulp and sugar and bring to a boil over medium heat stirring frequently to prevent sticking to the bottom. Boil 30 minutes and seal in sterilized jars.
Note: Use a heavy bottomed pot when preparing this.
Mrs. Dee Bowers

PRESERVED KUMQUATS

2 quarts kumquats
2 pounds sugar

1 cup water
2 teaspoons soda

Soak fruit in soda and water to cover. Let stand overnight. Next day pierce each kumquat several times with a needle. Put kumquats in kettle and cover with cold water. Boil for 15 minutes. Drain and repeat process two more times. Make syrup with sugar and water. Boil slowly until transparent. Put in jars and cover tightly; let stand 30 minutes until plump. Seal.
Mrs. A. S. Brandt (Eunice)

CALAMONDIN CONSERVE

4 cups calamondins   1 teaspoon soda
4 cups sugar

Wash and scald fruit with 1 teaspoon soda and boiling water to cover. Seed
and grind fruit using coarse blade. Place fruit in kettle, add sugar, and barely
cover with water. Boil until fruit is tender and syrup has thickened. Pack in
sterilized jars and seal.
Mrs. Ben Redding (Dee)
Mrs. Warren Middlemas (Martha)
Mrs. Ray Wagner (Nancy)

ELDERBERRY JELLY

3-4 quarts elderberries   4½ cups sugar
1 package Sure-Jell

Wash berries well in a colander. Place berries in a Dutch oven and barely
cover with water. Cook the juice out of the berries. Strain juice and reserve 3
cups of juice. Strain the 3 cups of juice again and bring to a rolling boil. Add
Sure-Jell and stir continuously until Sure-Jell has dissolved. Add sugar and
continue to stir skimming off foam. Cook until a drop of jelly will cling to the
spoon. Seal in hot sterilized jars. Makes 3 pints.
Note: Be sure to use at least 1 quart green berries. These will contain the
pectin needed to make your jelly jell.
Mrs. Charley A. Gramling, III (Jo Ann)

STRAWBERRY FIG PRESERVES

3 cups figs, peeled   1 6-ounce package strawberry
3 cups sugar   gelatin

In a saucepan, combine all ingredients and mash with a potato masher. Bring
mixture slowly to a boil stirring constantly. Cook for 15 minutes. Pack in hot
sterilized jars. Seal jars. Set aside to cool. When cooled, tighten seals.
Variation: Blackberry, raspberry, black cherry, or other flavored gelatins
may be substituted for the strawberry.
Mrs. T. Woodie Smith (Lois)

MAYHAW JELLY

3 pounds Mayhaw berries
4 cups Mayhaw juice

1 box Sure-Jell
5 cups sugar

Wash berries thoroughly. Place berries in boiler adding water to cover. Simmer until berries pop, about 10 minutes. Mash with potato masher and strain through a pillow case and let drip. Do not squeeze case if you want clear jelly. Measure juice, adding water to make 4 cups. In a saucepan, combine juice and Sure-Jell. Bring mixture to a boil, stirring constantly with a metal spoon. Add sugar. Stir to dissolve and bring to a rolling boil for 1 minute stirring constantly. Remove jelly from heat, skim quickly to remove foam. Pour jelly into hot, sterilized jars to ⅛ inch from top. Wipe the top and the threads of the jars with a clean cloth. Place lid on jar and seal immediately. Invert each jar as it is filled and sealed. After all are sealed invert again to upright position and allow to cool. Yields about 5 half-pint jars.

Mrs. Sam Fleming (Irene)

SPICED FIGS

3 quarts figs
1 cup water
6 cups sugar
1 cup vinegar

¼ cup pickling spice
3 3-inch pieces cinnamon
8 whole cloves

Wash and stem figs; cover with boiling water, let stand 5 minutes. Make syrup of 1 cup water, sugar, vinegar, and spices tied in a bag. Drain figs and add to syrup. Boil *gently* for 10 minutes. Remove from heat; cover and let stand for 24 hours. Repeat boiling process for 3 consecutive days. On third day, pack in sterile jars and process in a hot water bath for 15 minutes. Makes about 5 pints.

Mrs. George Gore (Madelyn)

PEPPER JELLY

½ cup hot red or green peppers
1½ cups green pepper, chopped
3 cups cider vinegar
13 cups sugar, (5 pounds
    plus 3 cups

2 bottles Certo
Red or green food coloring

Seed and chop peppers, using gloves. Combine peppers, vinegar, and sugar. Cook 10 minutes. Strain. Add Certo and food coloring. Pack in sterilized jars and seal.
Mrs. Creed Greer (Selby)

CHILI PEPPER JELLY

24 hot, green, chili peppers
    chopped
2 cups green peppers, chopped

6 cups cider vinegar
12 cups sugar
2 bottles Certo

Place all peppers in blender. Pulverize and drain juice. In a large kettle, combine vinegar, sugar, and peppers. Bring to a boil and boil for exactly five minutes. Remove from heat, add Certo, and return to heat. Bring to boil and cook for one minute. Pour mixture into jars and seal. Good served with any meat.
Mrs. Jim Dunkerly (June)

PICKLED OKRA I

Fresh okra, small
Garlic cloves
Dillseed
Hot peppers

1 quart white vinegar
1 cup water
6 tablespoons salt

Into each pint jar place a clove of garlic, a hot pepper, and 1 teaspoon dillseed. Pack okra in jars (cut stems closely so they are open). Combine vinegar, water, and salt, and bring to a boil. Simmer for 5 minutes. Pour over okra. When it stops bubbling, seal, and pickles will be ready in two weeks.
Mrs. Joe Sain (Judy)

PICKLED OKRA II

2 teaspoons dillseed	4 cloves of garlic
2 10-ounce packages frozen okra	1¼ cups white vinegar
2 dried red peppers	3 tablespoons salt
2 cans chili peppers	½ cup water

Thaw and drain okra. Sterilize 2 pint jars and lids. Keep hot. Place 1 teaspoon dillseed into each jar. Pack okra into jars. Top each jar with ½ teaspoon dillseed, 1 red pepper, 1 chili pepper, and 2 cloves of garlic. Combine vinegar, salt, ½ cup water and bring to a boil. Pour hot mixture over okra into each jar. Cap jar and cool. Refrigerate at least 2 weeks before serving. Fresh okra may be used when available.
Mrs. J. M. Ros, Jr. (Rachel)

PICKLED EGGS

12 hard-cooked eggs	1 BAY LEAF
1 cup white vinegar	2 teaspoons mixed pickling
1 cup juice from canned beets	spices
1 clove garlic	1 small onion, sliced into rings
4 cups water	Salt

In a large jar, combine beet juice, vinegar, water, garlic, BAY LEAF, pickling spices, and salt; mix well. Add eggs and onion rings. Cover and refrigerate for several days.
Mrs. Curtis Bane (Ann)

CORN RELISH

1 cup vinegar	1 large onion, chopped
½ cup water	3 ribs of celery, chopped
1 tablespoon salt	1 large package frozen, mixed
2 tablespoons sugar	vegetables
3-4 carrots, chopped	1 can whole kernel corn

Bring to a boil the first 4 ingredients. Add chopped vegetables. Bring to a rolling boil. Add frozen vegetables and corn; boil 4 minutes. Serve chilled. Will keep several days in the refrigerator.
Mrs. Paul Gwinn   *Pine Bluff, Arkansas*

CRYSTALIZED GREEN TOMATOES

12 pounds green tomatoes, sliced
2 cups lime, sifted
1 cup alum
1 tablespoon alum
2 tablespoons ginger tea

12 pounds sugar
1 tablespoon whole mace
1 tablespoon cloves
6 sticks cinnamon, broken
Vinegar

Dissolve lime in 2 gallons water and pour over sliced tomatoes. Refrigerate for 3 days in a porcelain or plastic container. On the fourth day, rinse tomatoes well, cover with water, and refrigerate for 24 hours. Drain water from tomatoes. Mix 1 cup of powdered alum with 2 gallons of water. Pour over tomatoes and soak for 3 days. On the eighth day, drain water from tomatoes. Mix 1 tablespoon of alum with 2 gallons of water, pour over tomatoes, and boil for 3 minutes. Drain water. Cover tomatoes with 2 gallons of water mixed with 2 tablespoons of ginger tea and boil for 3 minutes. Drain. Weigh tomatoes and for each pound of tomatoes, add 1 pound of sugar. Add the remaining spices for the entire recipe and sufficient vinegar to cover tomatoes. Boil for 4 minutes or until tomatoes are glazed. Pack tomatoes while still hot in sterilized glass jars and seal. Chill before serving. Yields 24 pints.
Mrs. H. Mack Lewis (Eleanor)

EYE-OPENING FRUIT DELIGHTS
. . .fun for breakfast—delicious dessert. . .

Bananas
1 can frozen orange juice

1 orange juice can of water

Slice bananas into small fruit bowls. Place frozen orange juice and water in blender and blend until frothy. Pour over bananas.

Fresh blueberries
Confectioners' sugar, sifted

Cantaloupe

Roll blueberries in confectioners' sugar. Cut cantaloupe in half; remove seeds. Fill each half with blueberries and serve one to each person.
Mrs. W. Gerald Harrison (June)

CRANBERRY RELISH

1 pound raw cranberries   1 large apple
1 orange   1½ cups sugar

Do not peel orange or apple but remove seeds. Grind cranberries, orange, and apple. Add sugar and bring just to a boil. Chill. Yields 1 pint.
Mrs. Curtis Bane (Ann)

NOODLES AND CHERRIES
...an old Dutch recipe...

6 ounces egg noodles   2 1-pound cans of sour, tart
1 tablespoon butter   cherries
1½ cups sugar   8-12 slices bread

Cook egg noodles in salted water. Drain well and mix with margarine or butter. Cook cherries with sugar. Cut bread into cubes and toast in butter in a hot skillet. To serve, place croutons on dinner plate, spooning noodles over them. Top with hot cherries and juice. HMMMM!
Note: This is light and different for Sunday lunch or evening meal.
Mrs. Foster H. Kruse (Helen)

CURRIED FRUIT
*... For something different,
serve for brunch with Eggs Benedict...*

1 No. 2 can pineapple   1 tablespoon curry powder
1 No. 2 can pears   ½ cup melted butter
1 No. 2 can apricots   1 cup brown sugar

Place drained fruit in a deep casserole, allowing about 4 pieces of fruit per serving. Combine remaining ingredients and pour over fruit. Bake at 375 degrees for about 40 minutes. Serve hot. Serves 8.
Mrs. C. L. Jinks, Jr. (Mary Catherine)

HOT FRUIT COMPOTE

This dish is delicious with ham or turkey.
Try it next Thanksgiving or Christmas.

1 can applesauce mixed with
   ¼ cup instant flour
1 can blue plums or bing cherries
½ cup pecans, chopped

1 can pineapple chunks
2 bananas, sliced
½ cup brown sugar
Butter

Butter a small casserole with ½ stick butter. Layer fruit with brown sugar and butter between each layer. Cover top with brown sugar and pecans. Bake until heated. Can be prepared a day ahead and heated at time of serving.
Marguerite Fleming Bryant

HOT FRUIT MEDLEY

1 8¼-ounce can sliced
   pineapple
1 No. 2 can peach halves
1 jar apple rings
1 No. 2 can pear halves

1 No. 2 can apricot halves
2 tablespoons flour
½ cup brown sugar
1 stick of butter
1 cup sherry

Drain all fruit. Half pineapple slices. Arrange fruit in layers in medium deep dish. Combine butter, sugar, flour, and sherry in double boiler. Cook, stirring until smooth and thickened. Pour over fruit, cover, and let stand in refrigerator overnight. Before serving, heat in a 350-degree oven until bubbly.
Mrs. Gordon Hindsman (Helen)

GLAZED BANANAS

6 green-tipped bananas
¼ cup margarine
¼ cup brown sugar

2 teaspoons lemon rind, grated
¼ cup fresh lemon juice
½ teaspoon cinnamon

Peel bananas and cut in half lengthwise; place in shallow baking dish. Combine remaining ingredients and pour over bananas. Bake at 325 degrees for 15 minutes. Serves 6.
Variation: Substitute orange juice for lemon. Sprinkle with coconut.
Mrs. C. Edward Miller (Mary Ola)

WATERMELON RIND PICKLES

3 pounds watermelon rind
(about 10 cups cubed)
2 teaspoons salt
7 cups sugar

2 cups vinegar
½ teaspoon oil of cinnamon
¼ teaspoon oil of cloves
Cloves

Prepare rind by removing all red and green. Cut in one-inch cubes. In kettle, gently boil rind in 3 quarts salted water, uncovered, just until tender (about 10 minutes). In large saucepan boil sugar and vinegar gently about 5 minutes after sugar has dissolved. Remove from heat; stir in oils and, if desired, a little red or green food coloring. Drain rind well and place in a quart bowl. Add syrup. Weight rind down with plate so syrup covers rind. Refrigerate overnight. Next day, drain syrup into saucepan and bring to boil. Again pour over rind, weight down, and refrigerate overnight. On third day, drain syrup, add cloves, and bring to a boil. Place rind in five or six pint jars, covering with hot syrup. Cool, cover, and refrigerate. Will keep several weeks. To keep longer, sterilize jars. Bring rind and syrup to boiling point. Immediately ladle into hot, sterilized jars. Cover with hot syrup and cap as manufacturer directs.

Mrs. Wesley Zuber (Bea)

CHOW-CHOW

1 gallon cabbage
1 gallon green tomatoes
4 green peppers

4 sweet red peppers
1 quart onions

Chop well; salt and let stand overnight. Next morning press water out and add:

4 tablespoons ground mustard
2 tablespoons powdered ginger
1 tablespoon cloves
1 tablespoon mace

1 tablespoon cinnamon
3 pounds sugar
3 quarts vinegar
1 teaspoon tumeric

Combine all ingredients and cook until tender. Mix tumeric with a little hot water or vinegar and add to above. (Tumeric is for color.) Put in hot sterilized jars and seal. Serve cold.

Mrs. Harold L. Ross (Sarah)

TOMATO-APPLE CHUTNEY

3 medium onions, quartered
4 medium tart apples
1 rib of celery, cut into pieces
2½ cups white vinegar
¾ cup seedless raisins
2 tablespoons mustard seed
1 tablespoon ground ginger

2 ounces candied ginger,
   finely chopped
1 tablespoon salt
3 cups light brown sugar
4 large ripe tomatoes, peeled
1 sweet red pepper, minced

Core apples and tomatoes and cut each into eighths. Force the first three ingredients through coarse blade of food chopper. Place in a kettle with remaining ingredients, except pepper. Bring to a boil and simmer, uncovered, stirring frequently for 1¾ hours. Add pepper and simmer, stirring constantly for about 15 minutes. Pour into hot sterilized jars and seal. Makes 4 pints.
Mrs. C. H. Beach (Pat)

CRANBERRY CHUTNEY

4 cups fresh cranberries
2¼ cups brown sugar
1 cup golden raisins
1 cup water
½ cup toasted almonds, coarsely
   chopped

¼ cup candied ginger, snipped
¼ cup lemon juice
2 teaspoons salt
1 teaspoon onion, grated
¼ teaspoon ground cloves

Combine all ingredients in a large saucepan, bring to a boil, stirring constantly. Simmer over low heat for 15 minutes. Pack in hot, sterilized jars. Seal at once or refrigerate. Makes about 5 half pints.
Mrs. Philip Cotton (Salie)

ROAST RELISH

Cherry tomatoes
Hearts of palm
Avocado, sliced
½ cup oil
½ cup tarragon vinegar

3 large cloves garlic, crushed
1 tablespoon caraway seeds
Salt
Pepper
Pinch of sugar

Combine last 7 ingredients and place in refrigerator overnight. Pour over tomatoes, hearts of palm, and avocado before serving.
Robert LeNox

BREAD AND BUTTER PICKLES I

4 quarts medium cucumbers,
   sliced
6 medium white onions, sliced
2 green peppers, chopped
3 cloves garlic
½ cup ice cream salt

Cracked ice
5 cups sugar
1½ teaspoons tumeric
1½ teaspoons celery seed
3 cups cider vinegar
2 tablespoons mustard seed

Do not pare cucumbers. Slice thin. Add onions, peppers, garlic cloves, and salt (coarse). Cover with cracked ice. Mix thoroughly and let stand for 3 hours. Drain. Lift out cloves of garlic. Combine remaining ingredients. Pour over cucumber mixture. Heat just to boiling point. Seal in sterilized jars. Makes 8 pints.
Mrs. Sam Fleming (Irene)

BREAD AND BUTTER PICKLES II

3 quarts sliced cucumbers
½ quart sliced onions
½ cup salt
1½ pints vinegar

1½ pounds sugar
½ tablespoon tumeric
½ teaspoon mustard seed
½ teaspoon celery seed

Place cucumbers, onions, salt, and cold water to cover in a non-metal container and let stand for 3 to 4 hours. Drain and rinse. Bring vinegar, sugar, and spices to a full boil. Add cucumbers and onions and return to a boil. Remove from heat; quickly place in hot sterilized jars and seal. This usually fills 6 pint jars.
Mrs. William Boyle (Marise)

SQUASH PICKLES

8 cups yellow squash, sliced
2 cups onions, sliced
2 green peppers, sliced
1 tablespoon salt

1 cup cider vinegar
1¾ cups sugar
½ teaspoon celery seed
½ teaspoon mustard seed

Combine squash and onions. Sprinkle with salt. Let stand 1 hour. Combine peppers, vinegar, sugar, celery seed, and mustard seed. Bring mixture to a boil. Add squash and onions; bring to another boil. Remove from heat and pack in hot sterilized jars. Serve cold.
Mrs. E. Clay Lewis, III (Marsha)

OLD SOUTH PICKLES

7 pounds cucumbers, sliced
2 cups lime
2 gallons water
2 quarts vinegar

4¼ pounds sugar
1 tablespoon salt
Pickling spices

Dissolve lime in water and pour over cucumber slices. Soak cucumbers for 24 hours in lime water. Rinse cucumber slices 3 times in clear water. Soak cucumber slices for 3 hours in ice water. Drain water from cucumbers, make syrup of remaining ingredients except pickling spices, and pour over cucumbers. Soak overnight in syrup. Add pickling spices to taste. (Spices may be tied in cloth bag or added loose as desired.) Boil cucumbers for 35 to 40 minutes until pickles are tender. Pack pickles while still hot in sterilized glass jars and seal.
Mrs. Eugene Suggs (Betty)

DILLED SWEET SPANISH ONION SLICES

2 large sweet, Spanish onions
¼ cup sugar
2 teaspoons salt

½ teaspoon dillweed
¼ cup water
½ cup white vinegar

Slice onions into rings, ¼-inch thick. (Slice onions before peeling as the skins will slip right off the slices.) Pack the slices in a wide-mouthed quart jar that has a tight fitting lid. Combine all other ingredients in a saucepan; heat to boiling. Pour over onion slices at once. Cover tightly and refrigerate overnight. These will keep for several days.
Mrs. A. D. Teal, Sr.   *Mobile, Alabama*

PEAR RELISH

1 peck *green* pears
6 onions
4 green peppers, seeded
3 red peppers, seeded

1 teaspoon whole spice
1 tablespoon salt
5 cups vinegar
2 pounds sugar

Peel and core pears. Place in cold water to prevent turning dark. Feed pears, onions, and peppers through food chopper. Place in large boiler. Add whole spice, salt, sugar, and vinegar. Boil 30 minutes, stirring occasionally. Allow to cool slightly and pack into hot sterilized jars; seal.
Mrs. Casper E. Harris (Sue)

PURPLE PLUM MINCEMEAT

4 pounds purple plums	1½ pounds light brown
2 pounds Bartlett pears	sugar
1 pound seedless raisins	⅓ cup cider vinegar
1 tablespoon lemon rind, grated	1 teaspoon salt
¼ cup lemon juice	1 tablespoon ground cinnamon
2½ tablespoons orange rind,	2 tablespoons gound cloves
grated	1 teaspoon ground nutmeg
½ cup orange juice	½ teaspoon ground allspice

Quarter and pit plums. Core and dice unpeeled pears. Combine fruits with remaining ingredients in a large kettle and bring to a boil. Reduce heat, cover, and simmer for 30 minutes. Remove cover and simmer for 1 hour until slightly thickened, stirring occasionally. Pour hot mixture within ⅛ inch of top of hot sterilized jars. Wipe tops and threads of jars with a clean, damp cloth. Put sterilized lids on jars and screw bands tightly. Place each jar as it is filled on rack in canner full of boiling water. Water should cover jars 1 to 2 inches. Put cover on canner and bring water to boil again. Process jars in boiling water for 25 minutes. Remove jars from canner and let cool for 12 hours. Remove bands and test lids for seal. If dome of lid is down or stays down when pressed, jar is properly sealed. Label, store in a dry, cool, dark place.
Mrs. Ray Wagner (Nancy)

BRANDIED GRAPES

Green grapes	Sour cream
Equal parts of brandy and honey	

Heat honey and blend in brandy. Cool. Pour over grapes and marinate overnight. Serve in sherbet or parfait glasses with sour cream.
Mrs. J. C. Harris (Ruby)   *Cove Hotel*

STUFFED PRUNES

½ box of dried prunes	1 3-ounce package
Mayonnaise to taste	cream cheese

Cook prunes until very tender (enough to remove seed easily). Cool. Cut top side of prune only enough to remove seed. Cream cheese until smooth and add mayonnaise to taste; stuff prunes. Store in refrigerator until ready to serve.
Mrs. Theodore G. Elchos (Jimmie)

STUFFED FRESH PINEAPPLE

1 fresh pineapple
Confectioners' sugar
1 8-ounce package dried apricots
1 cup pickled peach juice

1 cup golden raisins
Pinch of salt
1 cup pecans, chopped

Cut top off of pineapple and save. Scoop out the flesh; cut into bite-sized pieces and sprinkle with a little sugar. Cook apricots until tender. Mash and add peach juice. In a small amount of water, simmer raisins a few minutes; drain. Combine apricots, pineapple, raisins, salt, and pecans. Stuff shell with fruit mixture and replace top.

Mrs. Florence Hood   Moultrie, Georgia

PINEAPPLE SOUFFLÉ

...good as an accompaniment with barbecue or as a dessert...

6 slices bread, cut into 1-inch
  cubes
1 stick margarine
2 eggs

2 tablespoons flour
1 16-ounce can pineapple chunks
  and juice
1 cup sugar

Melt margarine in a large skillet. Stir in bread cubes until margarine is absorbed. Beat eggs slightly. Add sugar, flour, pineapple juice, and pineapple. Layer in a 2-quart casserole dish beginning with pineapple mixture and ending with bread cubes (about 4 layers). Bake at 350 degrees for 1 hour.

Mrs. Ray Syfrett (Ann)

ROSEY APPLES

8 Winesap apples, peeled and
  cored
½ pint whipping cream

2 cups sugar
1 bottle red or green
  food coloring

Fill a frying pan half full with water. Add sugar and bring to a boil. Add food coloring. Add apples and cook until tender (about 15 minutes). Turn apples and test by sticking a fork inside. Top with whipped cream. This is good served with Chicken Wiggle, tossed salad, and a light dessert.

Mrs. Sam Rowe (Nelle)

METRIC SYSTEM

1 teaspoon		5 cubic centimeters
1 tablespoon	3 teaspoons	15 cubic centimeters
¼ cup	4 tablespoons	59.1 cubic centimeters
1 cup		236.5 cubic centimeters
1 pint	2 cups	473 cubic centimeters
1 quart	2 pints	946 cubic centimeters
1 gallon	4 quarts	3.785 liters
1 pound	16 ounces	454 grams

250 degrees Fahrenheit = 106 degrees Centigrade
350 degrees Fahrenheit = 162 degrees Centigrade
450 degrees Fahrenheit = 218 degrees Centigrade

INDEX

S

Bay Publications

Post Office Box 404   Panama City, Florida 32402 (904) 785-7870

Please send _____ copies of *Bay Leaves* @ $14.95 $_____

Postage & Handling @ $2.00 $_____

FL residents add 6½% sales tax @ .98 $_____

*Check here for gift wrap ❑   Total enclosed $_____

Please send _____ copies of *Beyond the Bay* @ $14.95 $_____

Postage & Handling @ $2.00 $_____

FL residents add 6½% sales tax @ .98 $_____

*Check here for gift wrap ❑   Total enclosed $_____

Please charge my VISA ❑   MASTER CARD ❑

Card number_____

Signature_____ Exp. Date _____

Name_____

Address_____

City_____State_____ Zip_____

Bay Publications

Post Office Box 404   Panama City, Florida 32402 (904) 785-7870

Please send _____ copies of *Bay Leaves* @ $14.95 $_____

Postage & Handling @ $2.00 $_____

FL residents add 6½% sales tax @ .98 $_____

*Check here for gift wrap ❑   Total enclosed $_____

Please send _____ copies of *Beyond the Bay* @ $14.95 $_____

Postage & Handling @ $2.00 $_____

FL residents add 6½% sales tax @ .98 $_____

*Check here for gift wrap ❑   Total enclosed $_____

Please charge my VISA ❑   MASTER CARD ❑

Card number_____

Signature_____ Exp. Date _____

Name_____

Address_____

City_____State_____ Zip_____

Reorder Additional Copies

I would like to see *Bay Leaves* and *Beyond the Bay* sold in the following stores:

Store name _____

Address _____

City _____ State _____ Zip _____

I would like to see *Bay Leaves* and *Beyond the Bay* sold in the following stores:

Store name _____

Address _____

City _____ State _____ Zip _____

- -

I would like to see *Bay Leaves* and *Beyond the Bay* sold in the following stores:

Store name _____

Address _____

City _____ State _____ Zip _____

I would like to see *Bay Leaves* and *Beyond the Bay* sold in the following stores:

Store name _____

Address _____

City _____ State _____ Zip _____

Bay Publications

Post Office Box 404   Panama City, Florida 32402 (904) 785-7870

Please send _____ copies of *Bay Leaves* @ $14.95 $_____

Postage & Handling @ $2.00 $_____

FL residents add $6\frac{1}{2}$% sales tax @ .98 $_____

*Check here for gift wrap ❑   Total enclosed $_____

Please send _____ copies of *Beyond the Bay* @ $14.95 $_____

Postage & Handling @ $2.00 $_____

FL residents add $6\frac{1}{2}$% sales tax @ .98 $_____

*Check here for gift wrap ❑   Total enclosed $_____

Please charge my VISA ❑   MASTER CARD ❑

Card number_____

Signature_____ Exp. Date _____

Name_____

Address_____

City_____State_____ Zip_____

- -

Bay Publications

Post Office Box 404   Panama City, Florida 32402 (904) 785-7870

Please send _____ copies of *Bay Leaves* @ $14.95 $_____

Postage & Handling @ $2.00 $_____

FL residents add $6\frac{1}{2}$% sales tax @ .98 $_____

*Check here for gift wrap ❑   Total enclosed $_____

Please send _____ copies of *Beyond the Bay* @ $14.95 $_____

Postage & Handling @ $2.00 $_____

FL residents add $6\frac{1}{2}$% sales tax @ .98 $_____

*Check here for gift wrap ❑   Total enclosed $_____

Please charge my VISA ❑   MASTER CARD ❑

Card number_____

Signature_____ Exp. Date _____

Name_____

Address_____

City_____State_____ Zip_____

Reorder Additional Copies

I would like to see *Bay Leaves* and *Beyond the Bay* sold in the following stores:

Store name _____

Address _____

City _____ State _____ Zip _____

I would like to see *Bay Leaves* and *Beyond the Bay* sold in the following stores:

Store name _____

Address _____

City _____ State _____ Zip _____

I would like to see *Bay Leaves* and *Beyond the Bay* sold in the following stores:

Store name _____

Address _____

City _____ State _____ Zip _____

I would like to see *Bay Leaves* and *Beyond the Bay* sold in the following stores:

Store name _____

Address _____

City _____ State _____ Zip _____